I Want My MP3!

I Want My MP3!

How to Download, Rip, and Play Digital Music

Bill Mann

McGraw-Hill

New York   San Francisco   Washington, D.C.
Auckland   Bogotá   Caracas   Lisbon   London   Madrid
Mexico City   Milan   Montreal   New Delhi   San Juan
Singapore   Sydney   Tokyo   Toronto

McGraw-Hill

A Division of The McGraw-Hill Companies

2 3 4 5 6 7 8 9 0   AGM/AGM   9 0 4 3 2 1 0 9

P/N 0-07-212288-9

PART OF ISBN 0-07-212290-0

The sponsoring editor for this book was Michael Sprague and the production supervisor was Clare Stanley. It was set in Guardi by Patricia Wallenburg.

Printed and bound by Quebecor/Martinsburg.

Throughout this book, trademarked names are used. Rather than put a trademark symbol after every occurrence of a trademarked name, we use names in an editorial fashion only, and to the benefit of the trademark owner, with no intention of infringement of the trademark. Where such designations appear in this book, they have been printed with initial caps.

Information contained in this work has been obtained by The McGraw-Hill Companies, Inc. ("McGraw-Hill") from sources believed to be reliable. However, neither McGraw-Hill nor its authors guarantee the accuracy or completeness of any information published herein and neither McGraw-Hill nor its authors shall be responsible for any errors, omissions, or damages arising out of use of this information. This work is published with the understanding that McGraw-Hill and its authors are supplying information but are not attempting to render engineering or other professional services. If such services are required, the assistance of an appropriate professional should be sought.

 This book is printed on recycled, acid-free paper containing a minimum of 50% recycled, de-inked fiber.

Dedication

This book is dedicated to Patti & Jen: I don't know how you put up with these crazy writing projects—but I'm sure glad you do. I couldn't make it without your help and understanding.

Acknowledgments

I want to express my deep thanks to everyone involved in this project. Margot, my agent at Waterside Productions, who always believed I should, and would, do an MP3 book. Michael at McGraw-Hill for doing the deal. Jennifer and all the other pros at McGraw-Hill, who produced this book in record time, while adding more value than any editorial/production team I've ever worked with. Patty at TypeWriting, for those weekends and holidays you didn't enjoy because you were working on this thing.

But most of all I want to thank the people who produce the hardware, software, Web sites, and music that appear in the book. There isn't room (or time left in the schedule) to describe their individual contributions, but here are the names of the people or companies who gave us permission to include their stuff:

20-20Consumer, Andrew Hennessey & Solan Pan Cultural Productions, Atomsplit, Aureate Media Corp., BayCom GmbH, Boston Acoustics, Christopher Schmelnik, Creative Labs, Crunch Music, DailyMP3.com, Erik Ramsaur, Gene 6, Hostel Records/Karen Lawrence, Impy3 (CD Systems, Inc.), Innomedia, Jim Birch/Caffeinated Recordings, Johnna Morrow/Taiga Music/Skysong Productions, Inc., Joshua Kerr, Julian Kay (shift), Lance Records, Lawrence M. Jarquio/Kryptonic Productions, Listen.com, Lycos, Markus Babler & Toni Kaiser, Mediascience, Inc., MP3.com, MusicMatch, MySimon, Palavista, Paul Spaeth, Peacekeeper Enterprises, LLC, Peter Savstrom, Phil Frazier Management, Pontis Electronics GmbH, Pontoon Publishing, Proud Mary Entertainment, RioPort, Inc., Samsung Electronics, SavvySearch Limited, Sensory Science Corp., SouthWEST, swebmusic.com, Thomson Consumer Electronics, Tommi Prami & The Linear Team, Topica.

My deepest apologies to anyone I may have left out.

Contents

Contents

Introduction

Welcome to *I Want My MP3! How to Download, Rip, and Play Digital Music*. This book is about MP3 music, the hottest topic on the Internet today. It's so hot that the word "MP3" has even surpassed the word "sex" as the most searched for word on Internet search engines.

If you're already tuned into the whole MP3 scene, feel free to skip down to "Who Should Read This Book, and Why." If you are not yet up to speed on MP3, keep reading for a 5-minute introduction to the subject. When you're done you'll know what all the fuss is about.

What Is this MP3 Stuff Anyway?

MP3 is a way of encoding recorded sound so that it takes up much less storage space than it would otherwise. The term actually stands for a portion of an industry standard dealing with compressing motion pictures, but that doesn't really matter to most people. What does matter is that MP3 files are small enough to make it practical to transfer high-quality music files over the Internet and store them on a hard drive.

As a result, MP3 has become extremely popular as a way to distribute music. College students have been playing with MP3 files for years, and now the rest of us are catching on.

Why is Everyone so Worked Up about MP3?

MP3 sets off different groups of people for different reasons.

▪ Consumers like the fact that they can get a great variety of music (hundreds of thousands of songs are available in MP3 format), most of it free, and can listen to it in new ways. They are freed from the need to spend $17 on a CD to get the one song they like, and they get easy access to the vast amount of music that is not being pushed by the big record companies.
▪ Artists (some of them, anyway) like the fact that they now can distribute their music to a worldwide audience without dealing with the established music industry.

- Upstart Internet music publishers like the fact that MP3 opens up new opportunities for small, agile, and aggressive companies in the multi-billion-dollar music business.
- The big record companies hate MP3 because they don't have control over distribution, and can't guarantee a flow of money to themselves and their artists.

The big record companies do have one valid gripe about MP3. The MP3 format has no built-in way to prevent people from obtaining and distributing music illegally. How much of a problem this actually causes is open to debate, but the established music industry (and many of the newcomers) are not taking any chances. They have banded together and created the Secure Digital Music Initiative (SDMI), with the goal of imposing control on the way music is distributed.

This begs the question, "Is it legal to play MP3 files?" The answer is yes. It is perfectly legal to play MP3 files, provided that the copyright holder allows it. If you go to major sites like MP3.com, Crunch, Listen.com, and so on, you will find only legal MP3 files. It is also legal to rip (copy) music from your own audio CDs, encode it in MP3 format, and listen to it. It is not legal to distribute MP3 files without the copyright holder's permission.

Now all of this would be largely academic if not for a few interesting trends:

- The growth rate of digital music (primarily, but not exclusively MP3) is phenomenal. According to Media Metrix, the number of people listening to digital music in the United States in June of 1999 was 4 million. In June of 1998, the number was a few hundred thousand. In other words, the use of digital music is booming.
- According to the Jupiter Communications Plug-In conference, held in July 1999, more than 70% of 12- to 18-year-olds on the Net visit music sites, making such visits the number-one online activity for that age group.
- According to a report in the *Iconocast* newsletter for April 15, 1999, unit sales of music (not on the Internet) dropped by 2.4% in 1997, the last year figures were available.

■ One after another, industries are being shaken to their cores as Internet-based businesses and business models transform the way people live, work, and shop.

Put these trends together, and it is clear that the big record companies have something to be concerned about. These are interesting times indeed in the music business.

Who Should Read this Book and Why

I Want My MP3! is **your** guide to getting the most out of the MP3 revolution. It focuses on what today's computer-literate, Web-browsing consumer needs to know to get in on the MP3 action. If you spend a significant amount of time in front of a PC, and you like to listen to music, this book is written specifically for you.

Most MP3 software and music is available on the Net free of charge. Here is why you need a book on the subject:

■ I've been there already. I've used every piece of software and hardware in the book (except for some of the gizmos in Chapter 15, which hadn't arrived by my deadline). I've already spent hours trying to figure out why my new sound card wasn't making any noise, or why a particular piece of software trashed Microsoft Windows. There's no reason for you to go through the same hassles. *I Want my MP3!* guides you around the rough spots.

■ The number of MP3 Web sites has exploded. Finding quality sites calls for a lot of exploring, some of it in rather iffy territory. While researching this book, I encountered dozens of pirate music sites, got trapped by "music" sites that actually shunt you into endless mazes of XXX porno sites, and other lovely situations. I even had one site threaten to damage my hard drive unless I voted for it in some adult-site popularity contest. Stick with the sites covered in the book, and you won't have to deal with any of this junk.

■ Using the software and music included on the book CD can save you serious time. There is more than 60 MB of material on that CD. Even if you only use a quarter of what is available, how long would it take you to download 15 MB using your modem? How much is your time worth to you?

The Lay of the Land

I Want My MP3! is divided into five parts, each of which is described below. You don't need to read the book sequentially, so use these descriptions to decide which part has the information you are looking for, and start there. Once you satisfy your immediate needs, I do encourage you to read the rest of the book, as I bet you'll find something of use in every part.

NOTE

Make sure to bookmark Chapter 2, "Just the Facts, Ma'am: A Paper-Based FAQ." This chapter turns the book into a giant Frequently Asked Questions file by listing common questions, then pointing you to the spot in the book where you'll find the answer. When you just need that one answer, that one little bit of information to do whatever it is you're doing, turn to Chapter 2 first.

Part 1: Quick Start

If you want to get up and running right now, Part 1 is the place to start. Since most PCs today have all the hardware and power they need to play MP3s, *I Want My MP3!* gets right down to it. In Chapter 1, you'll get the Sonique MP3 player installed and running on your PC. Within 15 minutes of opening the chapter, you should be able to start playing the MP3 music that comes on the book CD. This short chapter is very detailed and includes numerous screen shots, so even if you have never installed software before, you can be playing MP3 music in minutes.

Chapter 2 is for readers who already have a player installed, but need some sort of information to get them moving forward. It is the book's equivalent of a Frequently Asked Questions (FAQ) file, addressing common questions you might have about MP3. For each question, the list contains a pointer to where the answer appears in the body of the book.

Part 2: The Software You Need

Part 1 showed you just enough to play some songs with Sonique, one of the top-notch MP3 player programs on the book CD. Part 2 covers two different approaches you might take to MP3. There's the component approach, where you mix and match this player with that ripper, the other encoder, and a number of utilities, giving yourself a custom solution. Then there is the all-in-one approach, where you choose a single program that plays, rips, encodes, and does all the rest.

The chapters in this part of the book give you the information you need to pursue either approach. The CD in the back of the book contains almost all the free and shareware (try before you buy) software you need to follow either approach. Lastly, since the software changes faster than I can write new books (or you can read them) there's a complete guide to finding (and downloading) the latest MP3 software from the Internet.

Part 3: Looking for Tunes in All the Right Places

MP3 means music. In this part of the book, you'll find out where to get your hands on thousands of songs. They're mostly free, and mostly from bands you've never heard of, but you can find great stuff from every genre and every corner of the globe. Starting at the beating heart of the MP3 movement, a Web site named MP3.com, these chapters lead you to the best places to find new music, and to the engines that let you track down the specific song or artist you're looking for. You'll also find useful information like how to tell when the music at a site is pirated, and which supposed MP3 site actually takes you to a XXX porn site.

Part 4: The Hardware You Need

The best software and the hottest music in the world won't do you any good if your hardware doesn't have the guts to do the job. This part of the book is your exhaustive guide to MP3-related hardware. It walks you through getting your PC ready to play music, including installing all sorts of components and using a CD-ROM burner to turn your MP3 music into audio CDs.

Another chapter takes you to the wonderful world of non-PC MP3 music. With equipment that's available or under development, you can listen to MP3 music anywhere you can listen to your radio or a CD: in the living room, in your car, or hiking up the side of New Hampshire's Mount Uncanoonic. Last but not least, there's a whole chapter dedicated to helping you shop the Net for the best deals on any hardware you might need.

Part 5: Keeping Up with the MP3 Scene

MP3 is a new technology, appearing in a boom economy, relating to a trendy industry, and existing primarily on the Internet, the hottest part of the global economy. No wonder people have trouble keeping up. Fortunately, there are information sources you can use to keep abreast of the ever-changing MP3 scene, without sacrificing hours a day to the task.

This part of the book introduces you to the best sources of MP3 information on the Internet. This includes the "I Want My MP3" electronic newsletter, delivering news, reviews, and who knows what else, direct to your electronic mailbox.

Appendix: MP3 on a Silver(y) Platter

This is your guide to the music and software on the enclosed CD. Thanks to the generosity of lots of software developers and artists, the CD contains top-notch software like Sonique and Music-Match Jukebox, along with great music from groups like Alien Fashion Show and Sci-Fi Lullaby.

Glossary

You'll run into some unfamiliar terms in this book. *Rip*, for example. Ripping a song from a CD means to copy the song from the CD to your PC, converting it to a particular format as you go. Unusual terms like rip are defined the first time they appear in the body of the book, and all of them appear in the Glossary.

PART 1

Quick Start

Whether you are a beginner wanting to play your first MP3 file, or an MP3 veteran with a nagging problem to solve, the chapters of Part I will get you up and running as quickly as possible. Chapter I is for anyone who does not have an MP3 player on his/her PC. It walks you through installing Sonique, a standalone MP3 player included on the CD-ROM in the back of the book. Assuming your PC is up to the task, you should be able to install Sonique and play one of the MP3s on the CD-ROM within 15 minutes of starting the chapter. With detailed instructions and plentiful screen shots, you should have no trouble getting the job done.

Chapter 2 is for readers who already have a player installed, but are stuck in some way. Designed like a Frequently Asked Question (FAQ) file, this chapter lists common MP3-related questions, and points you to where the answers appear within the book. In many cases, this question and answer format is a better way to find what you're looking for than the Table of Contents or the Index.

CHAPTER 1

15 Minutes
to Music

Are you new to MP3 music? If so, you're in the right chapter. Assuming your PC has the hardware it needs, the instructions in this chapter will have you playing your first MP3 file in 15 minutes or less. The software player you need is on the CD in the back of the book, and so are several MP3s you can play. Most PCs sold in the last couple of years are equipped to play music. So the odds are great that you'll be able to roll right through this chapter and be listening to all sorts of new music by the time you reach the chapter wrap up.

Here are the high notes you'll hit in this chapter:

▌ Figuring out if your PC is ready to play MP3s
▌ Installing an MP3 player
▌ Configuring your player
▌ Playing music.

Figuring Out if Your PC Is Ready to Play MP3s

The traditional way to figure out if your PC is ready to play MP3s is to compare system requirements for an MP3 player to your system configuration. But who wants to deal with that right now? You bought this book because you want to play music, not compare processor specs and available RAM.

Here is my quick and dirty approach to figuring out if your PC has what it takes to play MP3s. Just answer these questions:

1. Does your PC play music when Microsoft Windows starts or while you play computer games?
2. Does your PC have a CD-ROM drive?
3. Is your PC less than two years old?

If you answered Yes to all three questions, your PC almost certainly has what it takes to play MP3 music.

If you answered No to any of those questions, you probably can't be up and playing music in 15 minutes. In this case, your best bet is to turn to Chapter 12, "Pumping Up Your PC for MP3." There you'll find everything you need to determine whether your PC really does have what it takes, and what to do if it doesn't.

If you don't know the answer to any of the questions, assume that answer is Yes. The worst that can happen is that you spend 15 minutes working through this chapter, and the music won't play at the end. If that happens, you should head to Chapter 12 for help figuring out what's going on and fixing it.

If you're still reading at this point, you must be ready to go for the glory—or at least the music. The first step is installing an MP3 player.

Installing an MP3 Player

The CD-ROM in the back of this book contains, among other things, some MP3 players and MP3 music files. To get up and running quickly, you will install Sonique, a popular MP3 player. You're just going to cover the very basics of using Sonique here—Chapter 4 has an in-depth guide to this MP3 player. For now, just follow these instructions and let the music play.

Follow these steps to install Sonique:

NOTE

During the installation, you may see messages and dialog boxes flash across the screen that aren't discussed here. Don't worry about them. As long as you eventually get to the message or dialog box described in the step you're working on, everything is proceeding smoothly.

1. Close all Windows applications. Sonique will tell you to do this early in the installation process, so you might as well save yourself trouble and do it now.
2. Insert the book CD in your computer's CD-ROM drive.
3. Using Windows Explorer, browse the CD until you reach *X*:\Stand-Alone Players\Sonique, where *X* is the drive letter for your CD-ROM drive. If the drive letter for your CD-ROM drive is D:, you would browse to D:\Stand-Alone Players\Sonique.
4. Double-click the file named **S105wma.exe** to run it. This contains all the files needed to run Sonique. When you run S105wma.exe, it expands into all the files needed to install Sonique, and starts the Setup program. The first thing it does is display a dialog box asking if you want to continue the installation process (see Figure 1.1).

FIGURE 1.1

When this dialog box appears, click Yes to continue installing Sonique.

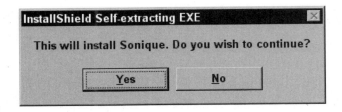

5. Click **Yes** to continue the installation process. When you do this, Setup goes about the process of getting ready to install the program (Figure 1.2). This can take a few minutes, so be patient. Eventually a Welcome dialog box appears (Figure 1.3).

FIGURE 1.2

Sonique Setup uses an InstallShield wizard to lead you through the installation process.

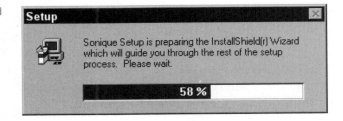

FIGURE 1.3

The Sonique Setup program's Welcome dialog box.

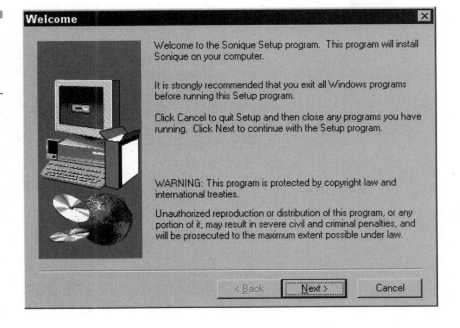

6. Click **Next** to continue. Setup displays the Software License Agreement shown in Figure 1.4.

FIGURE 1.4

Please read Sonique's software license agreement before continuing the installation.

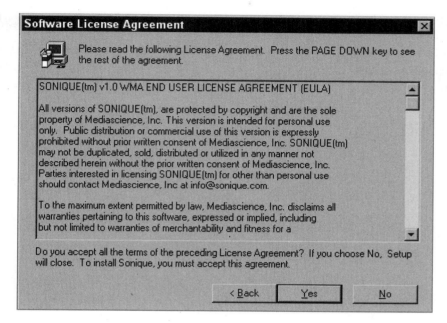

7. Read the license agreement then click **Yes** to accept the agreement, or **No** to abort the installation. If you click **Yes**, the Choose Destination Location dialog box appears, with a suggested Destination Directory appropriate for you computer (Figure 1.5).

8. Unless you have a good reason to do otherwise, click **Next** to let Setup install the program in the destination directory it suggests. When you do, the Select Program Folder dialog box appears. This dialog box shows a suggested folder for Sonique, along with a list of folders existing on your computer. The list in Figure 1.6 reflects some of the folders on my PC when I wrote this, and will include different folders on your computer.

9. As with choosing a Destination Directory, unless you have a strong reason to do otherwise, let Setup use the default folder it suggests by clicking **Next**. When you do, the Start Copying Files dialog box appears. As Figure 1.7 shows, this dialog box lists the settings Setup will use when actually

installing Sonique. Review these settings to be sure you're happy with them.

FIGURE 1.5

The Choose Destination Location dialog box lets you decide where to install Sonique.

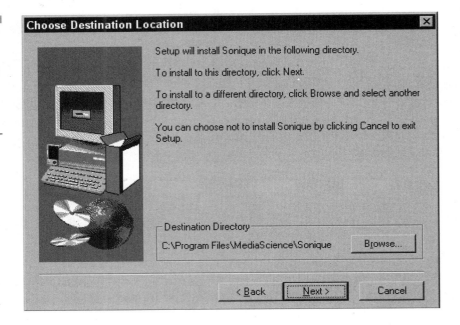

FIGURE 1.6

Use the Select Program Folder dialog box to tell Setup where to put Sonique's icons.

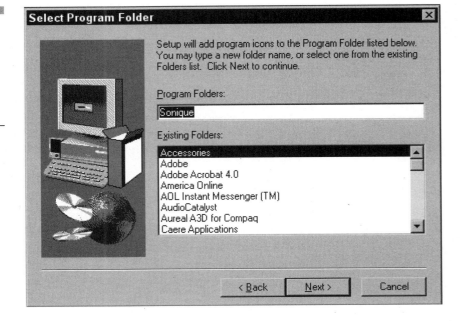

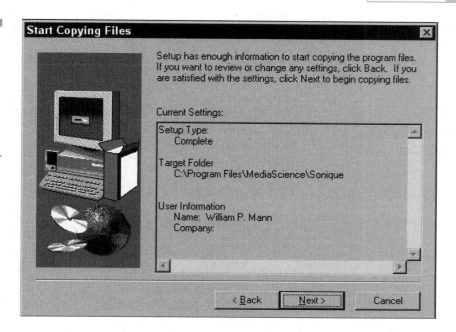

Click **Next** to continue. The Supported File Types dialog box shown in Figure 1.8 appears. Make sure the first two checkboxes, Mpeg audio files... and 'Modules'... are both checked. For now, leave the last two checkboxes unchecked. Once you have some experience with Sonique, you can decide whether you want to use it as your waveform audio file player and your audio CD player.

11. Click **Next** to continue. The Internet Connection Configuration dialog box in Figure 1.9 appears so you can select your Internet Connection Type. If your PC has a regular modem, and you have an Internet account, select the first option. If you have a cable modem or your PC is connected to a corporate network, select the second option. If you don't have any kind of access to the Internet, or have no idea, select the third option, "I do not have an Internet connection." If you eventually need to change this setting you can make the changes in Sonique's Setup Options pages.

FIGURE 1.8

*The Supported File
Types dialog box lets
you make Sonique
the default player for
certain kinds of
sound files.*

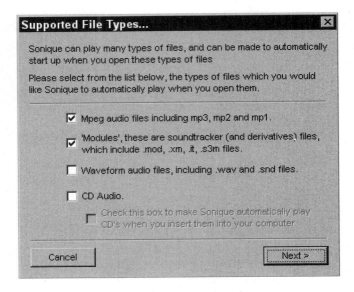

FIGURE 1.9

*Choose the
connection type
that matches your
equipment in the
Internet Connection
Configuration
dialog box.*

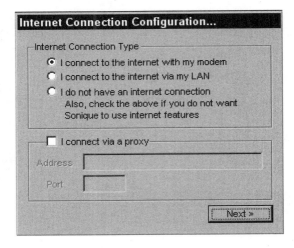

12. Once you've selected an Internet connection type, click **Next**
to continue. Setup now has all the information. Finally, just
when it seemed you would be clicking Next forever, Sonique
decompresses a bunch of information and copies it to your
PC (Figure 1.10). Once it finishes doing this, Setup displays
the Setup Complete dialog box in Figure 1.11.

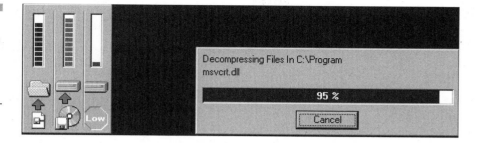

FIGURE 1.10

Setup will take a few moments to install the files it needs on your PC.

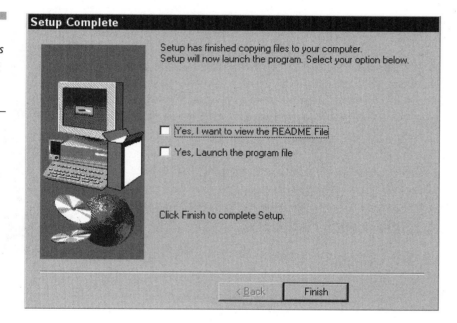

FIGURE 1.11

Setup has finished its work. You're almost ready to play some music.

13. If you have a Web browser on your computer (even if you don't have an Internet connection, your PC likely has a Web browser installed), check both checkboxes in the Setup Complete dialog box. If you don't have a Web browser or don't know, don't check the box that asks if you want to view the Readme file.

14. Click **Finish** to complete the installation process. Setup starts Sonique. If you elected to view the Readme file, Setup also starts your Web browser, and uses it to display Sonique's Readme file, a portion of which appears in Figure 1.12. Skim the Readme file to see if there are any issues of which you need to be aware.

15. If you have been looking at the Readme file, close your Web browser. That wild-looking gizmo (Figure 1.13) on your Windows Desktop—the one that looks like something out of a science fiction movie—is Sonique.

FIGURE 1.12

Even Sonique's Readme file is interesting.

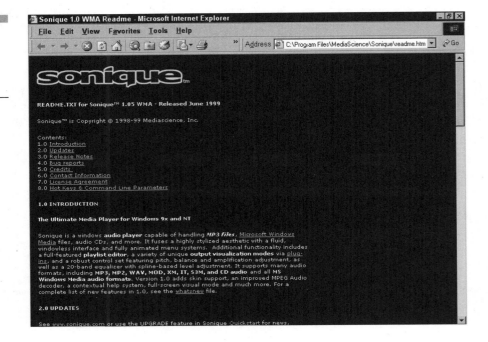

FIGURE 1.13

Sonique is not your run-of-the-mill Windows program.

Congratulations! You've installed your first MP3 player, and are only minutes away from playing your first MP3 file.

NOTE

Somewhere about now, if you told Sonique you have any kind of Internet connection in Step 11, it will try to connect to the Internet and look for available updates. You don't need to deal with this now. If Sonique asks you to connect to the Internet so it can look for updates, cancel that. If a dialog box like Figure 1.14 pops up on your screen, close it. Unless you specifically tell it not to, Sonique will periodically check with its home base on the World Wide Web and offer you the chance to install any available updates.

FIGURE 1.14

Sonique has found some updates you can install. Just click Close for now. You have some MP3s to play.

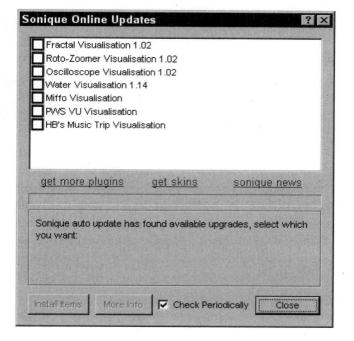

Playing Music

Sonique can play MP3 files whether they're on your hard drive or on a CD. To get your MP3 collection off to a good start, I've included a bunch of MP3s on the CD. As your very first track, I recommend "Rocket 95," by Alien Fashion Show. The Aliens play a combo of swing, cocktail, surf, and rockabilly that will get you off to a swinging start.

NOTE

Alien Fashion Show's self-named CD hit the stores in Summer of '98 and is distributed by Hollywood Records.

Follow these directions to get going:

1. Click the **Open File(s)** button on Sonique. You can do this by pointing the cursor at the various buttons and controls. As you move the cursor over these items, their names appear in the lower circle of the Sonique display. The Open File(s) button is the orange button on the left side of Sonique. When you click the **Open File(s)** button, the Open & Play Sonique Media dialog box appears.

2. Look for MP3s on the book CD. Click the down arrow on the right side of the Look in List box to display a list of drives and folders on your system. In this list, click the drive labeled **I Want My MP3!**. On most computer systems, this will be drive D: or E:. When you do this, the Look in List box closes, and a list of the folders on the CD appears.

3. Double-click the **Music** folder. This causes the Open & Play Sonique Media dialog box to fill up with the names of MP3 files available on the book CD (Figure 1.15). On this CD, the MP3 files are all named similarly: Band or Artist Name–Song.mp3. When dealing with MP3 files other than those on the book CD, you'll find that there are lots of different ways to name an MP3 file.

4. Find the MP3 named: Alien Fashion Show–Rocket 95.mp3.

5. Double-click the name of this MP3 file to start it playing. After a moment, the music should start playing, and you should see a bit of information about the track displayed in the lower circle of Sonique. If you're hearing the sounds of Alien Fashion Show, you're successfully playing your first MP3. Skip to the next section: "Playing Multiple Songs."

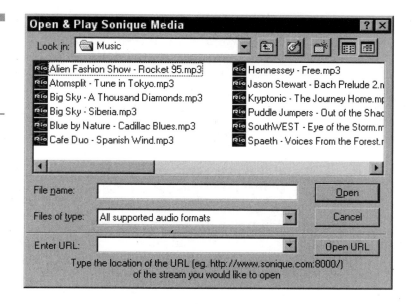

FIGURE 1.15
*Find tracks to play
with the Open &
Play Sonique Media
dialog box.*

What If It Doesn't Work?

If you don't hear any sound, but the timer at the top of the lower circle is counting, you may have some sort of hardware problem. There are a couple of things to try before turning to Chapter 12 for complete information on finding and fixing the problem.

Here is my quick and dirty approach to figuring out why your PC isn't playing MP3s even though you think it should. Just answer these questions:

1. Are your speakers or headphones plugged in to the PC?
2. If you have powered speakers, is their power supply plugged in to the wall?
3. If you have powered speakers, are they turned on?

If you answered Yes to all three questions, there's one last thing to try before heading to Chapter 12. While Sonique is trying to play an MP3, find the Sonique Volume Control Knob. This is a small yellow dial, located beneath the letters vol, on the right side of Sonique. Point at the dial with the mouse cursor, press and hold the left mouse button, then move the mouse back and forth to change the volume. Keep your fingers crossed that this works.

If you answered No to any of those questions, fix the problem and try playing the MP3 file again.

Playing Multiple Songs

Sonique lets you select multiple songs simultaneously from the Open & Play Sonique Media dialog box. To hear several songs, select the group, then click **Open**. You can use the standard Windows techniques to select multiple files, like holding down the Shift key while dragging the mouse over a series of songs, and holding down the Ctrl key while clicking individual MP3 files.

15 Minutes to Music Wrapup

You've reached the end of Chapter 1, "15 Minutes to Music." If all has gone as expected, you should now be listening to tunes in MP3 format. We hope it took you 15 minutes or less to get going. Regardless of how long it did take you to get here, you should now be ready to play MP3 files on your PC.

This chapter is for computer users who have little or no experience with MP3 files. Chapter 2, the other chapter in the Quick Start part of the book, is for users from all experience levels who are just looking for an answer to a specific question. Laid out like a Frequently Asked Question, or FAQ file, Chapter 2 directs you to answers to questions like: "Where can I shop for the hardware my PC needs to play MP3 files?," or "How can I listen to MP3s when I'm away from my desk." Chapter 2 tells you where in this book you can find the answers to these and dozens of other questions.

Even if Sonique is happily playing "Rocket 95" and other songs, you should at least take a look at Chapter 2. Sooner or later, you'll have a question, and you'll want to know where to go to find the answer.

CHAPTER 2

Just the Facts, Ma'am: A Paper-based FAQ

So many questions, so little time. "What the heck is an MP3 file?" "Should I install a new sound card in my PC?" "Where do I go to download some music, right now?" "What do I do with my huge CD collection?" "So, is this stuff actually legal?" If you picked up this book, you must have some questions about this MP3 music business. And the sooner you can get answers to your questions, the sooner you can start listening to MP3 music instead of fooling around with some book *about* MP3 music.

This whole book is designed to answer all your questions—including those you haven't even thought of yet. Read the book from end to end, and you'll get all answers. But if you just need that one little answer, that one tiny fact that'll get you moving in the right direction, you've come to the right chapter.

What Is a FAQ?

FAQ stands for Frequently Asked Question. FAQ files are common on the Internet, where they provide a convenient collection of answers to all sorts of questions about a Web site or other Net resource. This works out well for everyone concerned. The person with the question can get the answer required, right now, without having to ask someone and wait for a reply. For the someones who would otherwise have to answer all the questions, the benefit is the time and effort saved by answering the questions once, instead of dozens or hundreds of times.

This chapter is the printed equivalent of an Internet FAQ file. It lists all sorts of questions you might have about MP3. More important, it points you to the section of the book that has the answer to each question. The Table of Contents and the Index work well when you know the name or subject you're looking for. This paper-based FAQ does the job when you know the question, but don't have a clue to the answer. Here's an example:

You want to know the fate of your CD collection. Is this going to be like the switch from LP to CD, where you ended up getting rid of all your albums and replacing them with CDs? Finding the answer to a question like that is easy now. Just look through this chapter until you find the question that comes closest to yours.

Q: *What do I do with my huge CD collection?*

A: You can copy music from your audio CDs to MP3 files. Read Chapter 5, "Audio Catalyst and other Rippers and Encoders," or Chapter 6, "MusicMatch Jukebox and Ohter All-in-One MP3 Players."

While I've included every question I could think of in this chapter, I'm sure you and other readers will come up with ones I haven't. If you do, please e-mail your questions (and if the answers appear in the book) to me at **3manns@mediaone.net**.

General Questions and Answers

Q: *How can I get started with MP3 right away?*

A: If you have a CD-ROM drive, you can get started in minutes. See "Installing an MP3 Player," "Configuring Your Player," and "Playing Music" in Chapter 1.

Q: *How do I find out if my computer has what it takes to play MP3 music?*

A: Follow the instructions in Chapter 1, "15 Minutes to Music" to see if you can get the Sonique MP3 player up and running. If not, visit Chapter 12 for advice on figuring out what is going on.

Q: *Is it legal to make MP3 files?*

A: Yes! See the Introduction to get this common concern cleared up once and for all.

Q: *What is an MP3 file, anyway?*

A: See "What Is this MP3 Suff Anyway?" in the Introduction.

Q: *Why is everyone so worked up about MP3?*

A: This little file format is causing a big shakeup in the multi-billion dollar music industry. See the Introduction for more.

Q: *What do I do with my huge CD collection?*

A: You can copy music from your audio CDs to MP3 files. Read Chapter 5, "AudioCatalyst and Other Rippers and Encoders," or Chapter 6, "MusicMatch Jukebox and Other All-in-One MP3 Players."

Q: *Is ripping and encoding music legal?*

A: See "What Legal Tangles?" in Chapter 5.

Q: *Can I chat with other MP3 fanatics online?*

A: Probably the biggest place to hang out with other MP3 enthusiasts is in the Community section of MP3.com. See "Community" in Chapter 9.

Q: *Is it true that MP3 sites are full of pornography?*

A: Pornography is present on the Internet, regardless of what kind of site you are looking at. Most MP3 sites, like most of the people surfing the Net, avoid online porn. However, if you decide to search out MP3 Web sites on your own, you may get more than you bargained for. Read the sidebar titled "Web Surfers Beware: What You Click is Not Always What You Get" in Chapter 10.

If you stick with Web sites recommended in this book, you shouldn't run into any pornography.

Q: *How do I find porn-free MP3 music pages that aren't covered in the book?*

A: Stick with the major sites and you should be fine. If you want to poke around among the lesser sites, think about visiting the Pure MP3 site, which guarantees no porn on the sites it links to, or the sites they link to. See "Pure MP3" in Chapter 10 for more information.

Q: *Most of the music on the Web seems to be American. Are there places I can go to get European music?*

A: Of course there are. Try "WorldWideBands," "Crunch," and "swebmusic.com" in Chapter 10.

Q: *How can I tell if a file I find on the Internet is authorized or pirated?*

A: Read "Is This File Legal" in Chapter 11 for tips on how to tell if a file is authorized for MP3 distribution or is pirated.

Q: *Is there any way to search the entire Internet for a particular song?*

A: There are several Internet search engines that can do exactly that. See Chapter 11, "Finding that Particular Sound: MP3 Search Engines" for the full story.

Q: *Are there things I can do to make my PC a better MP3 player without opening the case?*

A: Chapter 12, "Pumping Up Your PC for MP3" shows you a number of things you can do to juice up your tired old machine without actually taking off the cover and poking around inside.

Q: *What is it really like to own a portable MP3 player?*

A: It is great. See "Living with Rio" in Chapter 15 for my impressions.

Q: *How can I find out what's new in the world of MP3 music?*

A: For general news, pick up any newspaper or magazine. For day-to-day action, go online. If you surf the Web, see Chapter 17, *MP3 News Web Sites*. If you don't have Web access, or would like the news delivered to your inbox, see Chapter 18, "MP3 Newsgroups, Mailing Lists, and Newsletters."

Q: *What's on the CD tucked into the back of this book?*

A: Loads of goodies to get you up and running right away. For more details, see the Appendix, "MP3 on a Silver(y) Platter."

Software Questions and Answers

Q: *What software do I need to play MP3 files?*

A: See Chapter 3, "Players and Other MP3 Programs."

Q: *What is a ripper?*

A: It is the software you need to convert songs on audio CDs into MP3 files. See "Rippers and Encoders" in Chapter 3.

Q: *What's a playlist?*

A: See "So, Tell Me More About Playlists" in Chapter 3 for the full story.

Q. *Will I run into problems if I have more than one MP3 player on my computer?*

A. Not normally. There is, however, one situation where you might have trouble. Read the "Who's in Charge Here" sidebar in Chapter 4 for more information.

Q: *I just want some software to play MP3s on my PC. Which programs do you recommend?*

A: You can find over 140 MP3 player programs on the Internet. To see which are my favorites, read Chapter 4, "Sonique™ and Other Standalone MP3 Players," and Chapter 6, "MusicMatch Jukebox and Other All-in-One MP3 Players."

Q: *What is a Sonique skin?*

A: A Sonique skin changes the look of the Sonique user interface. See "Installing and Using Skins" in Chapter 4.

Q: *What is an all-in-one player?*

A: An all-in-one player is software that combines an MP3 player with a ripper, encoder, playlist, and other utilities. See Chapter

6, "MusicMatch Jukebox and Other All-in-One MP3 Players" for some examples.

Q: *Ok. So what the heck is a normalizer?*

A: See "WavNormalizer" in Chapter 7 to learn what a normalizer does.

Q: *Is the term ID3 related to all this MP3 stuff in some way?*

A: Yes it is. See "ID3 Editor" in Chapter 7 to learn about ID3 tags.

Q: *Are there any cool utilities to make working with MP3 files easier?*

A: As a matter of fact, there are. Check out Chapter 7, "Cool Utility Guide."

Q: *Where can I get the latest MP3 software?*

A: The Internet is the home of all things MP3. See Chapter 8, "Finding MP3 Software Online."

Q: *Where can I find reviews and downloads of MP3 software?*

A: Go to MP3.com (Chapter 9, "The Heart of the Movement: MP3.com"), and any of the sites in Chapter 8, "Finding MP3 Software Online."

Q: *I hear a lot about FTP. What does it mean, and why do I care?*

A: Many sites let you download MP3 music files using FTP (File Transfer Protocol). For the whys, wherefores, and a program that'll make the whole thing simple, see "Downloading MP3 Files from FTP Sites" in Chapter 11.

Q: *What in the world is that roaring noise coming out of my computer?*

A: That's a program called Go!Zilla, letting you know that it has successfully downloaded another MP3 file from an FTP site. Go!Zilla is covered in Chapter 11, "Finding that Particular Sound: MP3 Search Engines."

Music Questions and Answers

Q: *Where can I download more music?*

A: Start with Chapter 9, "The Heart of the Movement: MP3.com." If you don't find what you're looking for there, try Chapter 10, "Other Sources of MP3 Files."

Q: *Is there any free MP3 music available from big name bands?*

A: Although the record companies may be resisting MP3, you can still get some free music in MP3 format from big-names like Alanis Morissette and the Grateful Dead. See "Free Music" in Chapter 10, and all of Chapter 11, "Finding that Particular Sound: MP3 Search Engines."

Q: *How do I find a specific song or band?*

A: See Chapter 11, "Finding that Particular Sound: MP3 Search Engines."

Q: *Do I have to check all those MP3 search engines one-by-one to find what I want.*

A: No. That's where meta MP3 search engines come into play. See "Meta MP3 Search Engines" in Chapter 11 for several that you can use.

Q: *Can I get personalized music recommendations?*

A: Yes, at MP3.com. This aspect of MP3.com is covered in Chapter 18, "MP3 Newsgroups, Mailing Lists, and Newsletters."

Hardware Questions and Answers

Q: *Can my computer play MP3 files?*

A: Most new machines can do so right out of the box. Older machines might need an upgrade. See "Figuring Out if Your

PC is Ready to Play MP3s" in Chapter 1. For more details, see "What hardware do I need?" in Chapter 12.

Q: *Do all CD-ROM drives work for ripping music?*

A: Most, but not all of them work fine. For more on this, see "CD-ROM Drive Peculiarities" in Chapter 5.

Q: *Where can I find reviews of MP3 hardware?*

A: There are quite a few places with useful information, if you know where to look. Try MP3.com (Chapter 9, "The Heart of the Movement: MP3.com"), and Chapter 16, "Finding Hardware Online."

Q: *Is there anything special I should know before opening up my PC?*

A: See "Things You Should Do" and "Tricks You Should Use" in Chapter 13.

Q: *What's the difference between CD-ROM drives, CD-R drives, and CD-RW drives?*

A: See "Burning Your Own CDs: The Basics" in Chapter 14.

Q: *How can I listen to MP3s away from my computer?*

A: See "Portable Players," "Home Players," and "Car Players" in Chapter 15.

Q: *My CD-ROM drive won't rip CDs. Do I have to replace it?*

A: Not necessarily. See "The MusicMatch Jukebox Phenomenon" in Chapter 12 for a trick you can try before spending any money on a new drive.

Q: *Can I play my MP3s on my stereo?*

A: No problem. See "Cranking It out Through Your Stereo" in Chapter 12, and "Home Players" in Chapter 15 for two approaches to the solution.

Q: *How do I add a sound card to my computer?*

A: For instructions and advice, see Chapter 13, "Working inside the Box."

Q: *Should I add a CD-ROM drive to my computer? Why? How do I do it?*

A: Yes, if you want to copy songs from your CD collection into MP3 format, or play with all the toys on the CD-ROM in the back of this book. See "Installing a CD-ROM Drive" in Chapter 13.

Q: *Can I use this MP3 stuff to make my own audio CDs?*

A: Yes you can. See Chapter 14, "Burning Your Own CDs."

Q: *Can I play my MP3 in the car?*

A: Yes, but it will cost you. See "Car Players" in Chapter 15.

Q: *How can I get a good deal on the hardware I need?*

A: Shop the Web. See Chapter 16, "Finding Hardware Online."

Q: *What is a shopbot site?*

A: Shopbots do your online comparison shopping for you. See "Shopbot Sites" in Chapter 16.

Q: *Can I buy portable MP3 players direct from the manufacturers?*

A: Of course. To understand the pros and cons of doing this, see "Manufacturers' Stores" in Chapter 16.

Q: *Where can I get advice and information on the latest PC hardware?*

A: Many of the online stores include buying guides and other useful information. See "CNET Shopper" in Chapter 16 for a great example.

Q: *Where can I get the best prices on portable MP3 players?*

A: Visit "20-20 Consumer" in Chapter 17 for the latest prices and availability.

PART 2

The Software You Need

This part of the book takes you beyond the basics and into more depth on the software available for playing MP3 files. You can take two basic approaches to MP3. In the component approach, you mix and match this player with that ripper, the other encoder, and a number of utilities. If you built your stereo component by component, or assembled your own PC, this approach should appeal to you. But there is also the all-in-one approach, where you choose a single program that can do anything you might want to do. If you are more concerned with getting some music on and getting back to the rest of your life, this approach should sound good.

One thing that struck me when I was writing Part 2 was the international nature of MP3 software. Countries of origin for the software in this part of the book include Australia, France, Germany, Greece, Indonesia, Israel, Korea, Norway, and United States.

Chapter 3 is your overview of the major kinds of MP3 software available. Reading it will help you decide whether to use a standalone MP3 player and go for the component approach, or use an all-in-one MP3 player and not have to deal with separate rippers, playlist editors, and all the rest.

Chapter 4 features Sonique, the player you installed if you read Chapter 1. In that chapter, you learned just enough about Sonique to be dangerous (that is, to play some music). This chapter takes a more in-depth look at Sonique, giving you the information you need to take advantage of the program. The chapter also covers two other standalone players: XingMP3 Player and RealPlayer G2.

Chapter 5 covers AudioCatalyst and other rippers and encoders. These are the programs you need if you are taking the component approach to MP3, and you want to be able to rip (copy) music from your audio CD collection into MP3 format.

Chapter 6 looks at the all-in-one programs and features MusicMatch Jukebox. You can install MusicMatch Jukebox from this book' CD-ROM, then follow along as the chapter explores the powerful features of this program. I think MusicMatch Jukebox is the ideal all-in-one MP3 program, but in case you want to check out the competition, I have included coverage of RealJukebox, the closest thing to MusicMatch Jukebox competition I've seen.

Chapter 7 covers the basic utilities you'll need if you follow the component approach to MP3. It also covers some of the interesting and unusual utilities available to enhance your MP3 playing experience.

You now know what kind of MP3 software is available, and are probably using some of the material that came on the book's CD-ROM. But MP3 software is evolving at blinding speeds. Chapter 8 shows you where to go on the Internet to get the very latest MP3 software. The Web sites listed in this chapter have the latest version of literally hundreds of MP3-related programs. Find what you want, download it (paying any required fees in the process), and go.

CHAPTER 3

Players and Other MP3 Programs

Did you know there is more to MP3 software than hot players like Sonique and MusicMatch Jukebox? Ever heard of rippers, normalizers, or ID3 editors? If not, as that old song says, "You need some educatin'." For all I know, you're listening to one of the MP3's on the book CD right now. But even if you are, you'll get more out of MP3 if you learn a bit about the variety of software floating around the Net.

This chapter gives you the straight story on:

- Standalone MP3 player programs
- Rippers and encoders
- All-in-one MP3 player programs
- MP3 utilities.

This chapter can help you decide if you want to go with the all-in-one approach to your MP3 music, or if you will assemble your system component-by-component. The first approach is probably best if your goal is to get a quality solution as quickly as possible. The second approach could be for you if you are the kind of person who builds your stereo systems out of carefully selected individual components, instead of just buying an entire system as a set.

Standalone MP3 Player Programs

The absolute minimum you need to enjoy MP3 music is a standalone MP3 player. Well over 100 players are available on the Internet, most of them freeware. Any standalone MP3 player can play any standard MP3 file. To stand out, standalone MP3 players compete on features, overall quality (does it sound good, work reliably, and do what you expect it to), and sheer coolness.

DEFINITION

A **standalone MP3 player** can play music and have many other capabilities, but lack the ability to rip tracks from audio CDs and encode them in MP3 format.

DEFINITION

Freeware is software that is copyrighted, but for which there is no charge.

To be a real competitor, any standalone MP3 player should do all these things:

- Play MP3s cleanly and accurately, without unduly bogging down your computer
- Work with few glitches or bugs
- Display the name of the song that's playing
- Include all the basic controls you would see on your CD player: Start, Stop, Pause, Next Track, Previous Track, and a Volume Control
- Include at least a minimal playlist editor (more on these in the Utilities section of this chapter)
- Be fun to look at.

Two players that fit the bill perfectly are Sonique and XingMP3 Player. Sonique is my favorite standalone MP3 player. It works flawlessly, sounds great, and looks wild. The user interface is a little funky (Figure 3.1), but once you get used to it, it's no problem.

FIGURE 3.1

Sonique is a quality standalone MP3 player and is included on the CD in the back of the book.

XingMP3 Player is a late arrival to the party, but don't let that bother you. Xing has been creating top-quality audio and video software for PCs for years. This standalone player is solid. While XingMP3 Player doesn't have the wild looks of Sonique, it is more fun to look at than most Windows programs (Figure 3.2). XingMP3 Player also has connections. With it, you're only one click away from AudioCatalyst, Xing's excellent combined CD ripper/MP3 encoder.

FIGURE 3.2

XingMP3 Player gives you all the basics you need, in a more conventional package.

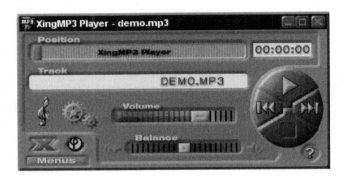

Even if you don't plan to follow the component approach to MP3, you should check out Chapter 4, "Sonique and Other Standalone MP3 Players" and give some of these toys a try.

Rippers and Encoders

One of the best things about MP3 is that it allows you to get music off an audio CD and into your PC. To do this, you must somehow convert the music from the format in which it is stored on the CD into MP3 format. Doing this is a two-step process. Step 1 is converting the music file on your audio CD into a kind of file that programs running on your PC can understand. Step 1 is done with a type of program known as a ripper.

A **ripper** is a program that can read an audio track from a CD and convert it into a file (a Windows WAV file, specifically) on your hard drive.

DEFINITION

There are many rippers on the Internet. One I like is Win-DAC32 (Figure 3.3). This program lets you rip tracks from audio CDs, as well as do some minor editing of those files.

FIGURE 3.3

WinDAC32 is a freeware ripper included on the book CD.

Track	Playtime	Starttime	Drivespace nee...	Copyprotection	Pre-Emphasis	Tracknumber
You Give Good Love	00:04:36.05	00:00:02.00	46.44 MB	Yes	No	1
Thinking About You	00:05:28.62	00:04:38.05	55.32 MB	Yes	No	2
Someone For Me	00:05:00.38	00:10:06.67	50.55 MB	Yes	No	3
Saving All My Love For You	00:04:01.25	00:15:07.30	40.60 MB	Yes	No	4
Nobody Loves Me Like You Do	00:03:48.00	00:19:08.55	38.36 MB	Yes	No	5
How Will I Know	00:04:31.62	00:22:56.55	45.73 MB	Yes	No	6
All At Once	00:04:29.13	00:27:28.42	45.28 MB	Yes	No	7
Take Good Care Of My Heart	00:04:22.12	00:31:57.55	44.10 MB	Yes	No	8
Greatest Love Of All	00:04:58.25	00:36:19.67	50.19 MB	Yes	No	9
Hold Me	00:06:02.68	00:41:18.17	61.05 MB	Yes	No	10

CD inserted | Playtime 00:00:29.61 h:m:s.f | Actual track : 01

Once you have copies of the music on your PC, you can play them with some of the standard Windows utilities. Even so, files that have only been ripped are of little use to you because they are huge. For example, Eye of the Storm, one of the songs included on the CD in the back of the book, occupies over 57 MB (megabytes) of disk space. As an MP3 file, this same song takes up only 5 1/3 MB of disk space. That's less than 1/10 the space of the file when it is first ripped from the CD. Converting the file from WAV format (the format files are usually ripped to) to MP3 format is Step 2. Step 2 is a job for type of program known as an encoder.

DEFINITION

An **encoder** is a program that can convert a Windows WAV file into MP3 format.

Although lots of encoders are available on the Internet, there is a catch: Thomson Multimedia and Fraunhofer IIS-A own numerous patents related to MPEG1 Layer-3 (a more technical term for MP3). Fraunhofer and Thomson offer licenses to use the patented technology, but most of the free encoders available today violate the patents and are not licensed. So while finding an encoder is easy, finding one that is legal isn't so easy. Fortunately, there are a few solutions to this problem. One is to use the example encoder Fraunhofer IIS-A makes available on their Web site. This encoder is slow, but does an excellent job of converting WAV files to MP3 files. The biggest problem with it is that it is relatively hard to use, as it was designed to demonstrate encoding, not for regular use by consumers.

Another approach is to use an encoder that someone has licensed from Fraunhofer IIS-A and Thomson. Xing's encoder, XingMP3 Encoder, works wonderfully, as does Xing's AudioCatalyst ripper/encoder (which includes Xing's encoder technology). The hitch with this is that Xing owes licensing fees to Fraunhofer and Thomson. As a result, these products are not free.

FIGURE 3.4
AudioCatalyst combines a ripper with the excellent XingMP3 Encoder, making it a complete CD-to-MP3 tool.

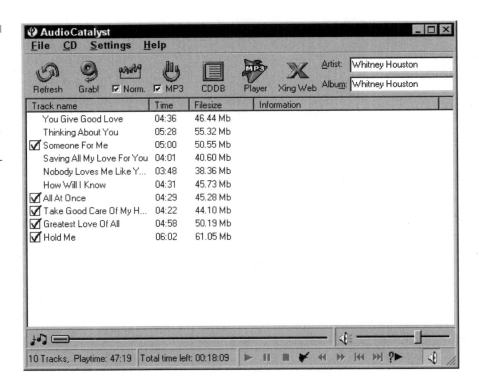

Fortunately, AudioCatalyst (Figure 3.4) is available as shareware, so you can try it before you actually have to spend any money.

DEFINITION

Shareware is software marketed on a try-before-you-buy basis. Test it out, see if you like it, then pay to register it if you decide to keep using it.

If you plan to take the individual component approach to MP3, you need to visit Chapter 5, "AudioCatalyst and Other Rippers and Encoders," where rippers and encoders are covered in detail.

All-in-One MP3 Player Programs

All-in-one MP3 players are the ultimate in MP3 software. As their name implies, all-in-one players can do virtually anything you want with an MP3 file. By definition, they include all of these things:

■ A player component that plays MP3 files—and usually other kinds of files—and audio CDs

■ Some sort of playlist editor to help you organize your music in ways that make sense for you

■ Rippers and encoders so you can record music from your audio CDs into MP3 format.

The top all-in-one players also include links to Internet resources (music Web sites, free online upgrades, things like that) and other added benefits. To my mind, the two top all-in-one players available today are MusicMatch Jukebox and RealJukebox.

DEFINITION

An **all-in-one MP3 player** is one that includes a playlist editor, audio CD ripper, and MP3 encoder, in addition to its ability to play MP3 files.

MusicMatch Jukebox (Figure 3.5) has everything you want in an all-in-one player. In addition to all the features listed earlier, it includes an automatic normalizer (see "MP3 Utilities" for more on normalizers) and when ripping music from CDs, will automatically get track information from CDDB, the world's largest database of CD information. MusicMatch Jukebox also takes advantage of the flexibility of the MP3 format to display album covers, lyrics, author bios, and other information for files that have this information included. A shareware copy is included on the book CD.

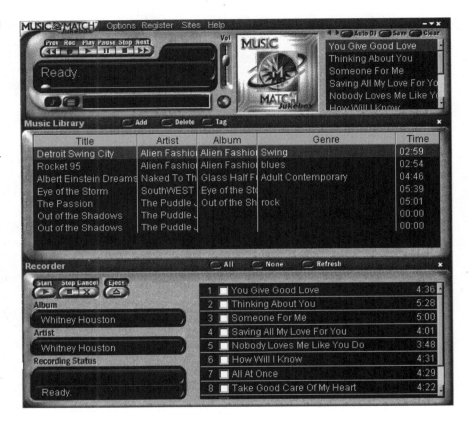

FIGURE 3.5

MusicMatch Jukebox combines a Player, Music Library, CD Recorder, and more into one professional package.

RealJukebox (Figure 3.6) is a new entrant in the all-in-one MP3 player competition. It too, does everything on the list and more. The RealJukebox Music Library lets you create playlists, but can automatically group your music by artist, album, or genre for you. RealJukebox has a large collection of links to Internet music sites and to the CDDB Web site.

If you're considering the all-in-one approach to MP3, head for Chapter 6, "MusicMatch Jukebox and Other All-in-One MP3 Players," where you'll get lots more information on MusicMatch Jukebox and RealJukebox.

FIGURE 3.6

RealJukebox is a new and exciting all-in-one player.

MP3 Utilities

Once you have an MP3 player and a ripper/encoder, you have everything you need to play existing MP3 files and create your own from your CD collection. However, well-chosen utilities can really improve your experience. Just ask all the people (maybe you're one of them) who buy packages like Norton Utilities to enhance their Windows computing experience. So the question is, How can I make MP3 even better than it already is, and can I get a utility to help? The answer is: People have come up with several ways to make MP3 cooler, and of course there are utilities to help.

Start by thinking about how you'll deal with your MP3 collection once you have hundreds of files. Just keeping track of what you have could be a problem. You won't want to let duplicate songs accumulate in your collection. And you'll probably get tired of manually choosing which files you'll listen to. You could let the MP3 player choose randomly, but suppose you want a particular mood. You might be looking for rowdy music to get you through a boring task. Or maybe you'll be in the mood for something mellow. Or maybe classical music helps you study. Whatever the case, keeping track of hundreds or thousands of files, and picking through them to find the particular ones you want to listen to is a pain.

> **So, Tell Me More About Playlists**
>
> A playlist is a list of songs grouped together for whatever reason suits you. You could create a rowdy playlist, a mellow playlist, and a classical playlist. You could also create a list of all the songs written by artists who changed their names into some unpronounceable symbol, or songs about Cleveland. A playlist utility lets you create and save playlists, then call them up and listen to them whenever you wish.

What you need is a playlist utility. See the sidebar "So, Tell Me More About Playlists" above for more details on exactly what a playlist utility is. Some standalone MP3 players and all-in-one programs (Sonique and MusicMatch Jukebox, for example) include basic playlist capabilities. Even so, you might want to investigate the capabilities of separate playlist utilities. To make that easy, the CD in the back of this book contains a copy of ShufflePlay, a superior playlist utility from flipTech Software. Figure 3.7 a shows the ShufflePlay home page, where you can read about the wide range of capabilities this program offers beyond basic playlist management.

FIGURE 3.7
flipTech Software is the home of ShufflePlay, a superb playlist utility.

When you rip a file from a CD, especially with some of the older rippers, you sometimes need to do a little massaging. That is, you sometimes need to do things like adjust the sound level of the recording or remove pops. Programs for adjusting the sound level of a file are *normalizers*. Normalizers typically work on the file after you copy it from the CD, but before you convert it into MP3 format. You can find a fine normalizer, WavNormalizer, on the CD in the back of this book.

Pop removers also work on sound files after you copy a song off a CD, but before you convert them to an MP3. The exact reasons for pops vary, but removers can eliminate pops for you.

One of the great things about MP3 files is the *ID3 tag*; a section added to the MP3 file that contains the name of the artist, the album the song came from, and other useful and interesting information. However, the tracks you rip from a CD won't include all that information. With an ID3 tag editor, you can enter that information yourself. For your ID3 tag editing pleasure, we've included a copy of ID3 Editor 1.0 (Figure 3.8), an easy-to-use, free ID3 editor, on the CD in the back of the book.

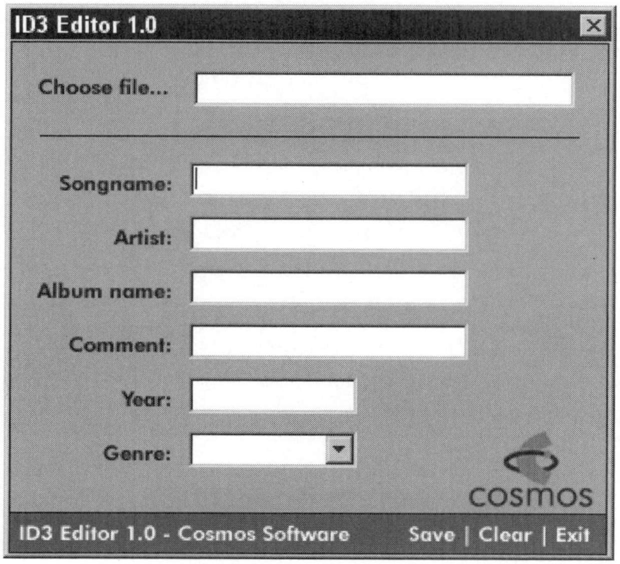

FIGURE 3.8

Add useful background information to your MP3 files with ID3 Editor 1.0.

Beyond the types of utilities you've just read about (playlist editors, normalizers, pop removers, and ID3 editors), there are all sorts of more specialized programs. If you want to be able to play particular MP3 files whenever you feel like it, but don't want to deal with creating playlists, one utility will let you click on the Windows desktop, click on an MP3 file, and start it playing. That utility is MP3 PopUp!, which puts an icon in the Windows System Tray on the right side of the Windows Status Bar. Once you have MP3 PopUp! configured, all it takes is a few clicks to start playing any MP3 file on your system.

The utilities described here are all covered in more detail in Chapter 7, "Cool Utility Guide."

Chapter Wrapup

There are two approaches to MP3 software. One is the all-in-one approach, where you choose a program like MusicMatch Jukebox, and let it do everything for you—ripping tracks from CDs, normalizing them, converting them to MP3 format, organizing them into playlists, and playing them back, an all-in-one player like MusicMatch Jukebox can do it. The other approach is the component-by-component approach, where you assemble your toolkit out of standalone rippers, encoders, players, and other tools.

The path you choose depends on your needs, interests, and personality. Whichever path you choose, this book has the information (and much of the software) you need to follow it.

For advocates of the component-by-component approach, the first thing you need is a standalone MP3 player. The next chapter features one player, Sonique, as well as some capable alternatives. Even if you're going to go with the all-in-one approach, give these standalone players a try first.

CHAPTER 4

Sonique™ and Other Standalone MP3 Players

The Web is flooded with MP3 players. DailyMP3, a Web site with a comprehensive collection of links lists around 140 MP3 players. Without help, choosing a top player could be tough. This chapter is primarily an in-depth guide to Sonique™, likely the most popular standalone MP3 player. Once you figure out Sonique's interface, you will find it to be capable, flexible, and flat-out fun to use.

A **standalone MP3 player** is an MP3 player that lacks the ability to rip tracks from audio CDs and encode them in MP3 format.

DEFINITION

But Sonique is not for everyone. The last part of this chapter covers two other standalone MP3 players with outstanding pedigrees: XingMP3 Player and RealPlayer G2.

Here are the high notes you'll hit in this chapter:

▌ Installing, configuring, and using Sonique
▌ XingMP3 player
▌ RealPlayer G2.

Sonique

Sonique is a powerful, capable, and flat-out fun media player from Mediascience, Inc.

TIP

Sonique stands out from the crowd of standalone players. Even ignoring that it works and looks good, the reasons for this include:

▌ Multiple screen modes
▌ Full range of audio controls
▌ Built-in playlist editor
▌ Sonique Online, with links to upgrades, music, news, and more, all from the player
▌ Sonique Contextual Help System, giving single-click access to mode-specific help

- Plug-ins that allow third parties to add new visual effects and support for new file formats
- Skins, allowing anyone to create wholly new looks for Sonique.

If you started with Chapter 1, you installed Sonique, and learned just enough about it to play the MP3s included on the book CD. Consider this chapter your guide to the middle levels of Sonique proficiency. By the time you finish it, you'll be able to play songs, adjust settings, change video modes, get help, and use plug-ins and skins. You can stop right there and know everything you need to know for happy use of Sonique as your MP3 (and audio CD) player.

NOTE

You can go much further with Sonique, learning all the tricks and tips, memorizing the keyboard shortcuts, creating your own skins, and generally immersing yourself in Sonique. But you'll have to do it on your own. The rest of us are getting off at the stop labeled, "Happy as clams playing our music and choosing skins."

Sonique System Requirements

To use Sonique successfully, your system must meet these requirements:

- Windows 95 or 98, or Windows NT 4.0 operating system
- Pentium 100 or better processor
- 16 MB of RAM
- 16-bit color
- Sound card
- Speakers or headphones.

Where to Get Sonique

Thanks to the people at Mediascience, Inc., we are able to include a copy of Sonique on the CD in the back of this book. Installing this version will let you get up and going right away. However, to get the best value out of the program, you need to visit the

Sonique Web site at **www.sonique.com** to get the latest version of Sonique, as well as to find plug-ins and skins to customize Sonique.

What Does Sonique Cost?

Sonique is freeware, so you can use it to your heart's content for free.

Installing Sonique

Follow these steps to install Sonique:

NOTE

During the installation process, Sonique will strongly recommend that you close all other Windows applications until you finish the installation. It would be a good idea to do so now, and save yourself the trouble of exiting Setup, closing everything, then restarting Setup.

1. Insert the book CD in your computer's CD-ROM drive.
2. Using Windows Explorer, browse the CD until you reach *X*:\Stand-Alone Players\Sonique, where *X* is the drive letter for your CD-ROM drive.
3. Double-click the file named **s105wma.exe**. This is a self-extracting executable file that does the actual work of installing Sonique on your system. The first thing it does is display a dialog box asking if you want to continue the installation process.
4. Click **Yes** to continue the installation process. When you do this, Setup goes about the process of installing the program. This can take a few minutes, so be patient. Eventually a Welcome dialog box appears.
5. Click **Next** to continue. Setup displays the Software License Agreement.
6. Read the license agreement then click **Yes** to accept the agreement, or **No** to abort the installation. If you click **Yes**, the Choose Destination Location dialog box appears.
7. Unless you have a good reason to do otherwise, click **Next** to let Setup install the program in the destination directory it suggests. The Select program Folder dialog box appears.

8. Let Setup use the default folder it suggests by clicking **Next**. The Start Copying Files dialog box appears.

9. Click **Next** to continue. The Supported File Types dialog box appears. Make sure the first two checkboxes, Mpeg audio files..., and 'Modules'... are both checked. For now, leave the last two checkboxes unchecked. Once you have some experience with Sonique, you can decide whether you want to use it as your waveform audio file player and your audio CD player.

10. Click **Next** to continue. The Internet Connection Configuration dialog box appears. Select your Internet Connection Type.

11. Click **Next** to continue. Finally, just when it seemed you would be clicking Next forever, Sonique copies information to your PC, and displays the Setup Complete dialog box.

12. If you have a Web browser on your computer, check both checkboxes in the Setup Complete dialog box. If you don't have a Web browser, don't check the box that asks if you want to view the Readme file.

13. Click **Finish** to complete the installation process. Setup starts Sonique. If you elected to view the Readme file, Setup also starts your Web browser, and uses it to display Sonique's Readme file. Read through the Readme file to catch any last minute issues.

14. Close your browser. You're ready to configure Sonique.

Configuring Sonique

In most cases, you don't need to do any additional configuration beyond the bit you do while installing Sonique. However, Sonique does support a full range of configuration options. It's worth taking a quick look at them, just so you know what is possible. You will do that later in this chapter, once you learn about Sonique's various display modes and how to switch between them.

NOTE

This chapter assumes that your PC is set up to play music. That is, that your PC has a sound card installed and configured properly, and that you have speakers or headphones properly connected to the PC. Most newer PCs are already set up this way and should have no problem playing music. If you know your system does not meet with these preconditions, stop now and read "Part 4: The Hardware You Need." If you aren't sure that your PC meets these preconditions, your best bet is to keep following the instructions that are coming up. If you follow these instructions and don't hear any sound, that's a good indication that your PC isn't ready to play music. Chapter 12, "Pumping Up Your PC for MP3" will help you determine where the problem lies and how to fix it.

Using Sonique

It's time to actually play some music. Start Sonique by double-clicking the Sonique icon on your Windows desktop. If this is the first time you run Sonique, you should see a splash screen (a welcoming screen that introduces the program and publisher) for several seconds, followed by Sonique itself. What you see on the screen will look very similar to Figure 4.1. If this isn't what you were expecting to see, don't panic. All will become clear soon.

NOTE

If you want to move Sonique around on the screen, point at the border around the outside of the Sonique window and drag it.

FIGURE 4.1

Sonique's Navigation Console gives you easy access to many of the key screens in the program.

What you see in Figure 4.1 is the Navigation screen of the Navigation console. The Navigation screen gives you access to the six screens that comprise the Navigation console. For now, don't worry about all those other screens. All you need to know is that the large area where all the text appears is the Visualization Display area, and that the music controls are grouped below and to the right of the Visualization Display area.

NOTE

If you ever forget which of the music controls is which, point at it with the mouse cursor for a few seconds. The name of the button will then appear for several seconds at the bottom of the Visualization Display area.

Playing a Song

There are three small buttons just below the Visualization Display area. These are, from left to right, the Open File(s) button, the Repeat Modes button, and the Shuffle Mode button. To play a song, all you need is the Open File(s) button. Click Open File(s), and Sonique displays the Open & Play Sonique Media dialog box. As Figure 4.2 shows, this dialog box is like a regular Windows File Open dialog box, with the addition of one section at the bottom. That section deals with streaming media, which is another of Sonique's capabilities, one you can explore on your own after you master playing MP3s on Sonique.

You can use this dialog box to find songs or playlists to play and apply new skins, but for now, your mission is to find an MP3 file to play. Your best bet is to insert the book CD in the CD-ROM drive and browse that CD until you find the Music folder. Rummage around in there a bit until you find an MP3 file name that looks interesting.

Double-click the file name to open the file you want to play. Once you open the file, Sonique starts playing it. If your system is set up right, you should now be hearing music. Congratulations!

You can adjust the volume by twisting the Volume Control knob. This is the small knob labeled **vol** in the right-hand corner of the Sonique window. To adjust the volume, point at the knob, hold down the left mouse button, and move the mouse left or right. I find this knob hard to adjust, but maybe you are more coordinated than I am.

FIGURE 4.2

Use the Open & Play Sonique Media dialog box to find songs anywhere on your system.

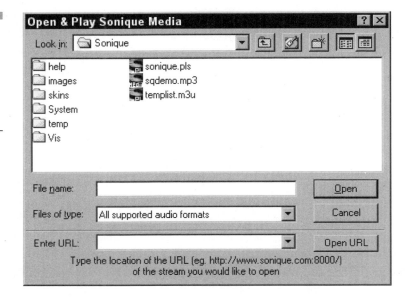

What if I Don't Hear Any Music?

If you're not hearing music, look at Sonique. The name of the song you selected should be scrolling across the bottom of the screen, and a counter should be busily counting off the seconds and minutes since you opened the MP3 file. If you don't see the counter counting, Sonique isn't playing the song.

If the counter is counting, make sure your headphones are plugged in, or your speakers are plugged in and turned on. If you still hear nothing, try turning up the volume on Sonique. If that doesn't work, it is time to head for Chapter 12 to figure out what the problem is.

Playing Multiple Songs

Sonique lets you select multiple songs simultaneously. To hear several songs, select the whole group, then click **Open**. You can use the standard Windows techniques to select multiple files, like holding down the **Shift** key while dragging the mouse over a series of songs, and holding down the **Ctrl** key while clicking on individual songs.

Adjusting the Sound

If you are hearing the song you selected, it should sound good without your having to do any fiddling around. However, if you want (or need) to adjust the sound, you can. To do this, you need to get to the Navigation screen.

Once Sonique displays the Navigation screen, click **Audio Controls** to open the Audio Enhancement screen. When you open this screen, Sonique automatically opens the Audio Enhancement control as well. This control has a 20-band graphic equalizer (known as Sonique EQ), with Amplitude (AMP), Balance (BAL), and Pitch knobs. Sonique displays a graph of the current equalizer settings in the Visualization Display area (Figure 4.3).

FIGURE 4.3

You can tweak the sound to perfection using the Audio Enhancement Screen.

The equalizer comes with five presets: Rock, Jazz, Classical, Dance, and Pop. You choose between them by clicking the left or right arrow at the bottom of the Visualization Display area. You can also create up to 10 presets of your own by adjusting the equalizer in a way that suits your needs. Use the Load and Save options at the bottom of the Visualization Display area to store and retrieve your presets.

You adjust the equalizer by changing the levels of each channel as you would on your stereo. The changes you make appear in the EQ graph, located in the Visualization Display area. But don't do it yet.

By default, the equalizer is not enabled. That means nothing you do to the equalizer has any effect on the sound that comes out of the player—until you click the Equalizer Enabled checkbox.

Also, notice that directly below the Equalizer Enabled checkbox is a Spline Tension checkbox, and that this checkbox is checked by default. The spline tension setting makes your life easier. When you adjust one of the equalizer channels, the spline tension causes the equalizer to change the settings for adjacent channels, so you have a smooth curve from point to point. Mediascience, Inc. believes that most people adjust their equalizers in curves anyway, so doing it for you just saves time and effort.

NOTE

If you are picky about the setting of each channel, turn off spline tension. When this is off, you can adjust each channel exactly as you wish, without it affecting, or being affected by, adjacent channels.

Now you know everything you need to know to start playing with the equalizer, but you still have those three little knobs you can adjust. The Amplitude knob adjusts the overall level of the songs by affecting the way Sonique decodes amplitude. It is ideal for songs that were recorded at low levels or are just too quiet even when you have the Volume knob turned up all the way. You can also increase or decrease the activity of the visual effects by adjusting the Amplitude knob. If you have a song that plays back at an acceptable volume, but that doesn't affect your favorite visual effect, use the Amplitude knob. Turn the amplitude up some, and the volume down. By playing with these two knobs, you should be able to increase the affect on the visual effect, without blowing out your eardrums or speakers.

The Balance knob adjusts the left-right balance of the sound. It works the same way the balance control on your stereo does: turn the knob left to push more sound through the left speaker channel, turn it right to push more sound through the right speaker channel.

The Pitch knob controls the pitch and tempo of the audio playback.

Doing a Little Exploring

Now that you know how to play a set of songs and adjust the playback to your liking, you can have a musical accompaniment while learning more about Sonique. As you read before, the Navigation screen connects you to the six other screens that comprise the Navigation console. It is time to learn about those screens. You navigate between the screens by clicking the name of the screen you want to see next.

To return to the Navigation screen from any of the Navigation Console screens, you click the Jump Back One Screen button (a left-facing arrow), which appears when you are on one of the Navigation Console screens. When you point the mouse at that button, the words Navigation Console appear at the bottom of the Visualization Display area.

NOTE

The Jump Back One Screen button is one of several buttons that make up the Navigation buttons. The exact buttons that appear in this group vary depending on which mode and screens Sonique is displaying. Whatever modes or screens Sonique is displaying, you should be able to find this group of buttons somewhere on Sonique's interface.

The six Navigation Console screens are: Music Download, Playlist Editor, Visual Mode, Setup Options, Info About, and Audio Controls.

NOTE

Sonique includes a large set of *hotkeys*, keyboard combinations that let you navigate the interface without using the mouse. You can find out more about Sonique hotkeys at the Sonique Web site.

Music Download

Music Download is actually a slightly misleading name for this page. From the Music Download page you can indeed find and download music. But you can also get music news on this page, as well as connect to Sonique specific news, upgrades, and a FAQ, all under the banner of Sonique Online.

Playlist Editor

Playlist Editor is a page where you can create and manage playlists. Playlists are described in detail in the sidebar "So, Tell Me More About Playlists" in Chapter 3. While Sonique's Playlist Editor is fully functional, I think you are better off using a separate playlist editor. Try ShufflePlay, a high-powered playlist utility that's available free of charge and is included on the book CD.

Visual Mode

Visual Mode is one place where Sonique really shines. When in Visual Mode, Sonique can display audio-sensitive graphics that occupy a portion of the Navigation Console background, the entire Navigation Console background, or your entire screen. Audio-sensitive graphics are graphics that change how they move depending on the music that is playing. Figure 4.4 shows one of the possibilities for Sonique when you click Visual Mode. The jagged lines that appear behind the text are one of the many possible visual effects. Those lines represent the sound waves that comprise the music playing, and they change their shape in time to the music. Note the Audio Enhancement controls (20-band equalizer and more) open at the bottom of the window. Normally, the controls are hidden as in Figure 4.1.

NOTE

Visual Mode is also known as Enlarged-Play mode.

Setup Options

Setup Options is the place you go to configure Sonique. There are two sets of settings: General Settings and Plug-in Settings.

FIGURE 4.4

In Enlarged-Play mode, Sonique gives you lots of information about the track, and still leaves room for visual plug-ins to do their magic.

General Settings   Click the general button at the bottom of the Setup Options screen to get to the General Settings screen. General Settings offers seven tabs that correspond to seven broad categories in which you can change settings. These are:

▌ **System Tab:** Controls whether Sonique appears in the Windows Taskbar and similar settings, as well as some aspects of how the playlist works. You normally won't need to touch these settings.

▌ **Audio Tab:** Controls where audio signals go after they pass through Sonique. Don't mess with this one unless you're sure you know what you're doing.

▌ **Visual Tab:** Controls the speed and smoothness of transitions between screens. You can safely experiment with this tab to see how it affects transitions.

▌ **File Types Tab:** Controls the types of files Sonique will play. You normally won't have to mess with these settings.

▪ **Vis FX Tab:** Controls settings that modify the way visual effects appear in Sonique. If you change some of these settings and a visual effect seems to be unaffected, it is because the author of the effect didn't design it to respond to these settings. You can safely experiment with these settings—in fact, we recommend it.

▪ **Internet Tab:** This tab lets you change the Internet settings you entered when you installed Sonique.

▪ **Skins:** Controls which skin Sonique displays as its user interface. More on this later in the chapter.

Plug-in Settings   Click the Plug-ins button at the bottom of the Setup Options screen to get to the Plug-ins Settings screen. This screen offers four tabs that correspond to the four major plug-ins currently included in Sonique. It is unlikely you'll ever need to touch these, so there will be nothing more said about them.

Changing Visual Modes

Remember that we told you not to panic if the way Sonique appeared was not the way you expected it to look? Here is why Sonique may have a different look than you expect.

Sonique has three display modes. The one you've been working in is Enlarged-Play mode. It is the largest of the three display modes, and includes the largest area for displaying audio-sensitive graphics. Figures 4.1 and 4.4 are both aspects of this mode.

If you point the cursor at the down arrow in the Navigation buttons, you will see its name: Jump Down once. Click this arrow to go from the Enlarged-Play mode to Mid-State Mode. Mid-State mode makes Sonique smaller. It takes up less screen space and has less room for visuals. However, Mid-State mode (Figure 4.5) has its own charms. How big Mid-State mode appears on your screen is determined by the video mode in which you run your PC. The best way to get a feel for how this mode could work for you is to run Sonique in Mid-State mode yourself and see.

Mid-State mode gives you virtually all the same controls as Enlarged-View mode, except that Enlarged-View mode has additional controls for the Visualization Display area. I suspect that most people run Sonique in Mid-State mode, and if Enlarged-View mode looked odd to you it was because you're used to seeing Mid-State.

FIGURE 4.5

Sonique in Mid-State mode; attention-getting looks without occupying a lot of the screen.

If you look closely at the Navigation buttons in Mid-State mode, you'll notice that there is an up arrow button (named Jump Up) and a down arrow button (named, not surprisingly, Jump Down). The Jump Up button takes you back to the Enlarged-View mode, while the Jump Down button takes you to Small-State mode.

In Small-State mode Sonique gets really tiny. As with Mid-State mode, you need to try this yourself to see just how small Small-State mode is. Put Sonique in Small-State mode and drag it below the icons that adorn the typical Windows desktop, and no one will even notice it is there. When Sonique gets this tiny, there isn't much room for controls. That's true, but the team at Mediascience, Inc. didn't let that stop them. When Sonique is in Small-State mode, and you point the mouse cursor at it, a little control panel pops out of the chassis. That control panel has the basic controls you need to play music, plus the Navigation buttons, so you can get into other modes. Figure 4.6 includes two views of Sonique in Small-State mode. The one on the left is how Sonique appears when you're not pointing at it. The view on the right is what Sonique looks like when you are pointing at it. Quite an inventive solution, isn't it?

FIGURE 4.6

In Small-State mode, Sonique can live on your desktop without your boss even noticing.

The Sonique Contextual Help System

As you've learned in this chapter, Sonique is a rich program, full of modes, options, commands, and capabilities. If you feel the need for help while you're working with Sonique, just click the question mark button (the Help button) in the Navigation buttons group. This activates the Sonique Contextual Help system.

Sonique's help system consists of HTML pages that correspond to the various pages and modes of Sonique. When you click the Help button, Sonique starts your Web browser and displays the specific help page that corresponds to the mode or page you are on. If you're on the Audio Enhancement page, Sonique displays help for that page. If you're in Small-State mode, Sonique displays help for that mode. Because the help pages are in HTML, the language of the World Wide Web, the help pages are as colorful and easy to navigate as the Sonique Web site. If you didn't know differently, you could easily believe that you are looking at the Sonique Web site when you are actually looking at help pages stored on your computer. Figure 4.7 shows part of the help page for Mid-State mode.

Getting Flashy with Plug-Ins and Skins

In its most basic form, Sonique is inherently flashy and fun. For even more flash and fun, you can delve into the world of plug-ins and skins. Plug-ins are capabilities you can add (plug in) to Sonique. Audio plug-ins give Sonique the ability to play new file formats beyond those it already supports. Visual plug-ins provide new graphics that can appear in the Visualization Display area. As already mentioned, skins are a way to give the Sonique user interface a new look. The next two sections show you how to install and use plug-ins and skins.

FIGURE 4.7

The Sonique Contextual Help System is as colorful and easy to navigate as the Sonique Web site.

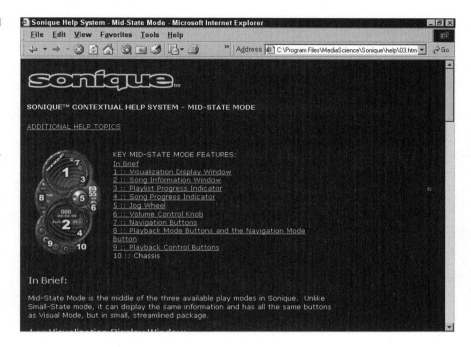

Installing and Using Plug-Ins

Right now, all the available audio plug-ins for Sonique get installed when you run the setup program. On the other hand, you can find lots of visual plug-ins on the plug-ins page (**www.sonique.com/plugs.html**) at the Sonique Web site. Follow the links to the Visual plug-ins, and browse the selections. For each plug-in, the site gives you a short description and two small pictures of what the vis (Sonique talk for a visual plug-in) looks like in action. Click a small picture to see a somewhat larger rendition of it.

Installing a vis is simple. Download any of the visual plug-ins you're interested in. When you download them, visual plug-ins come packaged as self-extracting executables. In plain English, this means they are files that, when run, extract and uncompress their contents. In the case of the Sonique vis, when you run the self-extracting executable, it extracts a set of files into the Vis folder under the Sonique folder, and displays a file containing information relevant to the vis. Some visual plug-ins have configuration options that you can use to tune the visualization. Any such configuration options should be described in the file that pops up when you run the self-extractor.

Follow these steps to install and use a visual plug-in:

1. Download the vis self-extracting executable to your hard drive. Make sure you keep track of where the Web browser puts the file.

2. Using Windows Explorer, open the folder the downloaded file is in.

3. Double-click the file to run it. After a moment, you should see a text file which describes the vis and includes any special instructions you might need.

4. If everything has worked properly, the files Sonique needs to display your new vis have all been copied to the Vis folder.

5. In Sonique, get into Visual Mode. Using the Page Up and Page Down buttons (the two large buttons with arrows on them, located in the bottom right-hand corner of the Sonique window), scroll through the available visualizations. The name of the current vis appears at the top of the Visualization Display area.

To the left and right of the vis name you can find additional buttons. Experiment with these. You'll like what you find. If you happen to end up in a mode where you can't see any controls (you'll know what I'm talking about when you get there) you can change the resolution of the display by pressing the plus or minus keys on the keyboard. Press the **Escape** key (**Esc**) to get your controls back. Have fun.

Installing and Using Skins

If you think visual plug-ins are hot, wait until you start playing with skins. With skins, you can change the whole look and feel of Sonique. Figure 4.8 shows Sonique wearing the Eight! skin in

Mid-State mode. It's hard to tell at first glance that this is still Sonique. And Eight! is relatively conservative.

FIGURE 4.8

Eight!, by Julian Kay from the UK, is clean, classy, and one of the more conservative skins to be found on the CD in the back of the book.

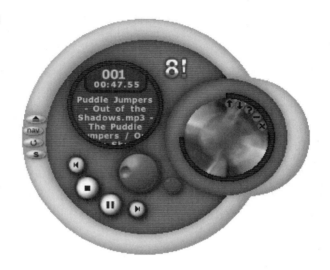

NOTE

You can find a massive collection of Sonique skins on the Web at **skins.sonique.com.** When you hit this Web site, check out the featured skins, then click one of the links that takes you to the skin archive. The archive contains over 100 skins contributed by Sonique staff and others. Click the detailed view link associated with a particular skin to see an enlarged view of that skin's Mid-State and Enlarged modes.

Skins are easy to install and use. Just follow these steps:

1. Download the skin to your hard drive from skins/sonique.com or the book CD. The quickest way to put the skin to work is to download it directly to the Skins folder. Assuming you let Sonique install to its choice of folders during setup, the path to the Skins folder is: C:\Program Files\MediaScience\Sonique\skins.

2. In Sonique, get into the Navigation screen.

3. Click **Setup Options** to open the Setup Options screen.

4. Click **General** to ensure that you are on the General Settings screen, then click **Skins**. A tiny picture of the Enlarged-State mode for the current skin appears in the Visualization Display area, along with the name of the current skin. Using the Page Up and Page Down buttons, scroll through the skins you have available.

5. When you find the skin you want to use, click the **Back One Screen** button to return to the Navigation screen. When you do, Sonique disappears for a second, then comes back wearing the new skin. Enjoy!

NOTE

There isn't really much anyone can do to make the Small-State mode look different, other than changing the color scheme. So don't expect skins to do much for you if you always use Sonique in Small-State mode.

Sonique Wrapup

You've reached the end of your guided tour of Sonique. You know how to make this flashy, fun, and unconventional MP3 player play music and do all sorts of other tricks. You can change display modes, plug in new visual effects, tweak the sound just the way you want it, even change the entire interface with skins. But this is just part of what you can do with Sonique. Remember, this is MP3 and the Internet we're talking about here. Who knows what the team at Mediascience will add to Sonique in the coming months? If you're going to make Sonique your MP3 player, you should really plan on making regular trips to the Sonique Web site at **www.sonique.com** (Figure 4.9). It's the best place to go to find out what's new and generally what's happening with Sonique.

FIGURE 4.9

The Sonique Web site (www.sonique.com) is the place to find newer versions of Sonique, related software, and tons of skins.

Checking Out Other Standalone MP3 Players

While I heartily recommend Sonique as my favorite standalone MP3 player, it never hurts to see what else is available. Especially when it's free. The rest of the chapter is a quick tour of two other standalone players you might want to investigate. You won't find nearly as much detail as you did for Sonique, but you will find enough information to install and test these other products.

XingMP3 Player

TIP

Now you can Xing your entire MP3 experience, from ripping and encoding to playing back.

One of the newest MP3 players comes from Xing Technology. Xing makes a top-notch ripper/encoder (AudioCatalyst), and in the Summer of '99, launched XingMP3 Player. Figure 4.10 shows the player's user interface. XingMP3 Player isn't as good looking as Sonique, and it doesn't have some of the fancier features, but it sounds great and many people find it easier to use.

FIGURE 4.10

The XingMP3 Player has a more conventional design than Sonique, making it easier to learn and use.

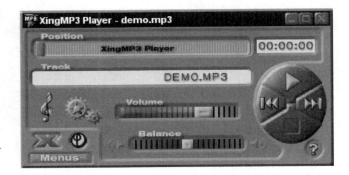

Besides being from a big name in consumer digital audio software (Xing has been publishing multimedia PC software since 1990), XingMP3 Player offers some interesting capabilities that boost it above the run-of-the-mill MP3 players, including:

- Built-in playlist editor
- One-click access to AudioCatalyst for ripping and encoding
- Links to the Web
- Ability to play other audio formats besides MP3, and also to play video.

System Requirements

To use XingMP3 Player successfully, your system must meet these requirements:

- Windows 95 or 98, or Windows NT operating system
- Pentium processor
- 32 MB of RAM
- Sound card.

Where to Get XingMP3 Player

You can download XingMP3 Player page on the Xing Technology Web site. The URL is **www.xingtech.com/mp3/player**. There you can always get the latest version of XingMP3 Player. In addition, the XingMP3 Player page has a link to the XingForum, an online discussion area where you can post questions and keep tabs on what's going on with XingMP3 Player and other XingMP3 products.

What Does It Cost?

XingMP3 Player is freeware. You get the full-power, unadulterated, timebombless, and nag-screenless player for free.

Installing XingMP3 Player

Follow these steps to install XingMP3 Player:

NOTE

During the installation process, XingMP3 Player will strongly recommend that you close all other Windows applications until you finish the installation. It would be a good idea to do so now, and save yourself the trouble of exiting Setup, closing everything, then restarting Setup.

1. Download XingMP3 Player from the XingMP3 Website.
2. Using Windows Explorer, browse to the folder where you download XingMP3 Player.
3. Double-click the file named **Mp3p10.exe** or whatever the file name is now. This is a self-extracting executable file that does the actual work of installing XingMP3 Player on your system. The first thing it does is display a Welcome dialog box asking you to close all other Windows applications before continuing the installation process.
4. Click **Next** to continue the installation process. Setup displays the Software License Agreement.
5. Read the license agreement then click **Next** to accept the agreement, or **Cancel** to abort the installation. If you click **Next**, the Choose Destination Location dialog box appears.
6. Unless you have a good reason to do otherwise, click **Next** to let Setup install the program in the destination directory it suggests. The Start Installation dialog box appears.

7. Click **Next** to continue. The Setup program copies information to your PC, and displays the Installation Complete dialog box.

8. If you have a Web browser on your computer, check both checkboxes in the Installation Complete dialog box. If you don't have a Web browser, don't check the box that asks if you want to Visit Xing on the Web.

9. Click **Finish** to complete the installation process. Setup displays the Readme file in Windows Notepad. Read through the Readme file to catch any last minute issues. If you elected to Visit Xing on the Web, Setup also starts your Web browser, and uses it to display the Xing Web site.

10. Close your browser and the Notepad window containing the Readme file. You're ready to start the player.

11. In the XingMP3 Player program group (that should now be visible on your Windows Desktop), double-click the **XingMP3 Player**. After a moment, the player should appear, with the name DEMO.MP3 scrolling across the Track window, and you should hear a short sound sample.

What if I Didn't Hear Any Music?

If you didn't hear any music, try this. Click the **Play** button (the top button in the circular set of buttons on the right side of the XingMP3 Player window). The name of the demo song should be scrolling across the Track window, the counter at the top right should be counting, and the indicator in the Position window in the top left part of the XingMP3 Player window should be changing. If you don't see these things, XingMP3 Player isn't playing the sound sample.

If the counter is counting, and the Position window is changing, XingMP3 Player is playing. Make sure your headphones are plugged in, or your speakers are plugged in and turned on. If you still hear nothing, try pushing the Volume slider on the XingMP3 Player window as far to the right as possible. If that doesn't work, it is time to head for Chapter 12 to figure out what the problem is.

XingMP3 Player shouldn't require any configuration on your part. If you heard the short demo track when you first started the program, you're good to go.

Using XingMP3 Player

XingMP3 Player is easy to figure out, despite the fact that it doesn't have the standard set of menus and toolbars most Windows programs sport. Like Sonique, XingMP3 Player only plays songs that appear in the Play List Editor window. You open the Play List Editor window by clicking the musical note that appears on the Player window. You can add songs or existing play lists to the Play List Editor window by clicking the open folder icon in the Play List Editor window, or by dropping files directly into the window.

The Play List Editor window has a set of play controls at the bottom left (Figure 4.11), so you can tell XingMP3 Player to play a song or a play list without ever leaving the window.

FIGURE 4.11

The XingMP3 Player Playlist Editor.

You control the volume and balance by dragging the appropriate sliders around on the player window. By dragging the Position slider you can move through a track to a favorite guitar riff or interesting spot in the lyrics.

The only part of dealing with XingMP3 Player that might be confusing is that bit about doing without standard menus and toolbars. Instead of these, XingMP3 Player has several icons and buttons embossed in the surface of the player window. Clicking them gives you access to the features they represent.

The icons do this:

■ The gears on the player window give you the Properties/Settings dialog box, where you can adjust general XingMP3 properties as well as Play List Editor properties.

■ The Menus button gives you a set of four menus you can choose from to do things like load files, launch the Windows volume control, or get help.

■ The Note icon, as already explained, starts the Play List Editor.

■ The blue 'X' icon is a link to the Xing Web site.

■ The round yellow button that looks like it has a pitchfork in it actually starts AudioCatalyst, if it is installed on this system. AudioCatalyst is a very capable file ripper and encoder from Xing Technology. Combine the two programs and you have almost all the functionality of an all-in-one player.

XingMP3 Player Wrapup

The XingMP3 Player is an easy-to-use alternative to Sonique. It does its job (playing play lists or individual MP3 files) smoothly and without calling attention to itself. But XingMP3 Player can also play different audio formats and even video clips. Combine these features with the Xing pedigree and the convenience of one-button access to the AudioCatalyst ripper/encoder, and you have an MP3 player with a promising future.

RealPlayer G2

TIP

RealPlayer G2 is an industry-standard streaming media player which does double duty as a decent MP3 player.

System Requirements

To use RealPlayer G2 as an MP3 player, your system must meet these requirements:

- Windows 95 or 98, or Windows NT operating system
- Pentium 90 processor or better
- 16 MB of RAM
- Sound card.

RealPlayer G2 has additional requirements if you intend to use it to play streaming media from the Net. You can find the full list on the RealPlayer G2 download page (see below).

Where to Get RealPlayer G2

The odds are good that RealPlayer G2 is already installed on your computer. You can find out if it is by clicking the **Windows Start** button, then **Programs**, and looking in the Programs list for a folder named Real. If you see RealPlayer G2 in that folder, you're in good shape. But see "Who's in Charge Here" before going any further.

Who's in Charge Here

RealPlayer G2 has a setting that might cause problems for people who want to try out more than one MP3 player. I believe this is a relic of an old battle between RealNetworks and Microsoft, and isn't meant to cause trouble for competing MP3 players. Regardless of the origin of this problem, you need to know about it and how to correct it.

The setting in question gives RealPlayer G2 your permission to make itself the default player for supported media types—including MP3 files and playlists—automatically, regardless of the settings you enter yourself in some other program. In other words, when this option is active, it is possible that you set Sonique as your default MP3 player, but when you double-click an MP3 file to play it, RealPlayer G2 starts running instead. I don't know the details of how this works, or the exact circumstances under which it occurs, but it is easy to ensure that this setting doesn't give you any trouble.

Follow these steps to ensure that RealPlayer G2 doesn't try to seize control of MP3 files from the player you select:

1. Start RealPlayer G2.
2. In the Options menu, click **Preferences**. The Preferences dialog box appears.
3. Click the **Upgrade** tab to see the Upgrade tabbed page. At the bottom of this page is a section named RealNetworks' Media Types.

continued on next page

4. In the RealNetworks' Media Types section, clear the checkbox named Reclaim RealNetworks' media types without asking.
5. Click **OK** to close the Preferences dialog box. RealPlayer G2 will no longer seize control of MP3 files without asking permission.

If you don't already have RealPlayer G2 installed on your computer, you need to download it. Go to the RealNetworks Web site at **www.real.com**. You should see a link that allows you to download RealPlayer G2. Make sure you're getting RealPlayer G2 and not RealPlayer Plus G2. G2 is free. Plus G2 is not.

If you don't see something that lets you download RealPlayer G2 on this page, look for a Products button and click that. Once you reach the Products page, you should have no trouble finding RealPlayer G2. Follow the instructions that appear on the screen (and get past the ads for RealPlayer Plus G2 and other products) and download the player to some folder you can find again later. Remember the name of the file you are downloading, as it might have changed between now and when I wrote this chapter.

NOTE

The RealPlayer G2 Minimal download provides everything you need for playing MP3 files, and takes the least time to download, so I suggest you use that.

What Does RealPlayer G2 Cost?

RealPlayer G2 is free. RealPlayer Plus G2 is a version of the player with additional capabilities, including a graphic equalizer. If you want to use RealPlayer, and must have a built-in equalizer, it will cost $29.99.

Installing RealPlayer G2

Follow these steps to install RealPlayer G2:

NOTE

During the installation process, RealPlayer G2 will strongly recommend that you close all other Windows applications until you finish the installation. It would be a good idea to do so now, and save yourself the trouble of exiting Setup, closing everything, then restarting Setup.

1. Using Windows Explorer, browse to the folder where you downloaded RealPlayer G2.

2. Double-click the **RealPlayer G2** file. This self-extracting executable file installs RealPlayer G2 on your system. It immediately does some preparations for the installation, then displays a Setup of RealPlayer G2 dialog box containing a software license agreement.

3. Read the license agreement then click **Accept** to accept the agreement, or **Cancel** to abort the installation. If you click **Accept**, a new dialog box appears. This dialog box asks for your e-mail address and the directory in which you want to install the program.

4. Enter your e-mail address. Unless you have a good reason to do otherwise, let Setup install the program in the destination directory it suggests.

5. Click **Finish** to let Setup copy files to your hard drive and configure your system to use RealPlayer G2. Once this is done, you should see the RealPlayer window as well as a dialog box named Configuration of RealPlayer. This is actually an electronic registration form plus some real configuration information.

6. Enter the speed of your modem when the appropriate dialog box appears, then click **Next**. A dialog box appears that talks about media types. Figure 4.12 shows what this dialog box looks like today.

7. Think carefully about the settings in this dialog box. The first checkbox, which makes RealPlayer G2 the default player for supported media types is no big deal. It makes RealPlayer G2 the default player for various media types, including MP3 files and playlists. If you try RealPlayer G2 and decide you want to use another MP3 player, you can always set the other player to be the default MP3 player using its configuration options.

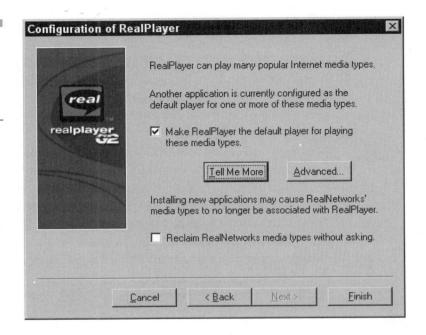

The checkbox that talks about reclaiming media types without asking can be a problem. Checking this means that RealPlayer G2 has the ability to make itself the default player for MP3 and other media types even if you decide to use a different MP3 player. You can manually set Sonique, or MusicMatch Jukebox, or anything else as the default MP3 player, and RealPlayer G2 has your permission to undo your settings and make itself the default player. I can't tell you exactly how this option works, or precisely when it tries to reclaim control of MP3 files, but I strongly recommend that you clear this checkbox before continuing the RealPlayer G2 installation. Then you won't have to worry about it at all.

8. Click **Finish**. RealPlayer G2 connects to the Net, transfers your registration information to RealNetworks, then plays a short sound and video clip. If your Web browser starts and takes you to the RealNetworks Web site, take a look at what they have to offer, then close the browser and get ready to play some music.

> ### What if I Didn't See Any Video or Hear Any Sound?
>
> If you didn't see or hear anything emanating from the RealPlayer G2 window, try this. Click the **Play** button (the arrowhead facing right on the left side of the RealPlayer G2 window, just below the Real logo in Figure 4.13). The indicator to the right of the Play button should be moving, the counter in the lower right corner should be counting, and video should be playing in the large window on the right side of the RealPlayer G2 window. If you don't see these things, RealPlayer G2 isn't playing the sound and video sample.
>
> If the indicator is moving, the counter is counting, and the video is changing, RealPlayer G2 is playing. Make sure your headphones are plugged in, or your speakers are plugged in and turned on. If you still hear nothing, try pushing the Volume slider in the RealPlayer G2 window up as far as possible, then play the clip again. If that doesn't work, it's time to head for Chapter 12 to figure out what the problem is.

FIGURE 4.13

RealPlayer G2 can play individual MP3 files or playlists, as well as other audio and video formats.

Using RealPlayer G2

Because it is primarily a streaming media player, RealPlayer G2 has relatively limited capabilities as an MP3 player. You can play an individual MP3 file simply by dragging it to the RealPlayer G2 window and dropping it there, or by using the Open File command on the File menu.

RealPlayer G2 also works with MP3 playlists generated by programs like ShufflePlay. If you plan to use playlists, you should go to RealPlayer G2's View menu and select **Clip Info and Playlist**. These commands add two additional toolbars to the RealPlayer G2 window. The Clip Info toolbar allows you to see the information RealPlayer G2 knows about the clip, while the Playlist toolbar lets you scroll through the files in the playlist.

NOTE

ShufflePlay is included on the CD in the back of this book. You can learn more about ShufflePlay and find instructions for installing and using it in Chapter 7, "Cool Utility Guide."

RealPlayer G2 Wrapup

RealPlayer G2 is a powerful streaming media player that doubles as a basic MP3 player. While it lacks some of the features of Sonique or XingMp3 Player, RealPlayer G2 produces high-quality output, and is fine for light-duty MP3 playback, particularly when combined with a good playlist editor utility.

Chapter Wrapup

This chapter covers three of the 140+ MP3 players floating around in cyberspace. Most of the focus is on Sonique, probably the most popular standalone MP3 player on the Net today. The first two-thirds of the chapter cover many aspects of Sonique, from where to get it, to installing and using it. While the text doesn't go into the more esoteric aspects of Sonique (coding vis plug-ins, for example), it does cover using vis plug-ins as well as skins.

The last third of the chapter is devoted to two other standalone MP3 players: XingMP3 Player and RealPlayer G2. There's enough information to get each of them installed on your computer, and get you on your way to exploring their capabilities. Between the three of them, you should find one standalone MP3 player that suits your needs.

One thing distinguishes standalone MP3 players from all-in-one MP3 players. The all-in-one players have the ability to copy (rip) tracks from audio CDs and convert (encode) them in MP3 format. If you want to be able to convert your CD collection into MP3s, you need this capability. But you don't have to switch to an all-in-one player to get it. Instead, you can install a ripper and an encoder and use them to suck tracks off your CDs, then play them back with your favorite standalone player.

CHAPTER 5

AudioCatalyst and Other Rippers and Encoders

In the last chapter you looked at Sonique and other standalone MP3 players. Those programs can play existing MP3 files, like those on the CD in the back of this book. They can also help you download MP3 files from the Web, and play those. But none of those programs can help you with the last source of MP3 music—your own collection of audio CDs. With the help of programs known as rippers and encoders, you can easily convert tracks from your audio CDs into MP3 format. This chapter is your guide to rippers and encoders. It shows you what's available, and helps you through some interesting legal tangles.

The featured program in this chapter is AudioCatalyst, from Xing Technology Corp. AudioCatalyst combines a ripper and an encoder in a single program, thereby simplifying your life. Even better, AudioCatalyst is not caught up in the legal tangles referred to earlier.

While I recommend AudioCatalyst for anyone who wants to do ripping and encoding, you may not want to follow that advice. For you difficult types, the chapter also covers a standalone ripper, Digital Audio Copy, and a standalone encoder, XingMP3 Encoder.

That should be all you need to rip and encode to your heart's content. But it's not. Anyone who wants to rip CDs needs to be aware of the kinks and quirks that afflict some CD-ROM drives. So the last part of the chapter is dedicated to CD-ROM drive peculiarities. Most of you won't ever have to worry about this, but you'll know where to go if you just can't seem to rip any tracks from CDs on your PC.

Here are the high notes you'll hit in this chapter:

▌ What legal tangles?
▌ AudioCatalyst
▌ Digital Audio Copy for Win32
▌ XingMP3 encoder
▌ CD-ROM drive peculiarities.

NOTE

This chapter assumes that your PC is set up for ripping music from audio CDs. That is, that your PC has a CD-ROM drive capable of playing music, has a sound card installed and configured properly, and has plenty of unused disk space to store the tracks you rip from your CDs. Most newer PCs are already set up this way, and should have no problem ripping music. If you know your system does not meet with these preconditions, stop now and read "Part 4: The Hardware You Need." If you aren't sure that your PC meets these preconditions, your best bet is to keep following the instructions that are coming up. If you follow these instructions and can't rip tracks, that's a good indication that your PC is not ready for ripping. Read "CD-ROM Drive Peculiarities" in this chapter to see if you can resolve the problem. If that doesn't work, Chapter 12, "Pumping Up Your PC for MP3" will help you determine where the problem lies and how to fix it.

What Legal Tangles?

There are many rippers and encoders floating around the Internet. They differ in many ways, but they have one thing in common: they all convert data to and from MP3 format. That seems pretty obvious, but what isn't so obvious is that the algorithms needed to convert to and from MP3 format are patented. The outfit that invented the MP3 format, the Fraunhofer Institute, owns the patents. They expect anyone who uses the algorithms for encoding data in MP3 format to pay a license fee. (Fraunhofer Institute could require license fees for ripping too, but does not do so at this time.) Most of the encoders on the Net do not pay the license fee, and so are illegal (at least in countries where the Fraunhofer Institute's patents are honored). As I indicated at the start, this is a real mess.

NOTE

I'm not a lawyer, and my understanding of the exact issues is imperfect. But it is clear that there are potential legal problems with most of the encoders available on the Net.

Some companies do pay the license fees required by the Fraunhofer Institute. One of them is Xing Technology Corp. If your encoder is from Xing, you can be sure it is legal.

The all-in-one players (which include encoders) covered in Chapter 6 are also legal.

NOTE

AudioCatalyst

AudioCatalyst is a high-performance ripper and encoder with lots of additional capabilities.

TIP

AudioCatalyst makes it easy to go from a track on an audio CD to an MP3 file on your PC by integrating the ripper and encoder. Both the ripper and encoder are high-performance tools that give you the best possible sound for any given track. Xing Technology Corp. pays license fees to the Fraunhofer Institute, so everything is legal.

Here are some of the features that make AudioCatalyst your best choice for ripping and encoding:

- Top-rated ripper and encoder integrated into one package
- Built-in normalizer
- Ability to get information from CDDB
- One-button activation of your favorite MP3 player
- Ability to play tracks before you rip them.

AudioCatalyst System Requirements

To use AudioCatalyst successfully, your system must meet these requirements:

- Windows 95 or 98, or Windows NT 4.0 operating system
- Pentium or better processor
- 16 MB of RAM
- Sound card
- CD-ROM drive supporting digital audio extraction
- Speakers or headphones.

Digital audio extraction (DAE) refers to the ability of a CD-ROM drive to transfer audio data (the song you are ripping) in digital format. If a CD-ROM drive supports DAE, it can transfer digital audio data without error.

DEFINITION

Where to Get AudioCatalyst

You can download a trial copy of AudioCatalyst from the Xing Technology Web site at: **www.xingtech.com**. When you reach the site, look for an AudioCatalyst link to click. If you don't find that, look for a link to MP3 audio or something similar. Just make sure to remember the folder you download AudioCatalyst to.

What Does AudioCatalyst Cost?

AudioCatalyst is shareware, so you can try it free. If you decide to continue using AudioCatalyst, you will need to register it. The registered version includes some features not found in the unregistered version, including the ability to select the tracks you want AudioCatalyst to rip.

Installing AudioCatalyst

Follow these steps to install AudioCatalyst:

During the installation process, AudioCatalyst will strongly recommend that you close all other Windows applications until you finish the installation. It would be a good idea to do so now, and save yourself the trouble of exiting Setup, closing everything, then restarting Setup.

NOTE

1. Using Windows Explorer, browse your hard drive until you reach the folder you downloaded AudioCatalyst to.
2. Double-click the self-extracting executable file that does the actual work of installing AudioCatalyst on your system. The first thing it does is display a Welcome dialog box, which asks you what kind of installation you want to do.
3. Select **Typical Installation**, then click **Next**. Setup displays the end-user license agreement.

4. Read the license agreement then click **Next** to accept the agreement, or **Cancel** to abort the installation. If you click **Next**, the Select Components dialog box appears.

5. By default, Setup will install both AudioCatalyst and XingMP3 Player. If you've already installed XingMP3 Player, clear that checkbox. Otherwise you need to decide if you want to try the player. Once you decide what you will do, click **Next**. Setup displays the Start Installation dialog box.

6. Click **Next** to begin the installation. Setup chugs away for a moment, copying files to your PC, creating an AudioCatalyst program group and doing whatever else it needs to do. Then the Installation Complete dialog box appears.

7. Set or clear the View AudioCatalyst Release Notes checkbox and the Visit Xing on the Web! checkbox, then click **Finish** to complete the installation process. If you elected to read the Release Notes, Setup displays them.

8. Read the notes, then close that window. You are now ready to use AudioCatalyst.

Configuring AudioCatalyst

AudioCatalyst's default settings should be enough to have you ripping and encoding right away. One configuration change you should make is to change the folder where AudioCatalyst stores files once it finishes converting them to MP3 format. To do this, follow these steps:

1. On the main menu, click **Settings**, then **General**. This displays the Settings dialog box (Figure 5.1). At the top of this dialog box is a text box that shows where AudioCatalyst will store the files.

2. To change the folder, click **Browse**, then browse to the folder you want AudioCatalyst to use.

3. Double-click the folder, then click **OK** to return to the Settings dialog box.

4. Click **OK** again to return to AudioCatalyst.

FIGURE 5.1

The AudioCatalyst

Settings dialog box.

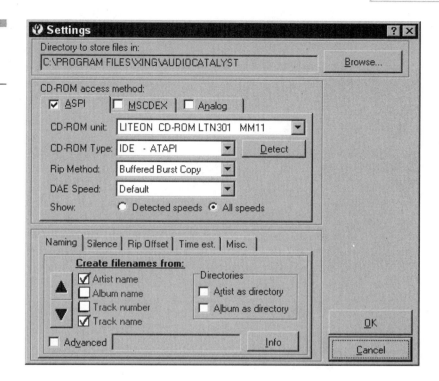

Using AudioCatalyst

Using AudioCatalyst is straightforward. There is, however, one thing to note. If you are using the shareware version of the program, you'll see the dialog box in Figure 5.2 every time you start the program. This reminder, known to us old shareware hands as a nag screen, serves to remind you to register the program. You'll just have to put up with it until you get around to registering the program.

To try your hand at ripping tracks, start the program, then pop an audio CD into the CD-ROM drive. After a moment, you should see a scene like that in Figure 5.3. AudioCatalyst is ready to rip eight tracks from the audio CD in the CD-ROM drive. In the shareware version of the program, the tracks to be ripped are selected randomly by AudioCatalyst. Each time you restart the program, it can rip a different group of tracks.

FIGURE 5.2

The unregistered version of Audio-Catalyst has some limitations, the most important of which is described in this dialog box, a.k.a. a nag screen. It pops up every time you start the unregistered version of the program.

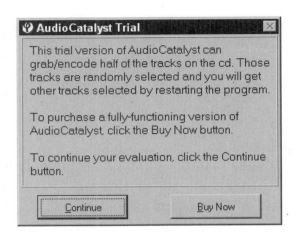

FIGURE 5.3

AudioCatalyst is ready to rip some randomly selected tracks from Out of the Shadows, by The Puddle Jumpers. (The title track for Out of the Shadows is included on the CD in the back of this book.)

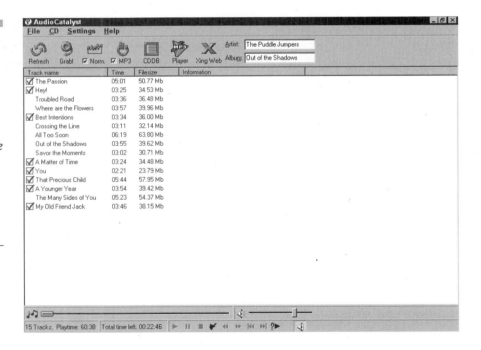

NOTE

If the tracks are identified as Track 1, Track2, etc., instead of by their real names, you can resolve the problem by opening a connection to the Internet, then clicking **CDDB** on the AudioCatalyst toolbar. This tells the program to try to connect to one of the CD Database servers on the Internet. These servers contain track and album information for most of the audio CDs that have been published.

To rip the tracks, set the checkboxes of the tracks you want, then click **Grab**. Immediately, AudioCatalyst sets to work, displaying its progress in the dialog box shown in Figure 5.4. If you look closely at the figure, you may be able to see that AudioCatalyst was reading the track at 8.94 times normal speed.

FIGURE 5.4

AudioCatalyst can often rip tracks eight or more times faster than the tracks normally play.

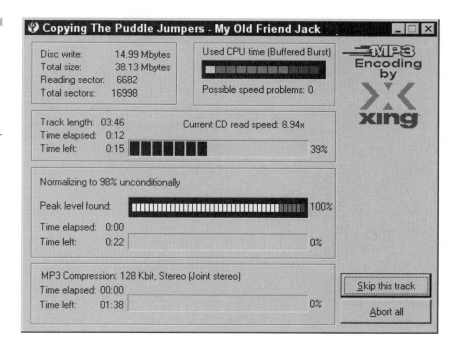

By default, AudioCatalyst goes through these steps when ripping a track and converting it into MP3 format:

1. Rip the track to Windows audio (.wav) format and store it on the hard drive.
2. Normalize the track. Normalizing is covered in detail in Chapter 7. For now, all you need to know is that normalizing a file adjusts the audio levels in the file to make the best use of the available audio range.

3. Encode the track in MP3 format, then save it in the specified folder.
4. Delete the old .wav file, as it is no longer needed.

Once AudioCatalyst finishes ripping the track, you should try to play it with any MP3 player you have installed. If the sound quality is poor, or you just have several minutes of silence, go to "CD-ROM Drive Peculiarities" for tips on resolving the problem.

Doing a Little Exploring

Now that you know how to rip and encode a track, you can take a few minutes to discover some of the other nice features of Audio-Catalyst. If you look back at Figure 5.3, you can see the additional controls you are about to explore.

You know about the normalizer and the CDDB buttons, but what about the rest of the toolbar buttons?

Here are all the toolbar buttons:

▊ **Refresh**, which refreshes the track list
▊ **Grab!**, which grabs (rips) the selected tracks
▊ **Norm.**, which, when checked, tells AudioCatalyst to normalize each track
▊ **MP3**, which, when checked, tells AudioCatalyst to create an MP3 file instead of just leaving the track in .wav format
▊ **CDDB**, which gets data from the CD databases on the Web
▊ **Player**, which starts XingMP3 Player or the MP3 player of your choice
▊ **Xing Web**, which links you to the Xing Technology Corp. Web site (**www.xingtech.com**).

Next to these buttons are the Artist and Album text boxes. AudioCatalyst fills those in with information from the audio CD, but you can change them if you feel the need. By default, Audio-Catalyst uses the artist's name when it creates the name of the MP3 file for a song.

You can change this using the Create filenames from the tabbed page in the Settings dialog box (click **Settings** then **General** then **Naming tab**).

NOTE

> While the Settings dialog box gives you a huge number of options to fiddle with, the default settings for most of them are sufficient for the vast majority of people. Experiment with these at your own risk.

At the bottom of the AudioCatalyst window is a set of controls that looks like they belong on a CD player program. They do. Select a track from the CD (click the name of the track to highlight it) and AudioCatalyst can play it. This allows you to preview tracks before you rip them.

AudioCatalyst Wrapup

That is all I have to say about AudioCatalyst. The program is easy to use and gives good results. It also saves you the hassles of ripping with one program, normalizing with another, then encoding with yet another. Furthermore, using AudioCatalyst lets you sidestep the legal tangles that surround the free encoders you can find on the Internet.

If, despite the above, you still want to use a separate ripper and encoder, here are some suggestions. Give Digital Audio Copy for Win32 a try. It is a quality shareware ripper. For normalizing, see WavNormalizer in Chapter 7.

As far as an encoder goes, there is only one I can recommend. XingMP3 Encoder is the only standalone encoder that I am sure includes the license fee owed to the Fraunhofer Institute. If you want to try some other encoder, go ahead, but I recommend staying legal and using XingMP3 Encoder.

Digital Audio Copy for Win32

TIP

> Digital Audio Copy for Win32 is a capable shareware ripper for anyone who doesn't want to use AudioCatalyst.

Digital Audio Copy for Win32 (also known as WinDAC) is a shareware ripper with all the features you could ask for. Unlike the shareware version of AudioCatalyst, WinDAC32 lets you rip any track on a CD. It does, however, display a nag screen after it rips each track, forcing you to click OK between each track.

System Requirements

To use Digital Audio Copy for Win32 successfully, your system must meet these requirements: Windows 95 or 98, or Windows NT 4.0 operating system

Where to Get Digital Audio Copy for Win32

The author of Digital Audio Copy for Win32, Christoph Schmelnik, has allowed us to include an unregistered copy of Win-DAC32 on the book CD. For the latest version of the program, be sure to visit the WinDAC32 home page at **www.windac.de**.

What Does It Cost?

You can try WinDAC32 free for 30 days. After that, you need to register it. Complete instructions for registering are included in the Register.txt file that comes with the program. The registration fee for WinDAC32 is about $23.

Installing Digital Audio Copy for Win32

Follow these steps to install Digital Audio Copy for Win32:

1. Insert the book CD in your computer's CD-ROM drive.
2. Using Windows Explorer, browse the CD until you reach *X*:\Utilities\WinDAC32, where *X* is the drive letter for your CD-ROM drive.
3. Double-click the file named **wdac149.exe**. This is a self-extracting executable file that does the actual work of installing WinDAC32 on your system. The first thing it does is ask you if you really want to install the program.

4. Click **Yes** to continue the installation process. The Setup program chugs away for a minute, installing the files and changing system settings as needed. Then the System Settings Change dialog box appears.

5. Click **Yes** to restart Windows. When you do so, WinDAC32will be ready to go.

To run WinDAC, click **Start** then **Programs** then **Digital Audio Copy**. In the list of files that appears, click **Digital Audio Copy** for Win32 to start the program. Until you register, a Register WinDAC32 dialog box will appear whenever you start the program. Enter your name and registration key then click **OK**, or click **Register Later** if you don't have a registration key yet. Once you get past an information box, you will see WinDAC32 itself (Figure 5.5).

FIGURE 5.5

Welcome to Digital Audio Copy for Win32.

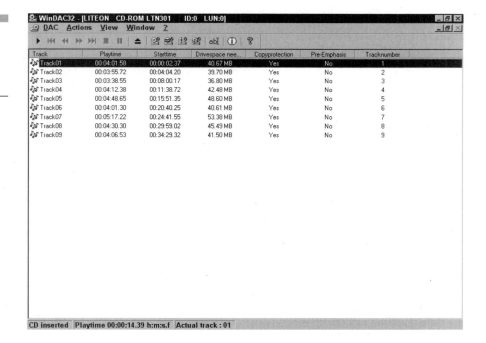

Configuring Digital Audio Copy for Win32

While WinDAC32 will work fine as installed, there is one configuration change you should do. Change where the program puts files after it rips them. Since the .wav files generated by a ripper are tens of megabytes long, you don't want to leave them on your system any longer than you have to. I suggest you create a folder named WAVs somewhere on your hard drive and tell WinDAC32 to put the files it rips into that folder. This way, you will know where to point your encoder, and where to go to delete the .wav files when you are done with them.

Follow these steps to point WinDAC32 to your WAVs folder:

1. In the WinDAC32 menu bar, click **DAC** then **Settings** then **General**. This opens the General Program Settings dialog box.

2. Click the **Output File** tab to display the Output File tabbed page (Figure 5.6).

FIGURE 5.6

Use this tabbed page to tell Win-DAC32 where to store those huge ripped files.

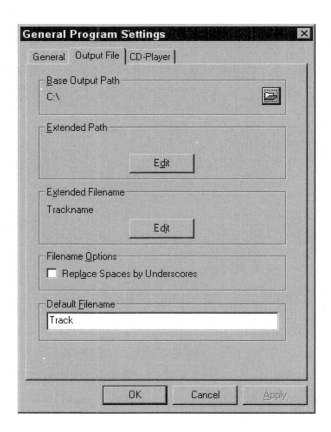

3. Click the **Folder** button in the Base Output Path area. This opens a Browse for Folder dialog box you can use to specify where WinDAC32 should put the files.

Using Digital Audio Copy for Win32

To use WinDAC32, start the program and insert an audio CD in the CD-ROM drive. Select the tracks you want to rip, then on the main menu, click **Actions** then **Copy Tracks**. You could get fancy and rename the tracks, but there is really no point. After all, ripping a file is only half the battle. To get it into MP3 format you'll need to encode it. You can save yourself a bit of work by naming the final MP3 file the way you wish, and not worrying about the .wav files created by WinDAC. Just be sure to remember from which CDs the tracks came.

Digital Audio Copy for Win32 Wrapup

You now know the basics you need to rip tracks from audio CDs using WinDAC. The program has various other capabilities, most of which you won't ever need to become involved with.

If you do decide to explore the other features of WinDAC, you need to be aware of the way this program provides help. Instead of normal online help, WinDAC32 comes with some additional files that take the place of a help system.

To see them, click **Start** then **Programs** then **Digital Audio Copy for Win32**. Besides the program, you should see a half-dozen other files. The Readme file and the FAQ file between them have information for using the program. Register tells you how to register the program. The Liesmich and Lisezmoi files are German and French versions of the Readme file.

XingMP3 Encoder

TIP

XingMP3 Encoder is a high-performance tool for converting audio files to MP3 format. It'll cost you a few bucks to buy it, but if you are interested in staying legal, it is well worth it.

System Requirements

To use XingMP3 Encoder successfully, your system must meet these requirements:

- Windows 95 or 98, or Windows NT 4.0 operating system
- Pentium processor
- 24 MB of RAM.

Where to Get XingMP3 Encoder

XingMP3 Encoder is a retail product. To buy it, go to the Xing Technology Web site (**www.xingtech.com**), and follow the links to the MP3 Audio page. There you will find a link to XingMP3 Encoder. This link takes you to an online store where you can buy the program and download it immediately.

What Does It Cost?

XingMP3 Encoder costs $19.95.

Installing XingMP3 Encoder

Once you download XingMP3 Encoder from the online store, you can follow these steps to install it:

NOTE

During the installation process, XingMP3 Encoder will strongly recommend that you close all other Windows applications until you finish the installation. It would be a good idea to do so now, and save yourself the trouble of exiting Setup, closing everything, then restarting Setup.

1. Using Windows Explorer, browse to the folder containing the copy of XingMP3 Encoder you downloaded.

2. Double-click the file named **Mp3en15.exe** (if Xing has released a new version of the encoder the file name will be different). This self-extracting executable file installs XingMP3 Encoder on your system. The first thing it does is display a Welcome dialog box asking you to close all other Windows applications before continuing the installation process. You also have the opportunity to select a typical installation or a custom installation. Use the typical installation.

3. Click **Next** to continue the installation process. Setup displays the end-user license agreement.

4. Read the license agreement then click **Next** to accept the agreement, or **Cancel** to abort the installation. If you click **Next**, the Start Installation dialog box appears.

5. Click **Next** to continue. The Setup program copies information to your PC, and displays the Installation Complete dialog box.

6. If you have a Web browser on your computer, check all three checkboxes in the Installation Complete dialog box. If you don't have a Web browser, don't check the box that asks if you want to Visit Xing on the Web.

7. Click **Finish** to complete the installation process. Setup displays the x3Readme file, as well as the Readme file. The x3Readme is for users of the command-line interface, and isn't covered in this chapter. Read the Readme file to find out about any last-minute issues. If you elected to Visit Xing on the Web, Setup also starts your Web browser, and uses it to display the Xing Web site.

NOTE

The command-line interface is useful if you want to have your ripper automatically call XingMP3 Encoder. If you end up doing a lot of ripping and encoding using WinDAC32 and XingMP3 Encoder, you will want to research this in each program's help files.

8. Close your browser and the windows containing the Readme files. You're ready to start encoding.

9. In the XingMP3 Encoder program group (that should now be visible on your Windows Desktop), double-click the XingMP3 Encoder. After a moment, an opening screen for the program will appear.

10. Click **OK** to start working with the encoder (Figure 5.7).

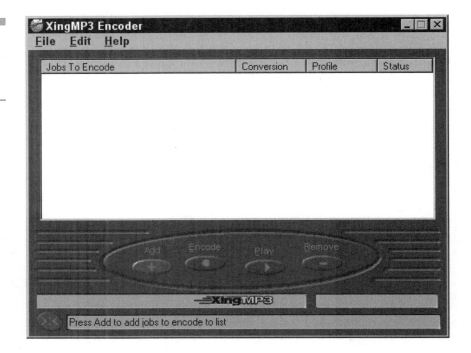

FIGURE 5.7

The XingMP3 Encoder is ready to go.

Configuring XingMP3 Encoder

Although you can use XingMP3 Encoder without changing any configuration settings, telling the program where to put the encoded MP3 files will save you time and effort in the future.

To set the file locations, follow these instructions:

1. In the main XingMP3 Encoder menu, click **Edit** then **Preferences**. This displays the Preferences dialog box. If the Encode tabbed page is not visible, click the **Encode** tab. Figure 5.8 shows the Preferences dialog box with the Encode tabbed page visible.

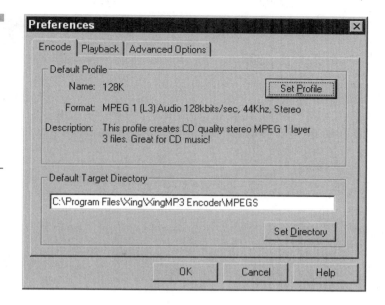

FIGURE 5.8

Use the Encode tabbed page of the Preferences dialog box to tell XingMP3 Encoder where to put the MP3 files it creates.

2. Click **Set Directory** in the Default Target Directory section of the Encode tabbed page. This displays a Browse for Folder dialog box.

3. Browse to the folder you want the program to put MP3 files in when it finishes encoding them.

4. Click **OK** to set this folder as the one in which XingMP3 Encoder will deposit MP3s by default.

Using XingMP3 Encoder

All you need to do to put XingMP3 Encoder to work is to tell it which .wav files you want convert to MP3 format. Follow these instructions to add a job to the encoding list:

1. Click the **Add** button that appears near the bottom of the MP3 Encoder window. This opens the Add Jobs dialog box shown in Figure 5.9.

2. In the Add Jobs dialog box, navigate around your system so the folder that contains the files you want to encode appears in the Look In text box. The contents of that folder will appear in the list below the Look In text box.

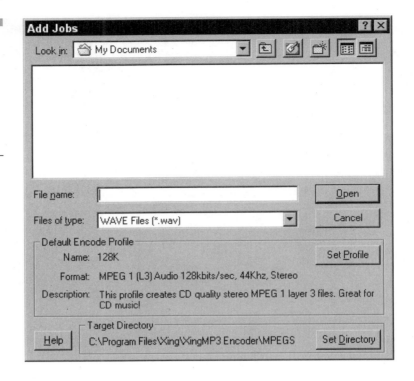

3. Select one or more .wav files to encode, then click **Open**.
    This closes the Add Jobs dialog box and adds the selected
    files to the Jobs to Encode list (Figure 5.10).

NOTE

Ignore all the other options in the Add Jobs dialog box. You can play with
them later if you wish, but the default has everything set to give you the best-
quality MP3 output the encoder is capable of creating.

4. Click **Encode** to start the process. XingMP3 Encoder can
    encode the files much faster than they would play back if you
    were listening to them, with the exact speed depending on
    the power of your PC.
5. Once XingMP3 Encoder finishes the job, click **Play** to hear
    the results. A mini-MP3 player appears and plays the songs.
6. When you are satisfied with the results of the encoding job,
    click **Remove** to remove the job from the list.

FIGURE 5.10

*XingMP3 Encoder
is ready to encode
two .wav files.*

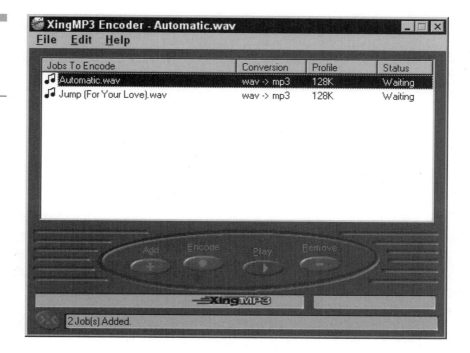

XingMP3 Encoder Wrapup

XingMP3 Encoder has various other options you can explore, including different encoding profiles, a command-line interface and several settings under the heading of Advanced Options. I'm leaving all those as exercises for the reader.

The key points are that XingMP3 Encoder works well, is fast and easy to use, and doesn't violate the Fraunhofer Institute's patents. It is the obvious choice for a standalone encoder.

CD-ROM Drive Peculiarities

The best ripping results come from using *digital audio extraction*. Unfortunately, not all CD-ROM drives are up to the challenge. Many older CD-ROM drives don't support DAE at all. Some newer drives claim to support DAE, but can't do it reliably or at full speed. If you can't rip tracks with AudioCatalyst or WinDAC, problems with digital audio extraction are probably the cause.

Strangely enough, you may be able to "fix" your CD-ROM drive without opening up your PC. MusicMatch Jukebox, the all-in-one MP3 player included on the book CD, configures your CD-ROM drive the first time you run the program. For example, one of my PCs couldn't rip tracks no matter what I tried.

Once I learned that MusicMatch Jukebox configured CD-ROM drives, I decided to install it on the problem machine. I let Music-Match Jukebox do its thing, and I can now rip tracks using that CD-ROM drive and any of my rippers.

Even if you don't want to use MusicMatch Jukebox as your ripper, encoder, and MP3 player, install and run it on any PC that has trouble ripping tracks. If your ripped tracks are still nothing but dead air after you run MusicMatch Jukebox, chances are good that your CD-ROM drive just doesn't support digital audio extraction.

In this case, the answer is to try *analog audio*. Analog audio is slower than DAE, and it might produce slightly less perfect sound, but you probably won't notice any difference. You can set Audio-Catalyst to use analog audio instead of DAE.

NOTE

WinDAC32 does not support analog audio. Your only choices in this case are to switch to another ripper, buy a new CD-ROM drive, or not to rip tracks from CDs.

Follow these steps to set AudioCatalyst for analog audio:

1. Start AudioCatalyst.
2. Click **Settings** then **General**. This displays the Settings dialog box.
3. Click the **Analog** tab to display the Analog tabbed page.
4. Click **OK**.
5. Try ripping and encoding a track. If you can hear the music, just stick with analog audio from now on.

What if you hear music, but it is full of skips, buzzes, and other strange noises? In this case, your computer may not have enough processing power to rip and encode tracks successfully.

The first thing you should do is close all other programs besides your ripper and encoder, and try the same track again. If that works, you know not to do other things while creating MP3s from your audio CDs. If that doesn't work, you need to give up on ripping, or start looking into upgrading your PC.

Chapter Wrapup

One of the best sources for MP3 files is your own audio CD collection. This chapter covered three programs to help you copy the music off your CDs (rip it) and convert it into MP3 format (encode it).

AudioCatalyst, from Xing Technology Corp., is the clear winner in this group. This shareware program combines a ripper and an encoder in a single program. It also includes a built-in normalizer, a utility that adjusts the sound levels of MP3 files for best results. And because Xing Technology pays the appropriate license fees to the Fraunhofer Institute, you don't have to worry about violating their patents.

If you are more inclined to build your MP3 environment component by component, you can give Digital Audio Copy for Win32 (WinDAC32) and XingMP3 Encoder a try. Between them, these two programs give you the basic capabilities of AudioCatalyst. Add a normalizer (WavNormalizer, a utility described in Chapter 7, and included on the book CD, is a great choice), write a few scripts to tie them all together, and you end up with about the same functionality.

Combine programs from Chapter 4 and Chapter 5, throw in a Web browser and some utilities from Chapter 7, and you have a fairly complete MP3 acquisition, management, and playback system. There is another way. Chapter 6 addresses all-in-one MP3 players. These programs include a ripper, encoder, MP3 player, normalizer, playlist editor (another very useful utility), audio CD player, and who knows what else, all in one package. If dealing with one program instead of half a dozen sounds appealing, you will enjoy Chapter 6.

MusicMatch™ Jukebox and Other All-in-One MP3 Players

If you're more interested in playing music than in playing with software, an all-in-one player is your best bet. These programs combine at least an MP3 player, playlist editor, CD ripper, and MP3 encoder in one product. That means you can do it all with one program: convert your CDs to MP3s, manage your music, and play it back.

All-in-one player is an MP3 player that includes a playlist editor, audio CD ripper, and MP3 encoder, in addition to its ability to play MP3 files.

DEFINITION

When you're looking for an all-in-one player, you should try MusicMatch Jukebox. This top-rated player has all the characteristics of all-in-one players, plus a normalizer, equalizer, the ability to display album covers and lyrics, and on and on. MusicMatch Jukebox is my recommendation for best overall all-in-one player.

However, as always, you might not agree with me, or you might just want to try some of the competition in this category. In that case, you'll like the last part of this chapter, which includes coverage of the one all-in-one player that appears capable of challenging MusicMatch Jukebox for the crown of champion all-in-one player: RealJukebox.

The high notes you'll hit in this chapter are:

▌ Installing, configuring, and using MusicMatch Jukebox
▌ RealJukebox

MusicMatch Jukebox

MusicMatch Jukebox is a do-it-all MP3 machine, for rippin' tracks and playin' them back.

TIP

If you're looking for one package that can do it all, rip tracks, encode them as MP3, play MP3s and CDs, even make like a jukebox, you're looking for MusicMatch Jukebox. This powerful and popular product offers multiple features that make it a clear choice for anyone seeking an all-in-one solution for dealing with MP3. Here are some of them:

- Built-in ripper and encoder
- Ability to listen to music while you record it
- Playlist editor and music library for tracking your tracks and playing them back the way you want
- Equalizer, normalizer, and many other music controls
- Variable bit rate (VBR) recording capability for the ultimate in playback quality
- Added cover art, lyrics, and more to go with your favorite songs
- Connection to CDDB to display CD track, artist, and more
- Links to online music sites and the CDNow online music store
- Themes, allowing you to change the look of the user interface.

This chapter covers all these features of MusicMatch Jukebox, plus minor details like how to play music with it.

MusicMatch Jukebox System Requirements

To use MusicMatch successfully, your system must meet these requirements:

- Windows 95 or 98, or Windows NT 4.0 operating system
- Pentium 166 or better processor
- 16 MB of RAM (32 MB for Windows NT)
- 30 MB available disk space
- Sound card
- Speakers or headphones.

Where to Get MusicMatch Jukebox

We've made arrangements with MusicMatch, Inc. to include the unregistered version of MusicMatch Jukebox 4.0 on the CD in the back of this book. Installing this version will let you get up and going right away. However, you should be sure to visit the Music-Match Web site at **www.musicmatch.com**. The Web site (Figure

6.1) will always have the latest version of the program, as well as news, information, music, and connections to related Web sites.

FIGURE 6.1

The MusicMatch Web site should be a regular destination for anyone who uses MusicMatch Jukebox.

What Does MusicMatch Jukebox Cost?

The standard version of MusicMatch is free. It allows you to rip an unlimited number of tracks from CDs, and play back an unlimited number of songs. However, the standard version can only record up to 96 kbps. This recording quality is known as *near-CD quality recording*.

To be able to record at *CD quality* (128 kbps or better), you need to upgrade to the enhanced version of MusicMatch Jukebox. This offers CD quality recording as well as VBR recording. You can buy the enhanced version for $29.99, or upgrade from the standard version for the same price at a later date.

Installing MusicMatch Jukebox

Follow these steps to install MusicMatch Jukebox:

NOTE

During the installation process, MusicMatch Jukebox will strongly recommend that you close all other Windows applications until you finish the installation. It would be a good idea to do so now, and save yourself the trouble of exiting Setup, closing everything, then restarting Setup.

1. Insert the book CD in your computer's CD-ROM drive.
2. Using Windows Explorer, browse the CD until you reach *X*:\All-in-One Players\MusicMatch Jukebox, where *X* is the drive letter for your CD-ROM drive.
3. Double-click the file named **mmjb4526.exe**. This self-extracting executable file does the work of installing Music-Match Jukebox on your system. After a couple of dialog boxes about unpacking files fly by, the MusicMatch Jukebox splash screen appears and the Setup program initializes a wizard to walk you through the rest of the installation. Eventually the Welcome dialog box appears.
4. Click **Next** to continue. Setup displays the software license agreement.
5. Read the license agreement then click **Yes** to accept the agreement, or **No** to abort the installation. If you click **Yes**, the Choose Destination Location dialog box appears.
6. Unless you have good reason to do otherwise, click **Next** to let Setup install the program in the destination directory it suggests. The Choose Music Folder Destination dialog box appears.
7. Choose a folder for MusicMatch Jukebox to save MP3s to when it records them from a CD. I recommend you change the default folder to something like C:\My Music. You can use a folder like that with any MP3 player you want, without risk of losing track of your music.
8. Click **Next** to continue. The Select Program Folder dialog box appears.
9. Let Setup use the default folder it suggests by clicking **Next**. MusicMatch Jukebox copies information to your PC, and displays a Question dialog box.
10. Click **Yes** to make MusicMatch Jukebox your default MP3 player. Another Question dialog box appears.

11. Click **Yes** to make MusicMatch Jukebox your default CD player. The Setup Complete dialog box appears.
12. Click **Finish** to complete the installation process. Setup creates a MusicMatch Jukebox shortcut on your Windows Desktop. Installation is complete.

Configuring MusicMatch Jukebox

If MusicMatch isn't already running, double-click its icon on the Windows desktop to start the program. First to appear is the splash screen, with its introductory message and graphics. After the splash screen, MusicMatch itself appears, looking something like Figure 6.2. What you see on the screen is actually a stack of three components. The topmost component is the Player. In the middle of the stack is the Music Library. The bottom component is the Recorder.

NOTE

Don't be concerned if you don't see all of the components when you start MusicMatch Jukebox. You can start the other components from the Player whenever you need them.

MusicMatch sets itself up to work just fine on your PC. However, it would be worthwhile to check some options before you start ripping and playing songs. These options are on the General and Recorder tabbed pages, which you reach by selecting the **Settings...** command on the Options menu.

Follow these instructions:

1. Click **Options** then **Settings**.
2. On the page that appears, click the **General** tab if the General tabbed page isn't visible.
3. On the General tabbed page set the checkboxes for using MusicMatch Jukebox as your default .mp3, .m3u, and CD player. This will ensure that MusicMatch Jukebox is the program that Windows activates to play MP3 tracks (.mp3), playlists (.m3u), or standard audio CDs.

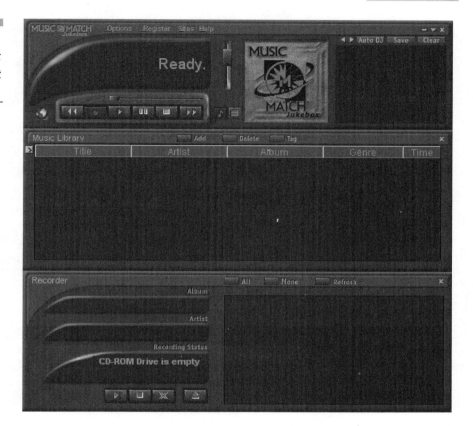

FIGURE 6.2
MusicMatch Jukebox as it appears the first time you start it.

4. Set or clear the Don't Ask Again checkbox in the Ask for Diagnostic Info Upload permission box. By default, Music-Match Jukebox periodically uploads diagnostic information about your copy of MusicMatch Jukebox to the MusicMatch computers. Technicians use this information if you ever need technical assistance. For some people, this function could be a privacy issue. The checkbox doesn't turn this function on or off. Instead, it controls whether or not MusicMatch Juke-box asks for permission before uploading your diagnostic information. If you clear this checkbox, MusicMatch Jukebox will always ask before uploading your information. You can then tell it no, if you don't want MusicMatch to have this information.

5. On the Recorder tabbed page, make sure the program is set for the optimum recording quality. If you have the standard version of MusicMatch Jukebox, the highest recording quality you can use is near-CD quality (96 kbps). If you bought the enhanced version, you can go to 128 kbps or higher. In most cases you won't notice any difference between 128 kbps and 160 kbps. Stick with 128 kbps for the best balance of quality versus file size. Ignore the custom quality settings. The VBR setting can yield extremely high-quality recordings, but isn't something for the casual user to get involved with. If you're really interested in this setting, check the MusicMatch Jukebox help system for more info.

That's all the configuration you need to do before you're ready to roll.

Using MusicMatch Jukebox

MusicMatch Jukebox is simple to use. Follow the steps in the MusicMatch Jukebox Quick Start section to get some music playing. Once you do that, you will be able to have a musical accompaniment while you look at the individual components a little more closely.

NOTE

The separate components of MusicMatch Jukebox even want to move as if they're part of a rack. Take a minute and drag the other components away from the Player component. Now they all move independently. Drag a component into position near the bottom of the stack of components. When you get it close to position, the thing will jump into place. This actually makes sense, but the first few times I saw it, I thought there was something wrong with my system.

MusicMatch Jukebox Quick Start

The basic approach to playing music on MusicMatch is to get songs into the Music Library. From there, you can move those you want to hear into the Playlist, then use the Player to control playback. The four techniques you need are:

- Adding MP3s to the Music Library
- Creating and playing playlists
- Ripping CDs into MP3s
- Putting the Auto DJ to work.

Adding MP3s to the Music Library

When you add MP3 files to the Music Library, you don't actually drag them to a new location on your hard drive. The Music Library really works more like a computerized card catalog. It contains records with information about your MP3s, including title, artist, album, genre, and play length (time). If you have a favorite place to keep your music, you don't have to worry about Music-Match messing up your system.

To add an MP3 file to the Music Library:

1. If the Music Library isn't already open, open it by clicking the music note button on the Player.
2. Click **Add** to open the Add Songs to Music Library dialog box.
3. Follow the directions in the dialog box to add one or more tracks to the Music Library.

Creating and Playing Playlists

A playlist is a group of tracks that MusicMatch Jukebox is playing, or will play. You can create playlists of favorite songs, or songs about New York, or whatever criteria you want. You create and manage playlists in the PlayList component of MusicMatch Jukebox.

To create and play a playlist:

1. Click the **Expand** button (the small arrowhead facing right on the Player, next to the button labeled Auto DJ) to expand the PlayList to its full size.
2. Open the Music Library if it isn't already open.
3. Double-click tracks in the Music Library to add them to the left-most column of the PlayList component. If you want to

add several tracks simultaneously, you can do so by selecting them (using the **Shift** and **Ctrl** key), then drag and drop them into the PlayList.

4. Once you have a playlist you're happy with, click **Save** to save that playlist. When you save a playlist, its name appears in the center column of the PlayList.

5. Select a playlist from the list of saved playlists, then click **Play** on the Player to listen to the playlist.

Ripping CDs into MP3s

One of the great features of MusicMatch Jukebox is its ability to automatically rip tracks from your audio CDs and turn them into MP3s, without relying on separate rippers, normalizers, and encoders. MusicMatch will even go onto the Internet and get information about the CD from CDDB, the world's largest CD database, automatically filling in track information for you (when it is available).

To rip CDs into MP3s:

1. Insert an audio CD into your CD-ROM drive.

2. Click the **Record** button (the button with the red circle in it) on the Player to open the Recorder. If it hasn't yet done so, MusicMatch Jukebox automatically configures your CD-ROM drive.

NOTE

I don't know what MusicMatch does when it autoconfigures a drive, but it actually "fixed" one of my PCs. For some reason, I could never rip CDs on that particular computer. I could play CDs, and I could play MP3s that came from some other computer, but I couldn't get the thing to rip CDs no matter what I tried. When I installed MusicMatch Jukebox on that machine, it did its "configure the CD-ROM drive routine" (Figure 6.3 shows the dialog box that tells you your system is being autoconfigured) and from that point on, I've been able to rip CDs, not only with MusicMatch Jukebox, but with every ripper I've tried.

3. If your PC has an active Internet connection, MusicMatch Jukebox connects to the Net and contacts CDDB to get any information available for the CD. MusicMatch enters whatever information it finds into the Recorder.

4. In the Recorder, select the tracks you want to record as MP3s.

5. Click **Start**. When MusicMatch finishes recording the tracks, they appear in the Music Library.

Putting the Auto DJ to Work

The Auto DJ creates custom playlists based on criteria you choose. The Auto DJ is easier to use than to explain, so follow these steps to create playlists with the Auto DJ:

1. Click **Auto DJ** to open the Auto DJ dialog box shown in Figure 6.4.

2. Enter the length of the playlist you want Auto DJ to create.

3. Select up to three criteria you want Auto DJ to use when creating your custom playlist. Look at Figure 6.4, or fire up Auto DJ yourself to see all the criteria you can use. As you enter the criteria, Auto DJ starts to create your playlist.

4. Once you finish entering playlist criteria, click **Preview** to see which songs Auto DJ has selected for you.

5. If you're happy with Auto DJ's selections, click **Get Tracks** to add those selections to the list of tracks to be played. If you're not happy with Auto DJ's suggestions, click **Cancel** and try again, or create a playlist manually.

6. If MusicMatch Jukebox isn't already playing music, click **Play** on the Player to start listening to the playlist. If MusicMatch

is already playing music, it adds Auto DJ's playlist to the end of the list already playing.

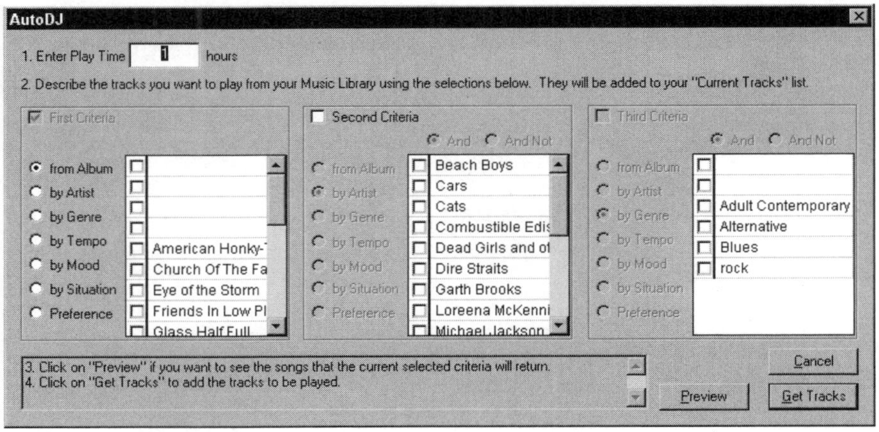

FIGURE 6.4

Answer a few simple questions, and the Auto DJ will create a custom playlist for you.

Going Deeper: The Main Screen (Player and Playlist)

The core of MusicMatch Jukebox is the Main screen (Figure 6.5). The Main Screen consists of two parts, the Player and the Playlist. The Player has the play control buttons, the volume control, track information and the graphics display area (the spot containing the MusicMatch Jukebox logo in the figure).

FIGURE 6.5

The Main screen is the control center of MusicMatch Jukebox.

The play control buttons work just as they do on any stereo, and the volume control is a simple slider. If you insert an audio CD into your computer, MusicMatch Jukebox automatically prepares to play it by loading all the tracks from the CD into the Playlist, and activating all the controls on the Player.

The button with the red dot in it is the Recorder button. Click it to open the Recorder screen and suck songs off audio CDs by creating MP3 copies of them on your hard drive. The button that looks like the globe opens your Web browser to the MusicMatch Web site. The one with the musical note opens the Music Library screen, while the one with the three horizontal lines opens the Track Information screen.

The graphics display area becomes interesting when you play an MP3 file that takes advantage of MusicMatch Jukebox's ability to display additional information stored in an MP3 file. In such a case, the graphics display area will contain an image of the CD cover for the current track, or some other relevant graphic.

If you want to keep MusicMatch Jukebox on your Windows desktop while you play music, but don't want it to be so obvious, you can shrink it. Click the down arrowhead in the upper right corner of the Main Screen to reduce the screen to a size just large enough for the play controls and the name of the track, as in Figure 6.6.

FIGURE 6.6
MusicMatch Jukebox gets small.

While the Player has the primary controls for the MusicMatch Jukebox system, the Playlist is where all the action is. For the Player to play a track, that track must appear in the Playlist. Unless you tell MusicMatch Jukebox not to play audio CDs, the tracks on any CD you insert in your computer automatically appear in the Playlist. You can also open MP3 files directly from the Player (by using the Options menu), and add them to the Playlist. Or you can drag one or more tracks from the Music Library (covered a bit later) into the Playlist. Or just double-click a single track in the Music Library to add it to the Playlist. While you can work with the Playlist as it appears in Figure 6.5, if you want to do anything more than just drag in songs and start them playing, you should expand the Playlist. The controls for doing this are the two little arrowheads that appear above the Playlist. Click the left arrowhead to put the Playlist into Integrated mode, as it appears in Figure 6.5. Click the right arrowhead to put the Playlist into Expanded Mode, where it appears as you see it in Figure 6.7.

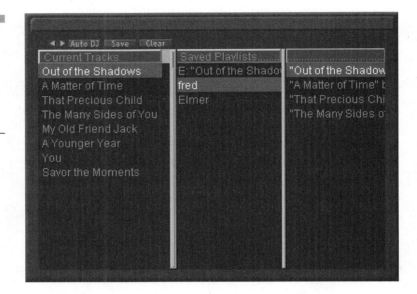

FIGURE 6.7

In Expanded mode, the Playlist screen gives you complete control over individual playlists.

In the expanded Playlist, the left column is the current playlist. This is where tracks go when you add them to a playlist. The middle column lists all your saved playlists. As you would expect, you can save any playlist and recall it later. Click the **Save** button to name and save the current playlist. It will then appear in the middle column. If you double-click a playlist in this column, Music-Match Jukebox copies its contents into the left column, making it the current playlist.

NOTE

Don't forget that you can also use Auto DJ to create playlists, as explained earlier in the chapter. If you need additional information on Auto DJ, there is a decent explanation of how it works in the Help system.

If you select a playlist in the middle column, the tracks that make up that playlist appear in the right column of the Playlist.

Music Library

The Music Library is a collection of pointers to your music. It resembles Figure 6.8, with a different set of tracks visible, of course. You can sort the tracks in the library by clicking the category you want to use for sorting. You can adjust the width of the columns by dragging the dividers between the categories.

FIGURE 6.8

The Music Library keeps track of your tunes, wherever they may be on your hard drive.

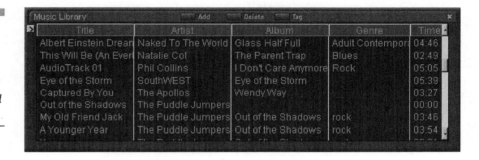

Add tracks to the library by clicking **Add**. When you do, the Add Songs to Music Library dialog box appears. This dialog box (Figure 6.9) is more powerful than the Open dialog box players usually use to add tracks, but has some quirks you need to know about.

Using this dialog box, you can explore your system, looking for MP3 files and other file types that MusicMatch Jukebox knows how to play. When you find a folder that contains the kind of file you're looking for, all such files from that folder appear in the Files list. If you want to add any of those files to the Music Library, you select them in this window, using standard Windows file selection commands. You can add any number of tracks from a single folder to your Music Library by selecting those tracks and clicking **OK**.

You can't manually select tracks from more than one folder at a time. However, if you check the Include subdirectories checkbox, MusicMatch Jukebox adds the songs you selected in the current folder, and every song in every subfolder of that folder, whether or not that song is already in the Music Library. While this is a powerful tool for adding songs to your Music Library when you first install MusicMatch Jukebox, you can easily mess yourself up.

While working on this chapter, I ended up with multiple copies of songs in the library and had to delete the whole thing and start over. Like all powerful tools, the Add Songs to Music Library dialog box can bite you if you misuse it.

FIGURE 6.9

The Add Songs to Music Library dialog box is a powerful tool for finding and tracking music on your PC.

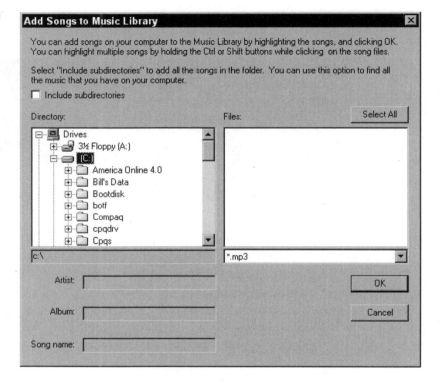

To delete a song from the Music Library, select the song, then click **Delete**.

You can also tag songs in the Music Library. Tagging a song means adding additional information about the song to the tag fields that MP3 files can contain. To tag a song, select it in the Music Library, then click **Tag** to open the Tag Songs dialog box shown in Figure 6.10.

This dialog box is another powerful but quirky tool. When you open it, it contains whatever information is available in the tag fields for the selected track. As Figure 6.10 shows, this can include massive amounts of information. Many of the fields are pull-down lists where you select the option that best applies to the track. When a field isn't a pull-down list, you just type the appropriate information.

FIGURE 6.10

The Tag Songs dialog box allows you to add background information, even graphics, to your MP3 files.

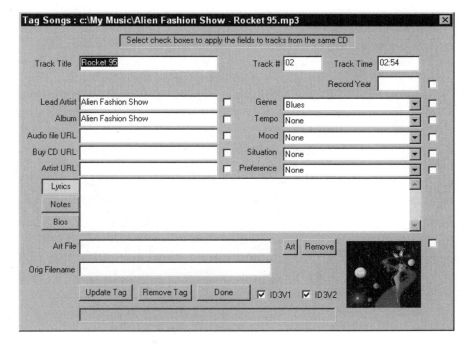

With the Art field, you can include cover art that appears on the Main screen in the graphics display area while the track is playing. You can download or scan art to appear in this location.

NOTE

You can get a more detailed explanation of tagging in the MusicMatch Jukebox help file. Look at the Tag topic under the MusicMatch Jukebox Components section in help.

You'll notice that there are white checkboxes next to many of the fields. You can save yourself lots of typing by checking any of these boxes to apply the information in that field to all tracks from the same CD. For example, I downloaded a track from the Alien Fashion Show CD and liked it enough to get the actual CD. Then I went into this dialog box and selected the white checkboxes for the fields I wanted to apply to other tracks from the same CD.

When I clicked Update Tag, MusicMatch Jukebox modified all the other Alien Fashion Show tracks listed in the Music Library, giving them tags with the selected information. It's quick and easy, once you figure out what you need to do.

Track Info

You probably noticed that there is space in the Tag Songs dialog box for a lot more information than appears in the Music Library, or on the Player. To see this additional information, you need to open Track Info. To open Track Info, go to the Player and click the button that has the three horizontal lines on it. Figure 6.11 shows Track Info with biographical information from the song "Detroit Swing City."

FIGURE 6.11

Track Info is the place to see lyrics, artist bios and notes for the current track.

Click the **Lyrics**, **Bios**, or **Notes** buttons to see this kind of information if it is available for the track. The **Tag** button opens the Tag Songs dialog box, while the **Buy CD** button launches your Web browser and connects you to the CDNow Web site where you can buy the CD from which the track comes.

NOTE

Any MP3s you download directly from the MusicMatch Web site will contain album art and lyrics.

Recorder

The last component to talk about is Recorder (Figure 6.12). As its name suggests, you use Recorder to record tracks from your CDs and convert them to MP3s. To record, insert an audio CD into the CD-ROM drive, start MusicMatch Jukebox, then open the Recorder by clicking the button on the Player with the red circle in it. If MusicMatch Jukebox hasn't already done so, the first time you open Recorder, the program automatically configures itself for the optimum recording.

FIGURE 6.12
Use Recorder to copy music off your CDs and onto your PC.

When you record tracks and are connected to the Internet, Recorder contacts the CDDB Web site and requests information on the CD you are recording. With this information, Recorder can fill in track information for you. If Recorder can't get track information from CDDB, you can still enter it yourself. To do so, click the number of the track you want to edit, then type the track name directly into Recorder.

You can choose the tracks you want to record by marking the checkboxes to the left of each track. You can also click **All** to record all tracks or **None** to clear all your selections. The Refresh button forces MusicMatch Jukebox to contact CDDB and refresh the track information for the current CD.

Before you start recording, you should decide where you want MusicMatch Jukebox to store the tracks you record. To do this, go to Player, and in the Options menu, select **Recorder**, then **Settings**. This opens the Recorder tabbed page on the Settings dialog box. Now click **Songs Directory** to open the New Songs Directory dialog box. Enter the path to the directory where you want MusicMatch Jukebox to store recorded tracks. For simplicity, I created a My Music folder, and directed MusicMatch Jukebox to put recorded tracks there. By keeping everything in one place, I'm less likely to create problems for myself or MusicMatch Jukebox by moving things around.

Another useful set of options in the New Songs Directory Options dialog box is in the Name Song File Using section of the dialog box. Set the options to have Recorder name tracks the way you want them named.

As you record each track, the progress of the recording appears next to the name of the track. If the track gets recorded cleanly, the box containing the track number turns green. If the track was recorded, but sound quality isn't optimal, the box turns yellow. Finally, if the recording failed for some reason, the box turns red.

Recorder automatically normalizes tracks as it records them, so you don't have to worry about levels varying from CD to CD or even track to track.

NOTE

MusicMatch Jukebox Wrapup

You've toured the components (Player, Playlist, Music Library, Track Info and Recorder) of this great all-in-one player, and gotten the information you need to use each component. You should be set to have MusicMatch Jukebox handle all your MP3 needs. But if you're feeling like doing some more experimenting, keep reading and give RealJukebox a try.

RealJukebox

Realjukebox brings all of RealNetworks' MP3 tools together into a single package.

TIP

Although MusicMatch Jukebox (**www.real.com/jukebox**) is my favorite all-in-one MP3 player, RealJukebox (Figure 6.13) (a new all-in-one player from RealNetworks) could give MusicMatch Jukebox a run for its money. The rest of the chapter takes you on a high-speed tour of RealJukebox.

RealNetworks are the people who gave the world the RealPlayer family of products. RealJukebox is built on solid technology and offers multiple features.

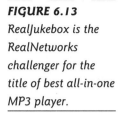

FIGURE 6.13

RealJukebox is the RealNetworks challenger for the title of best all-in-one MP3 player.

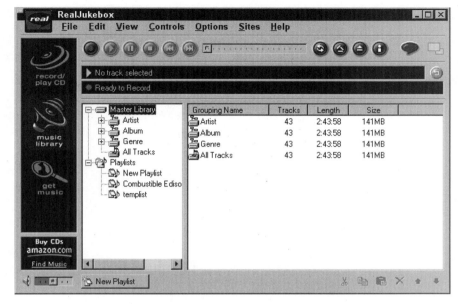

Features of RealJukebox include:

▌ Built-in ripper and encoder
▌ Ability to listen to music while you record it
▌ Playlist editor and music library for tracking your tracks and playing them back the way you want
▌ Links to online music sites and stores
▌ Automatic links to CDDB to identify CD track, artist, and album
▌ Wizards and tips to help you complete common tasks.

NOTE

When this chapter was being written, RealJukebox was still a beta product. That means it was available for people to use, but not yet released as a regular product. By the time you read this, RealJukebox is likely to be a fully functional released product. This has a couple of ramifications that affect how RealJukebox is covered in this chapter. First, the installation procedures will likely change, so they're not covered here. Second, I don't know what, if anything, the released version will cost. In some ways, the coverage of RealJukebox is less complete than you might like. But given how good the product is already, it may well be worth your time to investigate RealJukebox anyway.

System Requirements

To use RealJukebox successfully, your system must meet these requirements:

- Windows 95 with Service Pack 1 or Windows 98, or Windows NT 4.0 with Service Pack 4
- Pentium 200 processor or equivalent
- 32 MB of RAM
- 200 MB of free disk space
- 16-bit color video card
- Internet connection
- Sound card.

Where to Get RealJukebox

You get RealJukebox by downloading it from the RealNetworks Web site at **www.real.com**.

Using RealJukebox

Now that you've learned about MusicMatch Jukebox, RealJukebox should be easy to figure out. The components of RealJukebox are more integrated than those of MusicMatch Jukebox, so you do everything from the main RealJukebox window. You switch RealJukebox from one mode of operation to another by clicking the icons along the left edge of the window. Some of the controls, specifically those across the top and down the left side, are common to all modes. The controls are generally self-explanatory, but if you're not sure what one does, point to it with the mouse. If you hold the mouse pointer still for a couple of seconds, a tool tip appears, telling you what the control does.

Record/Play CD Mode

To record or play tracks from a CD, click **Record/Play CD**. When you do, the RealJukebox window will look something like Figure 6.14.

FIGURE 6.14

RealJukebox is ready to record or play tracks from the Out of the Shadows CD.

As with MusicMatch Jukebox, you click the button with the red dot in it to start recording. RealJukebox gets information from CDDB (assuming you have an active connection to the Internet when you insert the CD) to fill in the track names and lengths. You can choose which tracks to record by marking the checkboxes before specific tracks, or by clicking the **Check All** button (it looks like a checked box and is located below the track list) or **Check None** button.

Music Library Mode

To get to Music Library mode, click the **Music Library** icon on the left side of the main RealJukebox window. The lower right side of the window changes to allow easy file management, as Figure 6.15 illustrates.

RealJukebox organizes files around Groups. To create a Group, go to the Options menu then select **Preferences**. Click the **Master Library** tab in the Preferences dialog box to see the Master Library tabbed page. Choose any or all of the available Groups, then click **OK** to add those Groups to the main screen, under the

Master Library heading. In Figure 6.15, Artist, Album, and Genre are groups. So is All Tracks, which is the default group.

FIGURE 6.15

Managing your music is what the Music Library mode is all about.

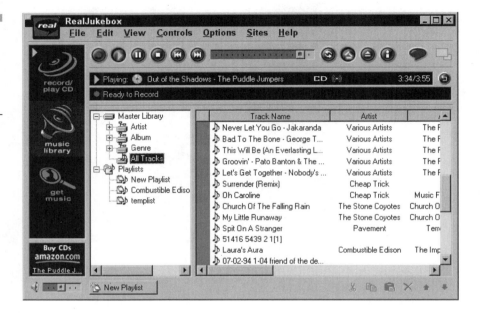

You can open a particular group (click the plus sign to the left of the group name) to choose among the subgroups it contains. For example, when I open the Genre group, I see subgroups like Alternative and Rock. If I select Rock, RealJukebox displays a list of all my tracks that fit that genre. I can select some or all of the tracks that appear, then click Play to listen to them. Or I can use Groups to make filling playlists easier.

To create a playlist, click the **New Playlist** button. RealJukebox displays a dialog box you can use to name the playlist. Your new playlist appears as a folder under the Playlists folder. In Figure 6.15, New Playlist, Combustible Edison, and templist are playlists I created.

Now select a Group that contains tracks you want to add to your playlist. Select tracks and drag into the new playlist folder. Continue dragging tracks into your playlist until you're happy with it. To see exactly what's in a playlist, click that playlist's folder. RealJukebox displays the contents of the playlist.

Get Music Mode

In this mode, instead of the Music Library or the tracks of a CD, the lower right part of the RealJukebox window is occupied by links to the Web. These links are divided into three tabbed pages, as shown in Figure 6.16.

FIGURE 6.16

In Get Music mode, RealJukebox gives you links to dozens of Web sites where you can download, search for, or buy music.

To take advantage of these links, just click the tab you're interested in, then click any of the links on the tabbed page that appears. This mode is an easy way to visit key MP3 Web sites.

RealJukebox Wrapup

While there is plenty more to RealJukebox that isn't covered here, you have enough information to put the program through its paces. By combining the information in the preceding pages with the general skills and techniques you learned for MusicMatch Jukebox, you'll have no trouble exploring RealJukebox.

Chapter Wrapup

When all you want to do is record and play MP3s, an all-in-one player is your best bet. You don't want to waste time selecting separate players, rippers, encoders, and playlist editors—you just want one program that will do it all. MusicMatch Jukebox does it all, and it does it all in a flexible, easy-to-use package. A few of the dialog boxes may have some quirks to them, but now that you know about them they shouldn't bite you. MusicMatch Jukebox is definitely the leader in this category.

RealJukebox is a worthy challenger to MusicMatch Jukebox. While it is still in beta, this all-in-one player is stable, functional, and built around proven technology from RealNetworks. You can't go wrong with either of these products.

In the last three chapters, you learned a lot about players, rippers, and encoders. That's only fitting, as these are the key tools you need in your MP3 toolkit. But they're not the only tools available. Just as with your home toolkit, there are times when having the right specialized tool makes your life much easier. This is particularly true for anyone using standalone tools instead of an all-in-one player like those covered in this chapter.

Whatever your situation, there are utilities that might be just what you need for handling MP3 files your own way. The next chapter looks at an assortment of such utilities.

CHAPTER 7

Cool
Utility Guide

If you're taking the component-by-component approach to MP3, this chapter is a treasure trove. With a standalone player (or more than one if you wish), a ripper, and an encoder, you have everything you need to play music and convert tracks from audio CDs into MP3s. But just because you have the basics doesn't mean your toolkit is full.

MP3 utilities are specialized tools that do things your players, rippers, and encoders don't, or that do them better than the functions built into your players, ripper, or encoders do. Here are the five utilities covered in this chapter, along with very short explanations of what they're for:

- MP3 PopUp! adds a pop-up menu to Windows, allowing you to click the name of an MP3 file and have it play.
- ID3 Editor lets you add track information right into MP3 files so that it can be displayed when the tracks play.
- ShufflePlay creates a playlist and manages your MP3 files, even if those files are on removable media like a backup tape or CD-ROM .
- WavNormalizer adjusts the level of the sound for files ripped from audio CDs, allowing you to compensate for differences between the ways CDs were recorded, and to take full advantage of the audio range of MP3 files.
- MP3 Renamer does exactly what you would expect—it renames MP3 files, a capability that can be very handy.

I've provided detailed instructions on installing and using each of the utilities listed here. Thanks to the authors of these utilities, I've also included a copy of each of them on the book CD. You should have no trouble putting these utilities to work.

MP3 PopUp!

TIP

MP3 PopUp! is a handy pop-up MP3 menu from Gene6, a French outfit.

MP3 PopUp! adds a special MP3 pop-up menu to your Windows 95 or 98 system. Select a song in this menu and MP3 PopUp! can direct your default MP3 player to play the song. There is no rummaging through your system looking for the folder that contains the song you want to hear. Just find it in the MP3 PopUp! menu and click it to hear it.

System Requirements

To use MP3 PopUp! successfully, your system must meet these requirements:

- Windows 95 or 98 operating system
- Any MP3 player to play the files selected with MP3 PopUp.

Where to Get MP3 PopUp!

MP3 PopUp! is included on the book CD. If your computer doesn't have a CD-ROM drive, you can download the latest copy of MP3 PopUp! from the Gene6 Web site at: **www.gene6.com/prod1.html**.

What Does MP3 PopUp! Cost?

MP3 PopUp! is freeware.

Installing MP3 PopUp!

Follow these steps to install MP3 PopUp!:

1. Insert the book CD in your computer's CD-ROM drive.
2. Using Windows Explorer, browse the CD until you reach *X*:\Utilities\MP3 PopUp, where *X* is the drive letter for your CD-ROM drive.
3. Double-click **Mp3setup.exe**. This opens the Installation dialog box.
4. The Destination text box suggests a destination folder in which to install MP3 PopUp!. You can accept the suggested

folder, click the **ellipsis** (...) to the right of the Destination text box to browse for a folder to install in, or directly edit the path in the Destination text box. Unless you have a specific reason to do differently, you should accept the suggested folder.

5. Click **Install** when you are happy with the location where MP3 PopUp! will be installed.

6. As the Setup program does its work, it gives you choices. If the destination folder doesn't exist, Setup asks permission to create that folder. Setup also asks if you want a desktop icon for MP3 PopUp!, and if you would like it to create a shortcut in the Windows Start menu. Click **Yes** for each of these questions to get the maximum benefit from MP3 PopUp!.

7. Finally, Setup asks if you want to launch MP3 PopUp! now. Click **Yes** to complete the installation and start the program.

Configuring MP3 PopUp!

Once you have MP3 PopUp! installed and running, you need to configure it. Follow these steps:

1. Right-click the **M** icon in the Windows System Tray. This opens the MP3 PopUp! pop-up menu. This menu closes after you select an option, so you will need to repeat this step for each option you set.

2. Select the **Drives** menu. Choose the drives you want MP3 PopUp! to scan for music files. Select **All Drives** to find every MP3 file on your computer.

3. Select the **Options** menu. Figure 7.1 shows the large set of options you have for configuring MP3 PopUp!. I recommend you choose the settings in the following table.

FIGURE 7.1

MP3 PopUp! adds a highly customizable pop-up music menu to your Windows PC.

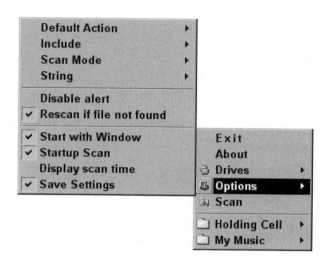

TABLE 7.1

Recommended MP3 PopUp! options

Option	Description
Rescan if file not found	Select this so MP3 PopUp! will automatically search for files that have moved since the last scan.
Start with Windows	Causes MP3 PopUp! to start whenever you start your computer.
Startup Scan	MP3 PopUp! scans for music as soon as it starts running. This is useful if you are actively collecting new MP3 files.
Save Settings	MP3 PopUp! automatically saves any changes you make to its settings.
Default Action	Select Play to direct your default MP3 player to play the selected file immediately.
Include	Select + Dir, + Subdir, + File Ext, + Icons, and Mp3 to search for MP3 files in every part of every folder in the disk drives you selected in the Drives submenu.
Scan Mode	Select Fast for quick scanning of files in every folder except those marked as Read Only in Windows.

Using MP3 PopUp!

Once you finish configuring MP3 PopUp!, you're ready to put it to work. Right-click the MP3 PopUp! icon in the Windows System tray. When the MP3 PopUp! menu appears, click **Scan**. A red "Mp3" appears in the icon while MP3 PopUp! scans your system. Once the scan is complete, the word Mp3 turns green if MP3 PopUp! finds any MP3 files. The MP3 disappears if MP3 PopUp! doesn't find any MP3 files on your system.

Now right-click the MP3 PopUp! icon in the Windows System Tray. If MP3 PopUp! found MP3 files, the bottom section of the pop-up menu will contain folders. Each of those folders contains MP3 files you can play. In Figure 7.1, Holding Cell and My Music are folders containing MP3 files.

To select the song you want to hear, point the cursor at one of the folders. After a couple of seconds, a new menu appears containing a list of all the MP3 files in that folder. Click one of the songs. If your default MP3 player isn't running, MP3 PopUp! starts the player and tells it to play the MP3 file you clicked. If your MP3 player is already running, and MP3 PopUp! tells your player to stop what it is doing and play the file you clicked. That's it. You're ready to use MP3 PopUp!.

ID3 Editor

TIP

Cosmos, a Norwegian outfit, gives us ID3 Editor for adding useful information to your MP3 files.

MP3 files can carry an additional chunk of information, known as an ID3 tag. This tag contains space for the following information about a song: Title, Artist, Album, Year, Genre, comment.

DEFINITION

The **ID3 tag** is a chunk of data attached to the end of many MP3 files, containing a range of information about the song and the artists.

ID3 Editor allows you to edit all the information stored in an MP3 file's ID3 tag. With ID3 Editor, you can clean up your MP3 files so they contain important information about songs, and so they work well with playlist programs.

NOTE

There is a newer standard for ID3 tags, one that adds types of information that ID3 Editor doesn't know how to work with. Some MP3 files, like those from the MusicMatch Web site, use these additional types of information. However, for now, for most MP3 files, ID3 Editor is fine.

System Requirements

To use ID3 Editor successfully, your system must meet these requirements: Windows 95 or 98 operating system.

What Does ID3 Editor Cost?

ID3 Editor is *bannerware*. A bannerware program is a program that doesn't cost anything to use. Instead, if you like the program, you should go to the author's Web site, and click on the advertising banner of one of the companies that sponsor the Web site. In this case, if you find ID3 Editor useful, you should go to **www.neutralzone.org/cosmos/** and click on the banner ad that runs across the top of the Web page. Investigate what the site's sponsors are offering. Who knows, you might find something you want or need.

Where to Get It

ID3 Editor is included on the book CD. If your computer doesn't have a CD-ROM drive, you can download the latest copy of ID3 Editor from the Cosmos Web site at: **www.neutralzone.org/cosmos/**.

Installing and Configuring ID3 Editor

Follow these steps to install ID3 Editor on your computer:

1. Create the following folder on your hard drive: C:\Program Files\MP3 Utilities\ID3 Editor.
2. Insert the book CD in your computer's CD-ROM drive.
3. Using Windows Explorer, browse the CD until you reach *X*:\Utilities\ID3 Editor, where *X* is the drive letter for your CD-ROM drive.
4. In this folder, select **readme.txt** and **ID3Editor.exe**, and copy them to C:\Program Files\MP3 Utilities\ID3 Editor. That's all there is to it. And since ID3 Editor has no configuration options to set, you are ready to edit ID3 tags.

Using ID3 Editor

Using ID3 Editor is almost as simple as installing it. Double-click the file ID3Editor.exe in C:\Program Files\MP3 Utilities\ID3 Editor to start ID3 Editor. The main window in the program looks like the one in Figure 7.2. As you would expect from looking at the figure, ID3 Editor is very simple to use.

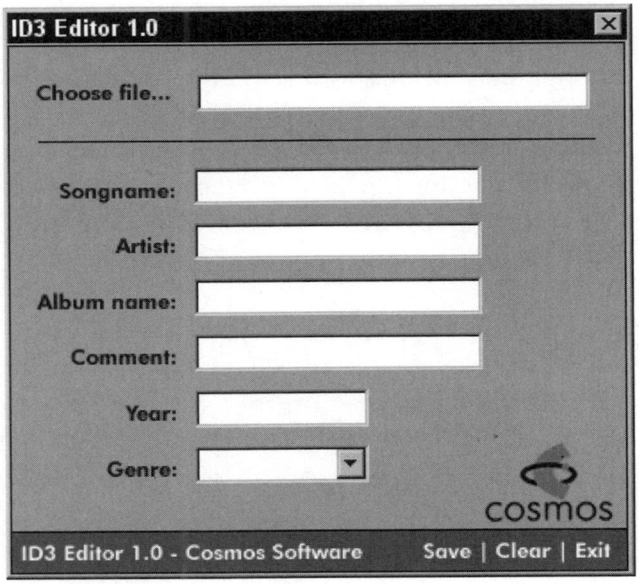

FIGURE 7.2

ID3 Editor makes it simple to modify information (like the title of a song or the artist who performs it) attached to an MP3 file.

Follow these steps to edit the ID3 information attached to an MP3 file:

1. Click the words **Choose file...** to open a standard Windows Open dialog box.
2. Find the file you want to work on and double-click its name to open it in ID3 Editor.
3. If the song you select has information in its ID3 tag, ID3 Editor displays that information in the appropriate fields of the ID3 Editor window.
4. If you want to clear the existing information in all the ID3 fields at once and start over again from scratch, click **Clear** at the bottom of the ID3 Editor window.
5. Edit any of the fields (except Genre) as required. To do so, just click in the text box next to the name of the field you want to edit.
6. To edit the Genre field, click the down arrow on the right side of the Genre text box, then choose one of the genres in the pull-down list that appears.
7. Make all your changes, then click **Save** at the bottom of the main window to apply the changes to the MP3 file on your hard drive.
8. Once you save the MP3 file with its new or modified ID3 information, you can work on another file (by clicking **Choose file...** again) or close ID3 Editor by clicking Exit on the main window.

ShufflePlay

TIP

ShufflePlay, a super playlist editor, comes from flipTech Software in Virginia.

ShufflePlay is a program you don't know you need until you've been doing the MP3 thing for a while. When you've only got a few songs to play, and you're still fooling around with your MP3 player, managing and selecting songs by hand is fun. But what happens when you've got hundreds, or even thousands of MP3s, and you want to listen to some rowdy tunes, or are trying to hit a particular mood? After 20 minutes of searching for that one song you must add to the mix, and selecting that perfect list of tunes, you'll probably give the whole thing up as a bad job and just play whatever is convenient.

That's no way to act, especially since your music lives right on your computer. What you need is a program that makes it easy to create and manage your playlists. ShufflePlay does that, and adds powerful features beyond those found in other playlist managers. Just one look at the ShufflePlay user interface in Figure 7.3 tells you that this is a power tool for your MP3 kit. The pane on the left side of the window is the Folders view. The pane on the right side is the Files view. The pane on the bottom is the Playlist view.

FIGURE 7.3

ShufflePlay packs all the tools you need to manage your MP3 files and playlists into one convenient bundle.

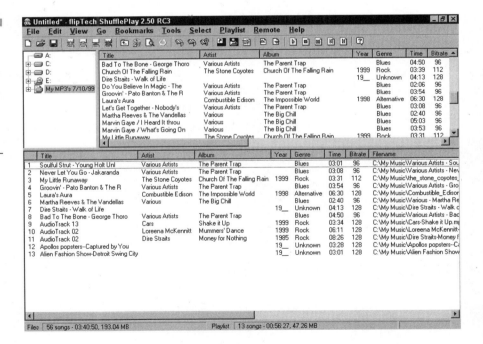

A particularly hot feature of ShufflePlay is virtual-drive support. *Virtual drives* are a way to represent information that may not be stored on your computer at all times. For example, if you record a few thousand songs onto a tape using your RaV6 drive, then remove that tape from the tape drive, what does your playlist program do? In most cases, if your music is on a tape (or any other removable storage medium) that isn't in the drive when your MP3 player or playlist program is looking for it, you're going to have problems.

ShufflePlay's virtual drives make this kind of problem go away. You can create virtual drives to keep track of all the relevant information from any storage medium, whether fixed in place (like your hard drive) or removable (like a CD-ROM). Each CD-ROM or tape cartridge can have its own virtual drive. When you want to create a playlist, or just find a particular MP3 file, ShufflePlay treats any virtual drives you create exactly as if they were real drives. The only time you need to insert the CD-ROM or tape that corresponds to a virtual drive is when you actually want to play a particular file.

Another particularly useful talent of ShufflePlay is the way it can serve as a front-end program for your MP3 player. This means ShufflePlay can, within limits, control your MP3 player program. You can create a playlist using ShufflePlay, then, instead of exiting ShufflePlay, starting your MP3 player, loading the playlist, and playing the playlist with the MP3 player, you can just tell ShufflePlay to play the playlist. Once you set it up, ShufflePlay can start most MP3 players and feed them a playlist to play, without your having to do any of the work.

ShufflePlay can do plenty of other things, some of which you will learn about in the next few pages. But Gary Calpo, the author of ShufflePlay, has created a slick features tour on his Web site, a guide to all the major features of the program complete with case studies like "Hiding your Spice Girls" that illustrate how you can put the features to use.

System Requirements

To use ShufflePlay successfully, your system must meet these requirements: Windows 95 or 98, or Windows NT 3.51 or 4.0 operating system.

Where to Get ShufflePlay

ShufflePlay is included on the book CD. If your computer doesn't have a CD-ROM drive, you can download the latest copy of ShufflePlay from the flipTech Web site at **www.pinoyware.com/ shuffleplay/**.

What Does ShufflePlay Cost?

The cost is $10, although you can pay more if you want to. ShufflePlay is *uncrippled shareware* that you have 14 days to evaluate. The uncrippled bit means that the version of ShufflePlay you get off the book CD has all the features and capabilities of the registered version. So what do you get for your $10? First off, you reward Gary for the work he put into creating the program. Secondly, you encourage him to write more quality software. Third, it's illegal to keep using the program after the registration period if you don't pay for it. After you use ShufflePlay for a week or so, I suspect you'll agree with me that it is easily worth the cost.

Installing ShufflePlay

Follow these steps to install ShufflePlay on your computer:

NOTE

During the installation process, ShufflePlay will recommend that you close all other Windows applications until you finish the installation. It would be a good idea to do so now, and save yourself the trouble of exiting Setup, closing everything, then restarting Setup.

1. Insert the book CD in your computer's CD-ROM drive.
2. Using Windows Explorer, browse the CD until you reach *X*:\Utilities\ShufflePlay, where *X* is the drive letter for your CD-ROM drive.
3. Double-click **Setup.exe** to begin the actual ShufflePlay installation. Setup directs you to close all other running programs (applications) before continuing the installation.
4. Click **OK** when you have closed all other running programs. The next setup dialog box appears.

5. Unless you have some strong reason not to do so, accept Setup's choice of installation directory by clicking the button with the picture of a PC on it. Setup begins to copy the required files to your hard drive and, if successful, displays a "setup was successful" message.

6. Click **OK** to complete the installation process.

Configuring ShufflePlay

Now that you have ShufflePlay installed on your machine, you need to do some configuring. If you haven't done so already, go to the Windows Programs menu (**Start**, then **Programs**) and click **ShufflePlay2**. The most important thing you can do to configure ShufflePlay is to tell it where to find your MP3 player. Here's how you do that:

1. If the Tip of the Day dialog box (Figure 7.4) is open, click **OK** to close it. Now press the **F12** key to open the Setup dialog box.

FIGURE 7.4

ShufflePlay even offers a Tip of the Day when you start the program.

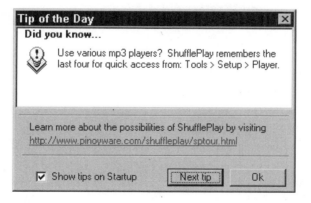

2. In the Player Configuration section of the Setup dialog box, enter the path to your MP3 player in the Player executable text box. Assuming you haven't memorized this path, click **Browse...** and use the Open dialog box to search for your player. You can typically find your player in a folder somewhere within C:\Program Files. Once you find the player,

select it and click **Open**. The Open dialog box closes, and the path to your player appears in the Player executable text box.

3. Click Okay to close the Setup dialog box and start using ShufflePlay.

NOTE

There are many other settings you can use in the Setup dialog box. To get at them, click on one of the pages in the Category list that appears on the left side of the Setup dialog box. But don't do this now. Wait to work with those settings until you've logged some time using ShufflePlay.

Using ShufflePlay

Since ShufflePlay can do so many things and since there is such a comprehensive tutorial on the Web site (click **Help**, then **Online**, then **Online Tour** to take the tour), all you get here is three topics: creating and playing a playlist, creating a virtual drive, and finding duplicate files. This is more than enough to get you started. Beyond that, you're on your own.

Creating and Playing a Playlist

Creating a playlist is the most basic capability for any program of this type. ShufflePlay builds on basic playlist generation with its ability to make your MP3 player play a list directly, as well as in its ability to shuffle the playlist before your player plays it. Changing the order of the songs in a playlist can be just the thing to keep the list from getting stale.

Follow these steps to create and play a playlist:

NOTE

These instructions assume ShufflePlay is running and that you configured it after you installed it. If you didn't, go back to "Configuring ShufflePlay" and finish the job before continuing.

1. In the Folder view, navigate the folders until you come to the one that contains the MP3 files you want to add to a playlist. When you select a folder that contains MP3 files, information about those files appears in the File view. ShufflePlay will

arrange the files in any order within this pane. Click the name of the column (Title, Artist, etc.) you want the files sorted by.

2. Drag a file into the Playlist view, and drop it there to add it to the playlist.

3. Repeat Step 2 for each file you want to add to the playlist.

NOTE

If you plan to let ShufflePlay shuffle the songs before playing them, you can skip Step 4.

4. When you finish adding files to the playlist, you can rearrange them. Select the file you want to move, then use the **Slide Up** and **Slide Down** buttons on the ShufflePlay toolbar (look for two pieces of paper, one with a green up-arrow head on it, the other with a red down-arrow head on it) to move the file to a new location in the playlist.

5. When you're happy with the order of the files, jump to Step 6 if you don't want to save this playlist, or click **Save** playlist on the toolbar (it looks like a floppy disk) to save it. Be sure to give it a good descriptive name, like Hard Rock or Smooth Jazz, so you can reuse it in the future.

6. It's time to play some music. In the ShufflePlay Playlist menu, click **Play** playlist to play the files in their current order, or click **ShufflePlay** playlist to play the current playlist in some random order. After a moment, your MP3 player should start running and begin to play the playlist.

Creating and Using a Virtual Drive

Creating and using a virtual drive is simple. Follow these steps to create a virtual drive for the CD-ROM that comes with this book:

1. Start ShufflePlay if it isn't already running, then load the book CD into your CD-ROM drive.

2. In the ShufflePlay menu bar, click **Tools**, then **Virtual Drives**, then **Add New Image**. ShufflePlay displays the Virtual Drive Wizard (Figure 7.5), which guides you through the rest of the virtual drive creation process.

FIGURE 7.5

Keeping track of music on CD-ROM or tape cartridges is easy with ShufflePlay virtual drives. The Virtual Drive Wizard does all the work for you.

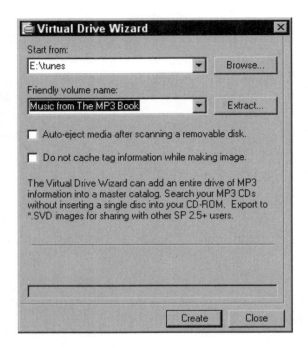

3. Click the **Browse...** button next to the Start From list box. This opens the Browse for Folder dialog box, which allows you to browse around your computer until you find the folder containing the music files you are interested in adding to a virtual drive. Navigate to the Music folder on the book CD. Select that folder.

4. Now you need to give this virtual drive a name. You can enter any name you want, although your best bet is to use something descriptive, so you'll recognize it later. Make sure you have some way to tell which CD-ROM or tape cartridge corresponds to this name. In cases where all the MP3 files on the virtual drive come from the same source, clicking the **Extract...** button will give you a volume name you can use to identify the removable media that corresponds to this virtual drive.

5. Once you have the Start From location and Friendly volume name you want, you can ignore the two check boxes in the wizard's dialog box and click **Create**. ShufflePlay quickly scans the drive for all relevant information about every MP3 file in the Start from folder and all of its subfolders. ShufflePlay cre-

ates the virtual drive beneath the related physical storage device (CD-ROM drive, tape drive, whatever) in the Folders view. You can now do almost anything with the virtual drive that you can do with a real drive. The only difference is that the actual MP3 files may not be available if you try to play them. So, make sure to insert the appropriate CD-ROM or tape cartridge when you want to play something from that drive.

Finding Duplicate Files

If you collect lots of MP3 files, you'll certainly end up with duplicate files eventually. ShufflePlay makes it easy to find and eliminate them. ShufflePlay offers five ways to filter out duplicate files. The author of the program recommends you have ShufflePlay scan by ID3 title. Here's how you do this:

1. In the ShufflePlay Folder view, select the folder that contains the largest portion of your MP3 file collection.
2. In the ShufflePlay menu bar, click **Tools**, then **Management**, then **Duplicate Finder**. This opens the Duplicate Finder dialog box.
3. On the General tabbed page, mark the Current Folder and Virtual Drives check boxes to look for duplicates in those location.
4. If ID3 Title does not appear in the Determine Duplicates Based On dialog box, select it from the pull-down list.
5. If Current folder does not appear in the Display Duplicates Pertaining To dialog box, select it from the pull-down list.
6. Click **Start**. ShufflePlay searches for duplicate files based on the settings you entered in the Duplicate Finder dialog box.
7. If ShufflePlay returns any duplicates, examine their information carefully. Ask yourself, "Is this really a duplicate file, or does it just seem that way to the Duplicate Finder?"
8. If you do find duplicates, right-click one of them in the Duplicate file list in the Duplicate Finder dialog box. You have several options, including options to play the file, copy it, move it, or delete it.
9. Click **Close** when you finish dealing with duplicate files.

WavNormalizer

TIP

WavNormalizer was created by Linearteam, a group of Finnish software developers dedicated to creating free utilities to make everyone's lives easier.

The volume level at which songs are recorded varies from audio CD to audio CD. When you rip songs from audio CDs, you can eliminate the volume differences by normalizing, or adjusting the peak volume level of, each song. WavNormalizer is an effective, easy-to-use freeware normalizer. Best of all, WavNormalizer is included on the CD in the back of the book, so you need not download it from the Web to put it to work.

To do its job, WavNormalizer must be used with a ripper that creates Windows audio files (files in the .wav format), and an encoder (a program that converts .wav files into MP3 files). The process works like this:

1. Rip the tracks you want, and store them as .wav files on the hard drive.
2. Tell WavNormalizer which files you want normalized.
3. WavNormalizer modifies the .wav files "in-place." It adjusts the levels of the files and writes the new values back into the same file. By doing this, WavNormalizer eliminates the need to store the normalized version of the file, delete the original, and rename the normalized version as the old version.
4. Using an encoder like XingMP3 Encoder, convert the normalized .wav files into MP3 files.

System Requirements

To use WavNormalizer successfully, your system must meet these requirements: Windows 95 or 98 operating system, or Windows NT 4.0.

Where to Get WavNormalizer

WavNormalizer is included on the book CD. If your computer doesn't have a CD-ROM drive, you can download the latest copy of WavNormalizer from the Linearteam Web site at **linearteam.iwn.fi/normalizer.html**.

Even if you get WavNormalizer from the CD, you'll want to visit the Linearteam Web site, as WavNormalizer 2.0 is due out before the end of 1999.

What Does WavNormalizer Cost?

WavNormalizer is freeware. However, the author, Tommi Prami, asks that if you use WavNormalizer you send e-mail or a postcard. And if you do want to make a small contribution to the cause, Tommi will certainly accept it.

To contact Tommi, send e-mail to: **tommi.prami@kno.fi**, or write to:

Tommi Prami
Jussintie 7 B8
71800 SIILINJARVI
Finland

If you do write or e-mail, please let Tommi know that you found WavNormalizer in this book.

Installing WavNormalizer

Follow these steps to install WavNormalizer on your computer:

1. Create the following folder on your hard drive: C:\Program Files\MP3 Utilities\WavNormalizer.
2. Insert the book CD in your computer's CD-ROM drive.
3. Using Windows Explorer, browse the CD until you reach X:\Utilities\WavNormalizer, where X is the drive letter for your CD-ROM drive.
4. In this folder, select **readme.txt** and **Norm10.exe**, and copy them to C:\Program Files\MP3 Utilities\WavNormalizer. That's it. You're ready to configure WavNormalizer.

Configuring WavNormalizer

WavNormalizer is easy to configure. Once you start the program, you should see three tabbed pages on the lower left side of the main window. For most uses, the default settings on the Preferences tabbed page are fine. The only thing you will normally want to do to configure WavNormalizer is to tell it where to find your MP3 encoder. (Remember, after normalizing the .wav file, you need an MP3 encoder to convert the .wav file into an MP3 file.)

Follow these steps to configure WavNormalizer to work with your MP3 encoder:

1. With WavNormalizer running, click the **Enc** tab to display the Encoder tabbed page (Figure 7-6).

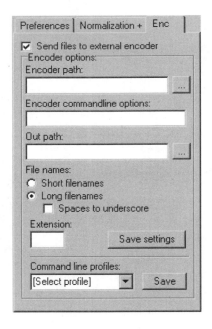

FIGURE 7.6

Filling in WavNormalizer's Enc (Encoder) tabbed page is normally the only configuration you need to do to put this utility to work.

2. Set the Send files to external encoder checkbox. If you do not do so, WavNormalizer prevents you from entering additional information on this page.
3. Enter the path to your MP3 encoder, or click the **...** button next to the Encoder path text box to browse for your encoder.

4. If you are using the XingMP3 encoder, you don't need to do anything else to configure WavNormalizer. If you are using a different MP3 encoder, you need to check the documentation that comes with that encoder to determine if you need to set any more configuration options on this page.

5. You are now ready to start normalizing files.

Using WavNormalizer

The easiest way to use WavNormalizer is to start the program (double-click **Norm10.exe** in the C:\Program Files\MP3 Utilities\WavNormalizer folder), then drop .wav files into the file list on the right-hand side of the main window. Figure 7.7 shows the full WavNormalizer interface with two .wav files already added to the file list.

FIGURE 7.7

Drop files into WavNormalizer's file list, then click Go... to normalize them.

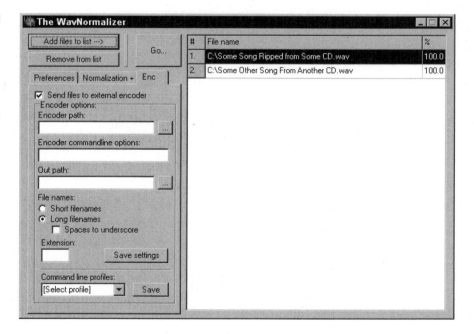

Once you drag all the files you want normalized into the WavNormalizer file list, just click **Go....** A Normalization in Progress... dialog box appears to inform you how the normalization is going. When the Normalization Completed message appears in this dialog box, click **Close**. Your files are now normalized, and, if you configured WavNormalizer to do so, have been sent off to your MP3 encoder for conversion into MP3 files.

MP3 Renamer

TIP

Tired of MP3s with names like "this%20band-live%20a%20little%28 remix%29.mp3?" MP3 Renamer, a product of Digital Dreams in the Netherlands, can fix such strange files names for you automatically.

Unfortunately, there is no standard way to name MP3 files. Each program does things its own way. Artist's name first, song first, separated by an underscore (_) or a space, on and on. And when you download files from Web sites, it can be even worse. Sometimes when you download an MP3 file, the file name it ends up with look something like: "this%20band-live%20a%20little %28remix%29.mp3." What can you do with that? Not much, so you're forced to change the file name manually, if you can figure out what it should look like.

The team from Digital Dreams has come to the rescue with a great little utility called MP3 Renamer. Keep reading to get the full story.

System Requirements

To use MP3 Renamer successfully, your system must meet these requirements: Windows 95 or 98 operating system.

What Does MP3 Renamer Cost?

MP3 Renamer is freeware.

Where to Get It

MP3 Renamer is included on the book CD. If your computer doesn't have a CD-ROM drive, you can download the latest copy of MP3 Renamer from the Digital Dreams Web site at **www.dgdr.com**.

Installing and Configuring MP3 Renamer

Follow these steps to install MP3 Renamer on your computer:

1. Create the following folder on your hard drive: C:\Program Files\MP3 Utilities\MP3 Renamer.
2. Insert the book CD in your computer's CD-ROM drive.
3. Using Windows Explorer, browse the CD until you reach *X*:\Utilities\MP3 Renamer, where *X* is the drive letter for your CD-ROM drive.
4. In this folder, select **readme.txt**, **File_id.diz**, and **MP3Renamer.exe**, and copy them to C:\Program Files\MP3 Utilities\MP3 Renamer. That's all there is to it. MP3 Renamer requires no special configuration, so you're ready to start cleaning up screwy MP3 file names.

Using MP3 Renamer

When you first start MP3 Renamer, the main window looks like Figure 7.8. This is clearly another clean and easy-to-use utility. What MP3 Renamer does is look at a file and clean it up by applying some basic rules to the existing file name. It can turn file names like this: "this%20band-live%20a%20little%28remix%29.mp3" into file names like this: "This Band – Live A Little (Remix).mp3"

NOTE

If you want to know exactly what rules MP3 Renamer will apply to your file names, click **Help**, and look at the Functions tabbed page.

The easiest approach is just to set MP3 Renamer to do its thing automatically, point it at a folder, and let it run. This should clean up most of the file names in the folder, leaving you with only a few files that even MP3 Renamer doesn't know what to do with.

Naming the Unnamable

For files that even MP3 Renamer can't figure out, you have a couple of approaches. One way is to just listen to the thing and see if you can figure out which song it is. From there, you can rename the file following the form of your other MP3s. Another way to attack the problem is to open the file with a program like Sonique or MusicMatch Jukebox, one that looks at the ID3 tag to display the file name and artist while the track plays. With that information, you're set to rename the file.

FIGURE 7.8

With MP3 Renamer, it's easy to put sensible names on your MP3 files.

Follow these steps to rename your MP3 files with MP3 Renamer:

NOTE

If you want precise control over which files MP3 Renamer works on, create a temporary folder and copy (not move) into it the files you want MP3 Renamer to work on. Follow the steps listed below, but apply them to the temporary folder. If you're not happy with the results, you can just delete the files and revert to the originals.

1. Using Windows Explorer, browse to the folder containing MP3 Renamer (C:\Program Files\MP3 Utilities\MP3 Renamer) and double-click **MP3Renamer.exe** to start the program.
2. In the Folder to rename files in text box, enter the name of the folder you want MP3 Renamer to work on. You can type the file name in directly, or click **Browse** to look for the folder you want fixed. MP3 Renamer works only on the folder you specify, not on any subfolders of that folder.

3. If you would like MP3 Renamer to add a default artist name to every file that doesn't already have one, enter that name into the Default Artists text box.

4. Make sure *.mp3 is visible in the Filetype box.

5. Click **More** to expand the MP3 Renamer window. It should appear as in Figure 7.9 when expanded.

FIGURE 7.9

When you expand the MP3 Renamer window, you can change the way it renames files.

6. Make sure that the Auto Rename box is checked. When you set this option, you don't need to worry about the Presets, Replace, and With boxes.

7. Before checking or clearing the Capitalize Every Word box, think about the ramifications. If you check this box, MP3 Renamer will start every word in each file name with a capital letter. This includes file names that don't otherwise have anything wrong with them. For example, if MP3 Renamer comes across a file named, "Out of the Shadows.mp3," it will rename that file, "Out Of The Shadows.mp3." So, if that's a problem for you, be sure to clear this box. Note, however, that MP3 Renamer maintains a database of artists (like Run DMC or KC & The Sunshine Band) that capitalize their names a particular way, and capitalizes them the way the artists want it done.

8. There's only one thing left to do. Click **Rename** and see what happens. When it finishes its work, MP3 Renamer displays a Results dialog box, which contains a list of the files it has changed.

That's all you need to know to use MP3 Renamer.

Chapter Wrapup

MP3 utilities make life easier for you when you choose the component-by-component approach to your MP3 music. This chapter covered five such utilities, each of which offers you some benefit you won't get if you merely pull together a great player, ripper, and encoder. Thanks to the kindness of their authors, you can find a copy of each of these utilities on the CD in the back of the book. You don't need to install them now, as long as you remember what they do, and that they're available on the CD when you need them.

In the last four chapters you learned two ways to approach your MP3 music, and got your hands dirty by actually playing with MP3 players, rippers, encoders, and utilities, most of which are on the book CD. But things change fast in the MP3 world. Most of the programs covered so far are being actively maintained, and new versions are likely. In addition, programs and utilities that are valuable today can be displaced by something else tomorrow. So you need to know where to go to get the latest version of your old favorites, as well as where to download that hot new whatever that has suddenly appeared. Chapter 8 shows you where to go to find the latest and greatest MP3 software.

Finding MP3 Software Online

The CD that comes with this book is full of quality MP3 software, players, rippers, all-in-one applications, and utilities. But now we have an entire chapter on places to get still more MP3 software because MP3 competition is intense, potential rewards are immense, customers are fickle, the growth rate is practically vertical, media hype is rife, and all the action is on the Net where the playing field is flat and everything happens RIGHT NOW!

In other words, everything to do with MP3 is changing constantly, and new versions of everything on this CD are likely to appear before you can say "MPEG 1 Layer 3." Besides, you never know when some MP3 player or utility is going to pop out of some lone genius's PC and take the Net by storm. When and if that happens, you can turn to this chapter and find out where to download a copy of whatever it is that's causing all the fuss.

The Web is the place to go to get the latest MP3 software. You might find what you're looking for in a newsgroup or mailing list, but your safest and most convenient source for the latest software is one of the Web sites in this chapter. Download from one of these places, and you can be confident that you've got a legitimate copy of an authorized version of the software.

NOTE

The exact contents of the sites in this chapter will surely have changed somewhat between when I wrote this chapter and when you need it. The odds are good that at least one of these sites will have been completely redesigned. Please don't send angry e-mail if the descriptions you find here don't quite match the actual Web sites. Problems like this are unavoidable when things change so fast.

The Web sites covered in this chapter include: MP3.com, Daily MP3, MP3 2000, MP3 Place, MP3now, and RioPort.

While you could survive with only one source of new MP3 software, it can pay to shop around. These sites don't have exactly the same collection of software, don't update their collections at the same time, and sometimes disagree in their ratings of the software. Besides, these are all quality sites, and you won't know which one you like best until you check them out. Remember that this chapter only addresses the MP3 software sections of these sites. When a site is a great source of downloadable music or industry news, it's covered again in the appropriate chapter.

NOTE

The Fraunhofer Institute owns certain patents on MP3 encoding and decoding. While they are not apparently enforcing the decoder patents, they have contacted several developers of encoders, demanding that the developers obtain a license. What will come of all this is unclear, but you should know that free MP3 encoders, whether standalone or part of a ripper program, are likely in violation of Fraunhofer Institute licensing agreements.

MP3.com

TIP

MP3.com represents the heart of the online music revolution and is based in California.

MP3.com as a source of software isn't really covered here because it is so important, so central to the MP3 movement, that it has its own chapter. All I need to tell you here is that MP3.com has a huge collection of software, all of it rated from 1 to 5 stars. Top products in each category show up on the Featured lists, where you can see the interface and read a one-paragraph summary.

DailyMP3

TIP

DailyMP3 links a great variety of MP3 software run by Jimmy in Indonesia.

DailyMP3 (Figure 8.1) comes from Jimmy, who lives on one of the many islands that comprise the country of Indonesia. This site's strong point is its truly massive collection of links to MP3 software of all types. What's massive? One hundred and forty MP3 players alone is massive. If a piece of MP3 software exists anywhere, you're likely to be able to find it at DailyMP3.

To reach the DailyMP3 software collection, go to the home page at **www.dailymp3.com/main.html**, and look for the MP3 Software heading. Here you can find eight software categories: Players, encoders/decoders, CD rippers, Playlisters, Plug-ins, Skins, Other Utilities, and VQF/AAC.

While most of these categories should be familiar to you, a few require some explanation.

The Encoders/Decoders category covers programs that convert files between the Windows .wav format and .mp3 format. These can be useful when you aren't using an all-in-one MP3 program like MusicMatch.

Playlisters are programs for creating and managing lists of songs. ShufflePlay, one of the utilities included on the book CD, is a fine example of a playlister.

Plug-ins are programs that attach to another program to add capabilities. They can add new graphics effects or input capabilities to programs like Winamp, NAD, and Sonique.

Skins are new user interfaces for MP3 players. When I wrote this chapter, Sonique had only recently added the ability to use skins, so most of what was available in this category was for Winamp. By the time you read this, I suspect you can find plenty of Sonique skins here too.

The VQF/AAC category is for players that support these newer compression methods. Since this is an MP3 book, that is all I'm going to say about this category.

Within each category, DailyMP3 lists dozens of links to specific programs. As mentioned before, the Players category alone has 140 links. With the hundreds of software products listed at this Web site, it shouldn't be a surprise that DailyMP3 doesn't attempt to rate or review them. All you get is the size of the file you'll need to download, and a link to the program's download page at the publisher's site.

Another thing that's not a surprise is that there are some dead links here. Even so, DailyMP3 is worth a visit when you have a yen to try something you can't find at a site like MP3.com or Rio-Port.com, or are looking for something new, and can't find it elsewhere.

If you are looking for a new player (or anything else), your first stop should be the Last Updates page. The link to this page is next to the MP3 Software heading, or you can just go directly to **www.dailymp3.com/last.html**.

However you get there, when you do get there, what you see is a list of recent additions to the site, arranged by date instead of category. In June and July of 1999, the webmaster was adding 25 to 30 new links per week, so if the site has continued growing at that rate, it must be impressively large by now.

DailyMP3 also offers the DailyMP3 Search Tool, which lets you search for a particular word or phrase in four categories, including software. Unfortunately, this search engine won't be of much use if you want to download MP3 software. The engine searches online retailers like Computability, PC Zone, and CompSource. It won't find most MP3 software, which is usually free; the rest is sold direct from the publisher's Web site. If, however, you ever need to buy a word processor or something like that, this search tool could come in very handy.

MP3 2000

TIP

MP3 2000 is an MP3 portal crewed by a team spread across Korea, Israel, Australia, Canada, and the United States.

The MP3 movement is international in scope, and unconventional in its approach to doing business. Few sites illustrate this more clearly than MP3 2000. The team that runs this portal is spread across the planet. Members include a couple of Americans, a Russian émigré living in Israel, an Australian, a Canadian who is interested in Formula One racing, and a founder who runs the whole show from Suwon, Korea. Despite being scattered around the globe, this team has put together a fine Web site covering MP3 software, hardware, and news.

To reach the software section of the site, go to the MP3 2000 home page at **www.mp3-2000.com**. Then look down the Navigation Bar on the left side of the page until you come to the Software section. Choose one of the four categories: Players, Encoders, CD-Rippers, or Misc. Programs. In Figure 8.2 you can see the top of the Players page. This partial page has enough information on it to give you a good idea of how the main software pages are built.

For each product, MP3 2000 provides these things:

▌ A look at the program's user interface (if it has one)
▌ A brief description, which reduces MP3 2000's analysis of the product to a one-liner
▌ A full review (more on this below)
▌ A download software link that lets you get a copy of the program in the easiest way possible.

The full reviews are where you go when you want more than a one-liner about a program. Under full reviews, you will find a review that gives the product a rating of one to ten. Each review also offers a Key Features list and the pros and cons of that particular product. To top it off, each full review includes a link to the product's home page, as well as links to competing products that MP3 2000 has also reviewed.

FIGURE 8.2

MP3 2000, founded by Raphael Kang, provides full-blown reviews and ratings for the MP3 software it covers.

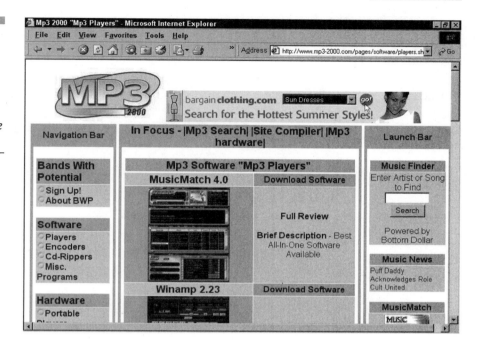

MP3 Place

TIP

MP3 Place is a small collection of MP3 software and Sonique skins, with ratings and short reviews by the MP3 Place team.

MP3 Place (**www.mp3place.com**) is another site that, among other things, reviews MP3 software. It's also a source for Sonique skins, although the collection at the Sonique site is much more comprehensive. Figure 8.3 shows the MP3 Place home page.

To reach the MP3 Place software pages, you can jump directly to the type of software you are interested in by clicking the type in the Site Menu that runs down the left side of the page, and lists five types of MP3 Software: Players, Encoders, CD-Rippers, WA Plug-ins, and Utilities.

Although you are familiar with most of these categories you probably aren't familiar with WA Plug-ins, which covers code you can add to the WinAmp player to give it visual effects different from those included with the basic product. This is exactly the same concept as the Sonique plug-ins covered in Chapter 4.

FIGURE 8.3

MP3 Place is a full-featured MP3 site that includes staff ratings and reviews of selected MP3 software and skins.

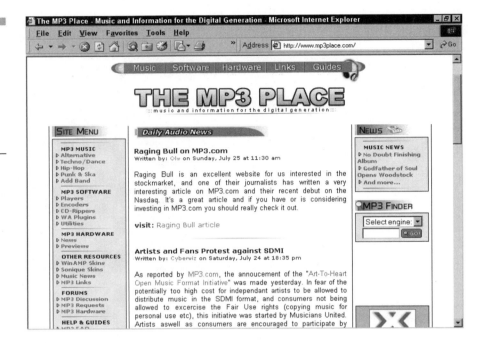

When you jump to a particular category, you get this information on every product covered:

- A picture of the product's user interface
- A rating of from 1 to 5 stars
- A link to the developer's home page, if it exists
- A short review of the product
- Pricing
- File size
- A link to the free download area, if a free download is available for this particular product.

DEFINITION

User interfaces are the way you interact with your software or hardware. Consider a user interface a fancy way of describing the controls and displays of a product.

Somewhere in the MP3 Place Site menu, you can find a collection of links to other resources. Among these links is one for Sonique skins. If you don't know what Sonique skins are, you should consider jumping back to Chapter 4 and learning about Sonique. Right now, the collection of Sonique skins is small, but it is likely to grow much larger as time passes.

The next time you're looking for a new piece of MP3 software, make sure you stop by MP3 Place and do a little comparison before you download anything.

MP3now

TIP

MP3now is an MP3 software guide with meaty reviews from Athens, Greece.

If you are looking for a new MP3 player, but aren't sure which one to try next, it would be great if there were some really meaty reviews of the various options, the kind that describe and rate different aspects of the software, and give you something to sink your teeth into. You can get that kind of review at MP3now. As Figure 8.4 makes clear, MP3now (**www.mp3now.com**) is a no-nonsense site, short on fancy graphics and long on real information.

While you can click the MP3 software link on the MP3now home page to get to the various types of software, there is a better way. Just click the name of the category of software you are interested in to go directly to a page of reviews and information. These category pages contain information about the product category, links to the sites where you can download specific products, as well as—for some MP3 players and encoders—links to MP3now product reviews.

On the product reviews pages you find a list of links to specific product reviews, as well as a description of the computer system used during the reviews. Each MP3 player review includes at least images of the player, an overall rating, and specific ratings in the following categories: sound quality, CPU usage, features, ease of use, user interface, and program support.

The encoder reviews tend to be less extensive, but still offer useful information. MP3now is definitely worth a visit when you are looking for new MP3 software.

FIGURE 8.4
MP3now gives you in-depth reviews of a range of MP3 software.

RioPort.com

TIP

The people at RioPort.com are the proud parents of the Rio PMP300, the little gizmo that really upset the record industry.

Diamond Multimedia launched RioPort, Inc. in June 1999. This wholly owned subsidiary got the rights to the Rio (now licensed back to Diamond so they can keep making and selling Rios), related software like Rio Audio Manager, and to RioPort.com, a major MP3 portal that provides music and spoken MP3 files, software, and news. If you can't find what you want at RioPort.com, the site provides links to a couple of hundred partner sites.

To reach RioPort.com's software section, go to the home page at **www.rioport.com**, find the Tools heading, and click one of the links below the heading. When you do, you end up on the Tools page, which has three sections: Software Players, MP3 Encoders, and MP3 Utilities. Each section lists one or more products. The page provides a summary of most of the software, but no ratings. The name of each product is a hyperlink to the home page of that particular product. For example, the Sonique link takes you to the official Sonique Web site.

When you click one of these hyperlinks, the Web site appears in a frame on the RioPort.com page. Aside from possibly looking odd when the design of the RioPort.com page clashes with the design of the product home page, using frames this way has two effects. First, the product home page doesn't get to use the full screen, so it may be harder to use. Second, if you are using an old Web browser that doesn't support frames, you could have problems. Your best bet is just to click the name of the product you're interested in. In the vast majority of cases, this should work fine.

NOTE

When I wrote this, RioPort.com was officially only a few weeks old. These folks have big plans (nine press releases on their first day as an independent company) and a hot-selling product to provide cash, so don't be surprised to find a lot more meat at this site than is described here.

Chapter Wrapup

When you are looking for new MP3 software, it pays to know which sites have good collections. In this chapter, you learned about a half-dozen sites from around the world that connect you to all sorts of MP3 software. Many of the files you download from these sites are available at all of the sites, while some only appear on one or two of these sites. It pays to visit several of the sites when on the hunt for new software to play with.

There is one other site you must visit if you are looking for MP3 software. That's MP3.com, the true heart of the MP3 movement on the Web. Whatever aspect of MP3 you are interested in, MP3.com covers it. MP3.com is the subject of the next chapter.

PART 3

Looking for Tunes in All the Right Places

Whatever it is that MP3 stands for (Motion Picture Expert Group blah, blah, blah), what it means to most people is music. Hundreds of thousands of songs are available on the Net in MP3 format. They are mostly free, and mostly from bands you have never heard of, but you can find great material from every genre and every corner of the globe.

As the importance of MP3 grows, more people you *have* heard of are experimenting with the format. You might have to pay something for some of them, but names like Alanis Morissette, Barry White, Merle Haggard, The Yard Birds, The Beastie Boys, Ella Fitzgerald, and so on are starting to appear on MP3s. Consider this part of the book as your guide to some of the best places to find quality music in MP3 format.

Chapter 9 takes you to the beating heart of the MP3 movement, a Web site named MP3.com. To give you some idea of this site's importance, shortly after MP3.com went public, the company's value peaked at nearly $7 billion on Wall Street. Whatever investors value MP3.com at today, it is a key part of the MP3 movement, and a site you have to visit.

Chapter 10 takes you to a baker's dozen other sites that offer MP3 files. Some sites include free content. Some charge for their content and pay the artists royalties. Some do both. But each of the sites offers something unique—music exclusively from Swedish artists, legal links to live performances by big-name bands, exclusive content.

Chapter 11 deals with MP3 search engines. These Web sites scour the Internet looking for MP3 files that match your search criteria. While these sites are powerful tools for finding the songs and artists you are looking for, they do have one important drawback: they can't really distinguish between legal and pirated music. Pirated music is the biggest threat to the acceptance and viability of MP3 as a means of distributing music. Chapter 11 includes a short guide on recognizing and avoiding pirated music.

CHAPTER 9

The Heart of the Movement: MP3.com

Sometimes a single thing can come to represent an entire industry. It could be a place: talk about movies, and people think Hollywood. It could be a company: mention computers, and most people think Microsoft. For MP3, it's a Web site: **MP3.com**. That's the place where people go to get their music, to find out what's new, and to download the latest software. It's also a place where people go to exchange messages with other diehard MP3 fans. For anyone interested in MP3 music, MP3.com is the starting point.

This chapter guides you through the rich collection of MP3-related material at MP3.com. The site is divided into several sections of which is covered in detal.

The high notes you'll hit on this tour include:

- Home Page, your starting point for exploring MP3.com.
- My MP3, a way to track and play your favorites and get recommendations based on your past selections.
- Music, a place to explore over 100,000 songs and download your favorites.
- News, where you can find out what's going on the world of MP3.
- Hardware, a place to find out about all sorts of hardware MP3 players, as well as speakers, sound cards, and other things you need to make your PC play MP3.
- Software, a prime source of software MP3 players, playlist editors and more.
- Community, a place where you can exchange messages and share your thoughts on aspects of the MP3 scene with other people who care as much as you do.

MP3.com Home Page

When visiting a major site like this, it's best to start at the beginning. Figure 9.1 shows the MP3.com home page at **www.mp3.com**. This page is chock full of content, but well-enough organized so that you can find things quickly and easily. Right on the home page, you have Featured Music and Artists, the Artists Only area, a Getting Started page, and assorted Cool Stuff at the MP3.com Store. The MP3.com home page also gives you direct links into the major sections of the site.

FIGURE 9.1

The MP3.com home page, the front door to a Web site that gets over 200,000 visits a day.

For even easier navigation, every page at MP3.com now has a navigation bar across the top, with links to the main page for each major section, as well as a search tool for when you know exactly what you're looking for. The rest of the chapter takes you to the major sections of MP3.com.

My MP3

My MP3 is a relatively new addition to MP3.com, and should be your first stop when you visit the site because My MP3 personalizes MP3.com to meet your needs and interests. So click the My MP3 link on the navigation bar at the top of the page and see what I mean.

NOTE

At the time I wrote this, My MP3 was up and running in the form described here. However, I believe this feature was still evolving, so by the time you read this it could look quite different.

The first time you follow this link, MP3.com displays an extremely short form asking for vital information like your e-mail address and the password you will use when you want to enter My MP3. Fill out the form, then click Go to My MP3 Page.

Figure 9.2 shows my (this author's) Favorites page in My MP3. Yours will look different, of course, but the basic structure should be the same. Note that the navigation bar at the top of the page has gained an additional section. This section gives you access to the specific areas of your My MP3 page. You start out in My Favorites. In case the type in the Figure is too small for you to read, the sections of My MP3 are: My Favorites, My Music, My News, My Info, and Recommendations.

FIGURE 9.2

Keep track of favorite songs from MP3.com on the My Favorites page.

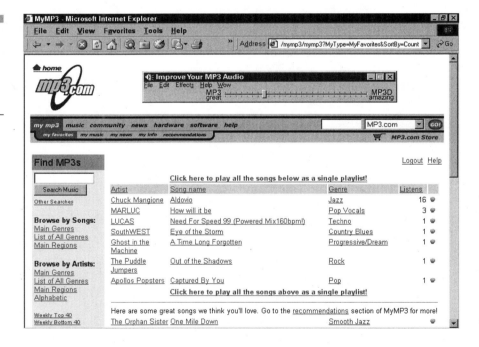

The first part of the page is a list of songs I have downloaded. Click the title at the top of any column to sort the songs by that column. Click an artist's name to go to that artist's page at MP3.com. Click a song name to download that song again (in case you lose the copy you downloaded in the first place). Click a genre to go to the main page for that genre. Finally, you can modify the list of songs and play the entire list as one giant playlist.

The bottom section of the page is a list of songs that MP3.com thinks you will like. The list is based on the songs you've previously downloaded, so chances are good that you'll like at least some of the recommended songs.

The My Music page is similar to the Favorites page, but contains more songs and a bit more information about them. The My News page lets you specify which, if any, kinds of e-mail you want to receive from MP3.com. At the moment, the options are the MP3.com Music Newsletter, MP3.com Special Offers, and General MP3.com Announcements.

The My Info page is a form containing all the information MP3.com knows about you. You can change any of the information here, so if you are concerned about privacy, you'll want to visit this page.

The Recommendations page (Figure 9.3) contains additional recommendations, beyond those that appear on the My Favorites page.

FIGURE 9.3

The My MP3 Recommendations page can point you to music that's similar to what you've previously downloaded.

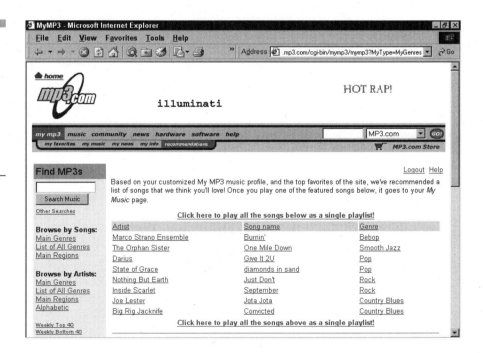

Now you know why I want you to visit My MP3 first. For the price of the few seconds it takes you to fill out a simple form, you gain personalized music recommendations and MP3 news.

Music

While MP3.com is the heart of the MP3 world, the Music section is the heart of MP3.com. This is where you can get your hands on any of the over 100,000 tracks stored on MP3.com's servers. To get here, click Music on the navigation toolbar at the top of the page.

Figure 9.4 shows the major features of the main Music page. From this page you can jump to a specific genre, browse songs by song or by artist, or check out the Daily MP3.com Top 40. The page also includes a list of new artists and new songs from across the entire collection. In addition, even though they're not visible in the Figure, you can jump to the Weekly Top 40 (MP3.com's version), Weekly Bottom 40 (ouch!), and the Top 10 DAM CDs. Every song in the Daily Top 40 list has a link to the song, as well as an Instant Play link.

FIGURE 9.4

The main Music page gives you access to all the genres of music at MP3.com.

The Instant Play link lets you listen to a RealAudio version of the song before spending the time to download it (this requires your PC to have a version of RealPlayer, which most machines have preinstalled). The quality of the RealAudio version is nowhere near the quality of the MP3 version, but you can listen to it without waiting for a long MP3 download.

What Is a DAM CD?

A DAM CD is a CD created by MP3.com's Digital Automatic Music (DAM) program. Priced by the artists as low as $5.99, these CDs contain MP3s and standard audio CD versions of each song. Follow the links to the DAM CD you want to buy, fill in the order form, and MP3.com burns you a CD and ships it off. You'll have it in a few days.

Say you want to browse country music, click **Country** on the main Music page. This takes you to the main Country music page (Figure 9.5), which is typical of the genre pages at MP3.com. The Country genre is divided into numerous subgenres, 10 of them in this case. There is also a link to the Country message board and RealAudio Internet Country radio station. Every day there is a new featured song. Beyond that, there's a long list of new songs in the genre, the Top 10 Country DAM CDs, and the Daily Country Top 40. The Subgenre pages are similar to the main Genre pages, but in place of the Daily Top 40, they have a list of the songs in the subgenre.

Eventually, you will probably want to download music. Click the name of a song, and off you go to the MP3.com page for the artists that perform the song. Figure 9.6 shows a portion of the SouthWEST MP3.com page, which is fairly typical. The page lists numerous songs, an audio CD, a way to e-mail the band, a link to their main (non-MP3.com) Web site, and information about the band.

FIGURE 9.5

This section of the main Country music page shows the volume of material you can find under each genre.

FIGURE 9.6

The SouthWEST page, a typical artist page at MP3.com

For each song on the page, you also have the option to Play or Save an MP3 version of the song, or Instant Play the song by immediately listening to the lower-quality RealAudio version. Not all MP3 players support the Play option. I recommend that you use Instant Play; then, if you like the song, Save it.

To save the MP3 version of a song, right-click the **Save** link. A shortcut menu appears. For Netscape Navigator, click **Save Link As…**, while for Internet Explorer, click **Save Target As…**. Either browser then displays a Save As dialog box that lets you tell it where you want the file stored.

That's all you need to know to download music from MP3.com. The songs are coming in faster than you can possibly download them, so get to work.

News

The News page (Figure 9.7) has a set of featured news stories. These aren't necessarily the latest news. Instead, they are stories that MP3.com finds particularly important.

FIGURE 9.7

Use the News page to keep track of goings-on in the world of MP3 music.

Beyond the featured news stories, the page offers artist profiles, press releases, daily industry news, and Michael's Minute, occasional commentaries by Michael Robertson, the head of MP3.com.

Hardware

The main Hardware page (Figure 9.8) features recent reviews of MP3 hardware. This means things like portable MP3 players, home and car MP3 players, and more. Near the bottom of the page you can find a link to the Hardware message boards, so you can ask questions and share your opinions on specific pieces of equipment. The page also links you to the seven subcategories of hardware reviewed and listed at MP3.com.

FIGURE 9.8

The main Hardware page includes product reviews and has links to subcategories or specific types of hardware.

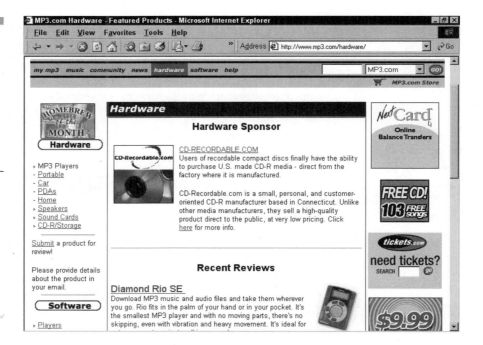

The pages for each subcategory resemble the main Hardware page, in that they offer reviews of featured products. In addition, the pages link to a complete list of hardware in that category, with information on make, model, price, and features.

Software

The Software section of MP3.com is very much like the Hardware section. It has 11 categories, covering things like Players, Playlist Makers, and Utilities. Most of these categories have multiple subcategories, with each subcategory representing a different operating system (Windows, Linux, Macintosh, and so on).

The main Software page (Figure 9.9) is also the Windows MP3 Players page. On the page are Featured Players, including Music-Match Jukebox, which is MP3.com's recommended MP3 player (I'm glad they agree with me on this). For each product reviewed, you get a summary, a rating (one to five stars), the size of the program, and a link to the author/publisher.

FIGURE 9.9

The main Software page connects you to coverage of hundreds of pieces of MP3 software, divided into nearly a dozen categories.

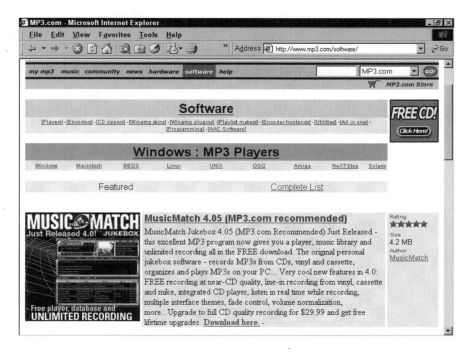

If you click Complete List, you get a page that contains a list of all the products that MP3.com has information for that sub-category. The list contains these columns:

- Name, where the product's name is a link to where you can download that product.
- Size, which is the size of the file you must download, not the final size of the product when installed on your PC.
- Author, which is a link to the Web site of the author/publisher of the product (if such a site exists).
- Price, which actually tells how the product is distributed: freeware, shareware, etc.
- Rating, which is MP3.com's rating of the product (one to five stars), if they have reviewed that product.

Community

The Community section of MP3.com consists of over two dozen message boards, divided into four categories: Music Genres, User Feedback, Artists Only, and MP3 General. Figure 9.10 shows the main Community page, with its links to each message board.

The Details links next to each category take you to a page dedicated to that category. Each board gets a one-line description, a count of the number of messages posted to that board, the date the last message was posted, and the name of the moderator responsible for that board. Just click the name of a message board and you're there.

As you might expect, the level of activity varies from message board to message board. I've seen a message board with 0 messages, while the General MP3 Questions board has over 14,000 of them. But the good thing about a community like the MP3.com message boards is the way you can take the initiative. If the board you're interested in doesn't have any messages, no problem. Just post a few of your own and see if you can fire up a few good discussions. These things feed on themselves, so you never know what you can get started.

FIGURE 9.10

The main Community page plugs you into more than two dozen message boards, so you can talk with other fans of MP3 music and MP3.com.

Chapter Wrapup

This is the end of the guided tour through MP3.com. You have been through all the major sections: My MP3, Music, News, Hardware, Software, and Community. If you haven't found more than a few things here that pique your interest, you may be reading the wrong book. MP3.com is one Web site that should be on every MP3 fan's Favorites list.

While MP3.com is definitely a key Web site for any reader of this book, it's not the only place to visit when you're online. MP3.com is like a giant department store, with a vast array of virtually anything you might need. For most of your MP3 "shopping," MP3.com is a great place to go. Sometimes though, it's better (or more fun) to shop at a specialty boutique, or even a competing department store. Chapter 10 takes you to some of those boutiques and competing stores in the quest for great MP3 music.

CHAPTER 10

Other
MP3 Sources

While MP3.com is the leading source of MP3 music, you shouldn't restrict yourself to the content you find there. Many other Web sites contain quality MP3 music. Some sites, like **Amazon.com**, offer a mix of exclusive and non-exclusive tracks. Others, like **MusicMatch.com**, offer a smorgasbord of fee and free downloads in support of their software or hardware players.

Then there are the specialty content providers. **Astrojams.com** provides free and legal copies of live performances by name like Phish, Grateful Dead, and the Dave Matthews Band. **Puremp3.org** collects links of MP3 sites that agree that pornography and MP3 don't mix, and are doing something about it. **swebmusic.com** (no, swebmusic isn't capitalized) is an artist-owned, online music publisher that sells music by Swedish artists. **Audible.com** owns over 15,000 hours of spoken content, and is beginning to make it available in MP3 format.

This chapter is divided into two parts: sites that offer primarily free content, and those that offer primarily content you must pay for. But don't expect a totally clear line between the two—most pay sites offer some free content, and many of the free sites offer some pay content.

That said, you'll find the following Web sites listed under the Free Music heading: Astrojams, AMP3.com, MusicMatch, Pure MP3, RioPort.com, and WorldWideBands.

Under the banner of content you must pay for, you will find: Audible, Crunch, Emusic.com, Listen.com, Riffage.com, and swebmusic.com.

Before you use your browser to hit the Web, you might want to know how to download music you find. As you explore the Web sites in this chapter, you will eventually come to links that point to MP3 files. These links are usually named "Download the song," or something similar. Don't just click them like you would a normal hyperlink. Right-click them instead. When you do this, both Netscape Navigator and Internet Explorer display shortcut menus. Use those menus to save the MP3 files to your hard drive. For Netscape Navigator, select **Save Link As...**, while for Internet Explorer, select **Save Target As....** Either browser then displays a Save As dialog box that lets you tell it where you want the file stored.

Before clicking Save to actually download the file, check the name. If the file name ends with .htm or .html, you're looking at a link to a Web page instead of at an MP3 file. So click Cancel to abort the save, and left-click the link you thought was a link to a song. This will take you to a Web page where, with any luck, you will find the link that points to the MP3 file you are trying to download.

I wish I could make it simpler, but everyone builds their Web sites slightly differently, so you need to be flexible when trying out a new site.

Web Surfers Beware: What You Click is Not Always What You Get

While you can certainly track down your own MP3 music sites, there can be a few minor pitfalls. As you are probably aware, not everyone on the Internet is honest and honorable. Some operators register domain names related to popular subjects (MP3, for example) and use them to redirect visitors to places they probably don't want to go.

While researching this book, I was trolling for MP3-related sites by entering URLs that someone involved with MP3 might register. While most such URLs led to the kinds of site you would expect, one immediately redirected me to an XXX pornography site. Beyond the time and effort you save by sticking to the MP3 sites you find in this book, you get the added benefit of avoiding close encounters of the obscene kind.

Free Music

If you want to drive someone from the record industry crazy, tell them you spend your days downloading free MP3 music from the Internet. The industry is rightly concerned about all the sites with pirated music, but if you look hard enough, you can find many sites that traffic only in legitimate free music. This section covers several such sites, mostly stocked with music from unknown, unsigned artists, but with a few big names mixed in for good measure.

NOTE

Remember that MP3.com (**www.mp3.com**) has the largest collection of MP3 music online. For complete coverage of this massive collection, take one giant step back to the beginning of Chapter 9, "The Heart of the Movement: MP3.com."

Astrojams

TIP

Astrojams provides free performances from Phish, the Grateful Dead, Dave Matthews Band, and others.

The Grateful Dead encouraged fans to make recordings at concerts and share them around. Other bands do too. But getting the recordings still isn't easy. Astrojams (**www.astrojams.com**) (Figure 10.1) provides the MP3 community with a central location for MP3 versions of free performances.

FIGURE 10.1

Astrojams is dedicated to providing a forum for the appreciation of free music.

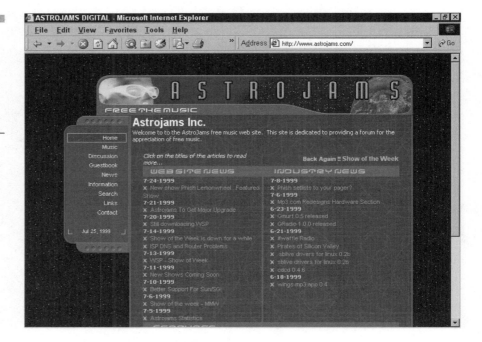

The Astrojams site includes MP3s of performances by more than 15 groups. The Show of the Week link takes you to a featured performance. The Music link on the left side of every page takes you to the main music page, where you get a description of the artists, including the number of performances available.

Click the name of the artists to go to a complete list of performances. For each performance, the list includes the date and location of the show, as well as a rating by the Astrojams staff. You download particular tracks by right-clicking the date of the performance.

NOTE

Astrojams has become so popular that the owners have had to put limits on the number of simultaneous users. The Show of the Week is always available, but everything else has limits on it. If you try to download a track and get a message that says you can't login to the server, or something similar, there are too many people using the site. Try again later.

AMP3.com

TIP

AMP3.com is a free music site where the artists get paid when you download their music.

One interesting thing about AMP3.com (**www.amp3.com**) is that it gives music away, while actually paying the artists every time their music gets downloaded. The money to do this, and to pay for the site, comes from advertising. But the banner ads plastered around the site aren't the only advertising. Each song you download from AMP3.com is preceded by a 5-second advertising jingle. You need to decide for yourself whether seeing that artists get paid for their work is worth the annoyance of an ad at the start of each song.

Assuming you don't mind the jingle, AMP3.com has a lot of music to offer. The music is divided into more than 40 genres, ranging from Alternative to Zydeco, with the list running down the left side of the AMP3.com home page. Click a genre. You get a list of songs and artists. Download a song and check it out. Or click the name of an artist and go to that artist's AMP3.com Web page. It is up to the artists to fill in the framework that AMP3.com provides, so expect a variety of content.

If you're looking for a particular band, head back to the main page and scroll down until you find the Click Here to Search for Your Favorite Bands link. This takes you to a basic search engine that searches the site for the band name you enter.

MusicMatch

TIP

MusicMatch offers a collection of free music that includes lyrics, graphics, and more that MusicMatch Jukebox users can view.

MusicMatch (**www.musicmatch.com**) isn't the first site to think of when you want to download music. The music collection here isn't really stressed, and the depth of the collection isn't obvious to a casual inspection of the site. But there is actually a good-sized collection of free music, and that collection has a key point in its favor.

The tracks you download from the MusicMatch site include additional information like cover art (which appears on the Player), lyrics, notes, and bios (which appear in the Track Info window). You can listen to the music and also get the background material MusicMatch Jukebox is designed to display.

On the MusicMatch home page, click the Music link. The Music page links to a range of music sources, including:

■ Free music
■ Free featured singles at the MusicMatch site
■ The MusicMatch Top 100
■ Featured MP3s from partner sites
■ The MP3.com Weekly Top 40.

The Free Music link and the Top 100 link take you to a page with three sections. The first part contains a link to the Music-Match Top 100, as well as featured singles. The second part of the page lets you browse the archive by genre, artist name, or home town. The third part of the page is a search engine, where you can enter the term you want to search for, and search by artist, location, song title, or across all of them.

All in all, the MusicMatch Web site's music collection may not be the easiest to find your way around, but the additional content that comes with the tracks makes it worthwhile for anyone using MusicMatch Jukebox as an MP3 player.

Pure MP3

TIP

Pure MP3 points you to MP3 sites that are porn free, but there's a catch.

As you are now aware, sometimes when you go looking for MP3 music, what you get is...pornography. Pure MP3 (**www.puremp3.org**) aims to do something about this situation. Here's how it works. Go to the Pure MP3 Web site and look around. What you find is a description of the Pure MP3 philosophy, which can be summed up as: Pornography and MP3 don't mix. If you want porn, go to a porn site, not an MP3 site.

Sites that agree with this philosophy can join Pure MP3 and display a Pure MP3 logo, as long as they don't include pornography on their sites, and don't link to sites that include pornography. When a site joins Pure MP3, it gets a link from the Pure MP3 page, so it is easy to find for people who want their MP3 site pure.

So far so good, but there is one catch. While Pure MP3 assures that sites don't have any pornography on them, it doesn't attempt to ensure that the sites have legal music on them. Keep this in mind if you decide to visit the members of Pure MP3. A quick survey of member sites showed that some do, indeed, carry pirated copies of music. See "Is This File Legal" in Chapter 11 if you need tips on how to distinguish authorized music from pirated music.

RioPort.com

RioPort (**www.rioport.com**) is a gateway to all things MP3 on the Internet, including legal musical and spoken content. To get access, just go to the bottom of the RioPort.com home page, and click the appropriate heading. Music is divided into 29 genres, while spoken content is divided into four categories at **Audible.com**.

DEFINITION

On the Web, a **gateway** is a site that gives you access to other sites.

To get an idea of how the musical content is organized at Rio-Port.com, click the Rock link. This takes you to the Rock genre page at RioPort.com. It should look very similar to Figure 10.2.

FIGURE 10.2

RioPort.com can connect you to featured tracks as well as to hundreds of sources of legal music on the Web.

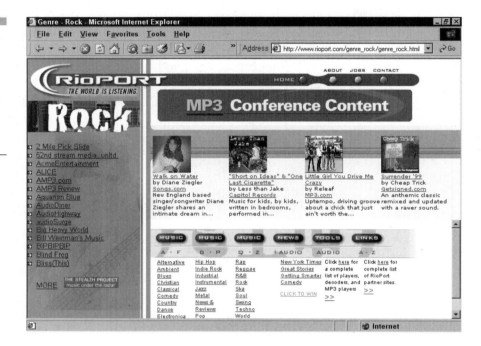

Most apparent on this page (and most other genre pages throughout RioPort.com), are four featured performers. For each, you get a picture of their latest CD, a short blurb on the artist, and a link to the track and the site where you can find it. A key thing to realize is that the tracks are not stored at RioPort.com. Instead, RioPort.com links you to a site that does store the track. The other site appears almost as if it were part of the RioPort.com site, but it is still a completely different site.

An advantage of this approach is that you get to see the tracks in their natural habitat, that is, at their home Web sites. These sites often have links to other songs, more information, and related resources.

A disadvantage of this approach is that the sites RioPort.com connects you to each do things their own way. Sometimes you even end up at sites like MP3.com or WorldWideBands. The look and feel of each site is different, possibly making things more confusing for you. Even so, access to hundreds of songs serving up legitimate MP3s is worth the small possibility of confusion.

WorldWideBands

TIP

WorldWideBands is a place to prospect for bands from around the world offering legal MP3s.

WorldWideBands (**www.worldwidebands.com**) is similar to RioPort.com, in that it connects you to sources of legal MP3 files. But what makes WorldWideBands stand out is its emphasis on music from around the world. With 16 countries represented so far, and the ability to search for music by country, as well as by other, more common criteria, WorldWideBands is a prime target for anyone interested in music from around the world.

One particularly useful page is Bands with MP3s, part of which appears in Figure 10.3. You get to this page by scrolling down the WorldWideBands home page until you can click the Bands with MP3s link. The page consists of one long list of links to bands and MP3s, organized by genre. When a band is not from the United States, its country of origin appears in the list.

Another approach to finding music from around the world is to click the Bands by Country link on the WorldWideBands home page. This link takes you to a page that contains a list of bands, organized by country. Using this list, you can troll for music from a particular place. The only problem with this approach is that there is no way of telling, short of searching each Web site, whether a particular site has MP3s you can download. This page is probably best reserved for days when you have time to do serious surfing, instead of quickly finding and downloading MP3s.

When you're looking for a non-American slant on music, try WorldWideBands.

FIGURE 10.3
Searching for legal MP3 tracks from around the world is easy at WorldWide-Bands.

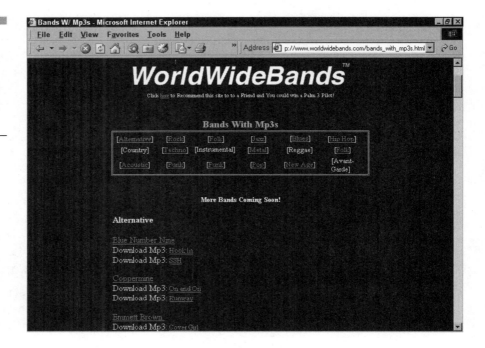

Content You Have to Pay For

The Web sites covered so far in this chapter have been those that provide primarily free content. But people do need to make a living, and artists do like to get paid for their efforts. So many of the music and spoken content sites on the Web charge for some or all of their content. If you are willing to part with a little cash in exchange for quality music or spoken content, check out the sites that follow.

Audible

TIP

If you're looking for spoken content in MP3 format, Audible is the place to start.

Audible (**www.audible.com**) is the source for spoken content on the Internet. The site maintains and sells more than 15,000 hours of spoken content. Until recently, none of that content was available in MP3 format. But times change.

Audible has begun to offer some of its content in MP3 format. Right now, Audible offers a sampling of its content, in such categories as Humor, News, High Tech, Personal Growth, Alt Rock and Jazz, and Literature. More content is being added all the time, with the company's stated long-range goal being that all of Audible's content be available to players that use the MP3 format.

Note that the goal is not for all of Audible's content to be available in MP3 format. My understanding is that Audible is working with manufacturers of hardware MP3 players to ensure that future versions of those devices can play Audible content, presumably in some secure format (in other words, not as MP3 files).

To get at the content that is available in MP3 format, click the Nomad owner or Rio owner links on the Audible home page. If you are not already a member of Audible, you will have to fill out a short form to get your free membership. Audible gives you access to the content, then e-mails you a username and password you can use in the future.

Once you are on the content page, click a topic to get access to whatever content is available for that topic. Download and play the content as you would any other MP3 file. With Audible's plans for making spoken content available on MP3 players, I recommend you check this site frequently to see what they're up to.

Crunch

TIP

Crunch Music Ltd. is an outfit selling dance tracks from the UK.

Are you a fan of Union Jack or BOM, but can't get their latest tracks because you're on the wrong side of the Atlantic Ocean? Longing to hear what people are dancing to in the UK? Or just interested in trying something new, and willing to part with 99 pence (less than $2.00) for the privilege? If so, it's time for a visit to Crunch at **www.crunch.co.uk**.

Crunch works deals with independent dance labels in the UK, then sells the individual tracks. When you shop at Crunch, you not only get legally distributed MP3s, you know that the artist and label are being paid for their efforts.

If you want to window shop at Crunch, there's no problem. Just go to the site and poke around. You can click Listen to Sample beneath the description of each track to listen to a 30-second RealAudio sample.

Actually buying something here isn't much more difficult. Start by browsing tracks (click the **Tracks** icon at the bottom of any page to enter the Tracks area). Figure 10.4 shows the Crunch home page, with Tracks and the other navigation icons visible at the bottom of the page.

FIGURE 10.4

Shop for the best in UK independent dance music at www.crunch.co.uk —the UK's premier MP3 resource.

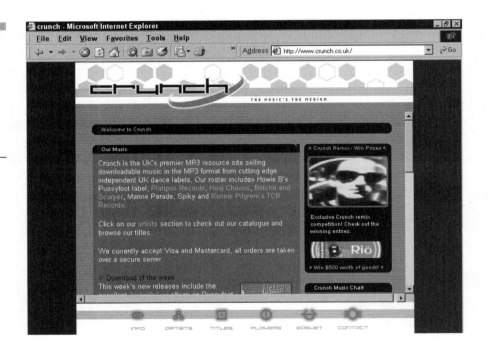

Spot something you like and click **Add to Basket** to include this track in your virtual shopping basket. Crunch takes you to your basket and shows you everything that is in it so far, along with a running total on how much it will cost you.

NOTE

If you want to remove a track from your shopping basket, click the word **Remove** to the left of the track.

Go back to the Tracks area and keep shopping until you have all the tunes you want for this visit. On the Basket page, click **Proceed to Checkout** to buy the tracks you put in the basket. Have your Visa or Mastercard number handy, and be ready for instant gratification. Give Crunch your billing info, and they'll give you your tunes as fast as you can download them. You don't have to download everything immediately—next time you come back, the tracks you paid for, but haven't downloaded yet, will be waiting. Shopping for music at Crunch makes even Amazon.com's overnight air delivery of CDs seem slow.

Crime Doesn't Pay

The Crunch info page makes a strong case for buying legal copies of independent UK dance music from them, instead of downloading pirate copies from somewhere else. To paraphrase, "Without royalties, artists don't get paid. Artists don't get paid, they don't eat. Artists don't eat, they die. Artists die, and you don't get any new tunes."

Listen.com

TIP

Listen.com offers a huge directory of legal music available on the Web in MP3 and other formats.

Listen.com (Figure 10.5) is another site that connects you to who-knows-how-many sites with downloadable, legal music. Not everything you find here is in MP3 format, and most of it requires you to pay for the privilege of downloading, but it is worthwhile to spend some time here.

Are you wondering if that band you just heard on the radio has any MP3s out there? Enter the band's name in the Find Music box that appears on every page of Listen.com, then click search. If that band has anything available legally on the Web, Listen.com will point you to it. The search will also return links to bands that sound like the one you're looking for.

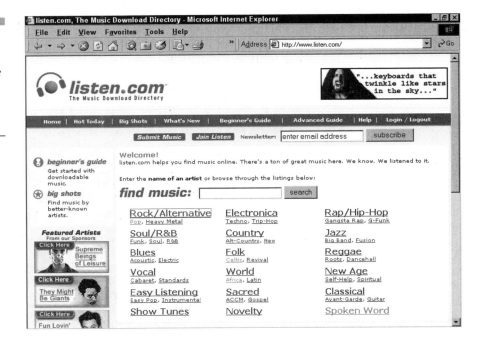

Are you a fan of a particular subgenre of jazz? Listen.com can connect you to legal downloadable music in 16 subgenres, like Bossa Nova and Jazz-Funk. Are you interested in a particular kind of Rock? Listen.com has more than 30 subgenres, including such exotic ones as Swamp Pop and Plunderphonic. Or you can just browse a particular genre and look for names you recognize.

However you navigate around Listen.com, eventually you get to the main listing for an artist. Each listing includes plenty of information:

❚ A description of the artist
❚ What other artists this one sounds like
❚ The subgenres where the artist's music is filed at Listen.com
❚ A link to the artist's home page (if one exists)
❚ One or more links to downloadable versions of the artist's music, with the file type identified.

Click a music link and Listen.com opens another Web browser window that shows the site that has the music. From there, it is up to you to figure out how to download the tracks you want, as each site Listen.com links you to may do things slightly differently. The next time you're looking for a particular artist or type of music, give Listen.com a try.

Riffage.com

TIP

Riffage.com is a personalized MP3 community by one of the fellows who brought you the Rio.

Some MP3 sites give you laundry lists of songs and artists. Others give you band info, ratings, and recommendations. This is all one-way material—the site put out the information, music fans take it in. Riffage.com isn't anything like that. You get band info, reviews, and recommendations here, but music fans and the bands themselves get their say. Riffage.com is a place to hang out at and contribute to, rather than just to pop in, pick off a track or two, then bolt for home. You can even generate playlists so that anyone who comes to the site can choose to hear your selection of songs.

The key to a personalized experience at Riffage.com is setting up a My Riffage account. On the home page, click **My Riffage** to start the simple registration process. You have to enter all the usual info: name, e-mail address, a login name and password, and type of connection to the Net.

You also have to answer a couple of questions so that the site can customize its presentation for you. Choose two types of music from the provided lists so that Riffage.com knows the basic types of music you like. Then, on a scale from 1 to 5, you have to tell the site how experimental you are. That is, how willing you are to try tunes from outside the favorite genres you selected. Finally, you need to choose at least four types of ad that you're interested in, or at least willing to put up with. Riffage.com provides lots of services and gives artists a great deal. The ads are the price you pay to support all the work that goes into this site.

Once you have your My Riffage account set up, you'll want to log in whenever you visit the site. Why? Because Riffage.com keeps track of the songs you rate, and makes recommendations to you based on your ratings, and the ratings of other My Riffage members. The more songs you rate, the more Riffage.com knows about your tastes, and the better the job it can do recommending other music you'll like.

With all of Riffage.com's features, you may almost forget about the music itself. One good way to explore the music is by browsing the genres. The Riffage.com home page has a set of tabbed pages running down its right side. Click the Genre tab and choose one of the thirteen genres. The home page for each genre includes a featured artist, a definition of the genre, A-Z lists of bands and songs, and a list of new arrivals in that genre.

Select the featured artist, or anything from one of the lists, and you eventually get to a particular set of tracks or a band's home page. When you reach a Traxx page, you get a list of all the tracks by a particular band. For each track, you can see how other My Riffage members rated the track, read detailed reviews (if available), play the track, e-mail it to someone, download it, add it to one of your playlists, or rate/review it yourself. Most of the music I found here was free, but bands can set a price for their songs if they like.

Band home pages live on Riffage.com, and provide a place for bands to give more information about themselves. They can post news and reviews, along with their calendar of events, so you can hear them live. Even more interesting is the upcoming ability to chat with, and send e-mail to, the bands and other fans.

Riffage.com has plenty of other features, like Top Ten and Top 40 lists, a site search engine, the ability to order band CDs and other merchandise. In other words, there is a lot to see, hear, and do at Riffage.com.

swebmusic.com

TIP

Try (and buy) Swedish music from swebmusic.com, an artist-owned, Internet-only music publisher.

One way for artists to sell their songs on the Internet is to sign up with a portal like MP3.com, or an online music vendor like Riffage.com. Another approach is to form a coalition and start their own online music publishing company. This second approach made sense to a group of Swedish artists, who banded together and created swebmusic.com, the "world's first record company owned by the artists themselves...." Figure 10.6 shows the clean and easy-to-use swebmusic.com site.

FIGURE 10.6

Buy Swedish music, direct from the artists themselves, at swebmusic.com.

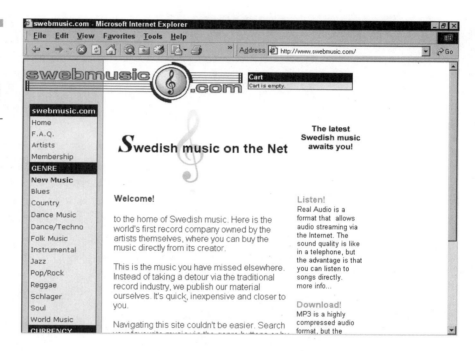

NOTE As Sven, the swebmusic swebmaster informed me, the name of this company is swebmusic.com, not Swebmusic.com.

swebmusic.com runs on an electronic commerce (e-commerce) system from a company named Forefront. This system accepts MP3s uploaded by the artists, and automatically makes a copy of them in RealAudio format. If you have a RealAudio player on your computer, a version of RealPlayer or RealJukebox for example, you can listen to a track to get an idea of whether you want to download it. The streamed sound you hear when you click Listen! isn't the full quality you get from an MP3 file, but you can certainly use it to tell whether you'll like the track or not.

While many tracks are available free as MP3s, others will cost money. Each track is clearly marked as to whether or not you have to pay for it. One of the nice touches here is that you can choose one of four currencies to work in. Go to the pull-down list under the Currency heading on the left side of the page to choose between: DEM (Deutsch Marks), GBP (British Pounds), SEK (Swedish Krona), and USD (United States Dollars).

Currently, if a song isn't free, it will cost $1.17. The actual buying process is simple, and based on the shopping cart model. The Cart, as it is called, is visible in the upper right-hand corner of almost every page at swebmusic.com. Each song's title appears in the Cart, along with a running total of what you're about to spend.

When you're ready to pay for your goodies, click Purchase in the Cart. Follow the onscreen directions to make your purchase. Note that the first time you shop here, you will need to fill out a short form in exchange for an access code. The site e-mails you the access code, which you must enter to reach the Download page and download your music. Give swebmusic.com a try and see what you think of the Swedish music scene.

Chapter Wrapup

The goal of this chapter was to introduce you to quality Web sites you can visit to find legally downloadable music and spoken MP3 content. The tour took you to comprehensive sites like Listen.com and RioPort.com, as well as to specialty sites like Pure MP3 and swebmusic.com. Somewhere along the line you should have discovered a site or two you will be going back to regularly, as you increase your MP3 collection.

All the sites covered in this chapter are built by people. That is, people choose the sites and the music that appear on any of these sites. People add value by reviewing the music, or entering short descriptions of the bands, or just making sure that nothing appearing on their site violates the philosophy of that site.

There is another type of site that helps you find music on the Web. *Search engines* rely on software that roams the World Wide Web, looking for particular kinds of content—in this case MP3 files. Just as there are advantages and disadvantages to relying on people to pick content, so are there advantages and disadvantages to the search engine approach. Chapter 11 tells you what you need to know about these advantages and disadvantages, then takes you on a tour of the best music search engines available today.

Finding that Particular Sound: MP3 Search Engines

The number of MP3 files on the Internet is staggering. MP3.com alone has well over 100,000 of them. Even so, you can't always find the songs you're looking for at MP3.com. One way to track down a really elusive song is to visit all the Web sites covered in Chapters 9 and 10, and search each one. That still might not get you what you're looking for. There are two reasons for this.

First, these sites depend on people to add songs to their sites, then catalog, organize and maintain them. The Internet is so huge, and there are so many people producing songs and posting them to the Net, that it is impossible to keep up with the volume.

Second, not all songs are posted on Web sites. Many songs appear at FTP sites instead of, or in addition to, Web sites. There are a variety of reasons for this:

DEFINITION

FTP is short for File Transfer Protocol. FTP is an earlier, simpler way to make files available on the Internet.

- An FTP site is simpler to set up than a Web site.
- Some people have Internet access, including FTP, but do not have Web access.
- Uploading and downloading files is faster with FTP than through a Web browser.

DEFINITION

With respect to the Internet, to **download** a file is to transfer it from some computer connected to the Internet to your computer. Similarly, to **upload** a file is to transfer it from your computer to some other computer that yours connects to through the Net.

Regardless of the reasons, if you want access to a full range of MP3 files, you need to be able to deal with FTP sites. To make that easier, I have included a utility called Go!Zilla on the book CD. It makes downloading from FTP sites simple. By the time you reach the end of this chapter, you will have all the tools you need to download the music you want, and you'll know some of the best places on the Net to find that music. You will hit these high notes in this chapter:

- Staying legal
- Downloading MP3 files from FTP sites
- Downloading with Go!Zilla
- Standard MP3 search engines
- Meta MP3 search engines.

Staying Legal

While MP3 search engines are powerful tools for locating MP3 files on the Net, they do have one big drawback—not all of the links they return lead to legal copies of songs. This is an unavoidable consequence of how search engines work.

NOTE

To use a time-honored acronym from Internet culture: IANAL—I Am Not A Lawyer. The information and guidelines in this section (or anywhere else in the book, for that matter) are not legal advice. They are, instead, common-sense observations and suggestions from a layman who has been knocking around the Net for years, and has been following the legal and political wrangling around MP3. This is the best advice I can give you—not a trained interpretation of the law.

When a search engine goes out on the Internet and finds an MP3 file, it doesn't have any way to tell if that MP3 file is posted legally. How could it know?

Whether through ignorance, disregard for the law, or other reasons I can't fathom, many people post illegal copies of songs on Web and FTP sites. This makes it hard for people like us, who want to download legal music. Fortunately, there are steps you can take to avoid pirated tunes when searching for a particular song.

1. Understand that most of the music you hear on the radio and see in the record store is NOT available in MP3 format. If you find the latest song by Madonna or Garth Brooks at an FTP site, the odds are very high that you are looking at a pirated copy. Some top performers (Alanis Morissette, 2 Live Crew, The Grateful Dead, and others) have made some music available in MP3 format free. But the vast majority have not,

so if you see something you're listening to on the radio, it is almost certainly pirated.

2. Look at the source of the music. If a song comes from an FTP site named something like "D:\Cool Music\...," it is probably hot. If it comes from RioPort.com, MP3.com, Listen.com, or other sites covered in this book, it is probably legitimate.

3. If the source of the song has "upload ratios," that's a bad sign. Most sites with upload ratios appear to be more interested in collecting music than in protecting the rights of the people who make the music.

DEFINITION

Upload Ratio: Some sites (primarily FTP sites) require you to upload a certain number of songs to their site before you can download any. You might be required to upload one song for every three you download, or something similar.

What You Click Isn't Always What You Get, Part II

In Chapter 10, I told you about the Web site that looked like an MP3 site but actually redirected me to XXX pornography site. Well, there is another, similar kind of trap you can get into.

In this trap, the site you visit spawns a slew of additional browser windows, all of which offer you pirated MP3s, or child pornography, or threaten to corrupt files on your PC if you don't vote for them in some porno site popularity contest. If you figure out what's going on in time, you should be able to use the Back arrow on your Web browser to get out of this. I did not realize what was going on until too late.

After about five minutes of clicking on windows full of threats, stolen software, and naked women, I was able to get all the extraneous browser windows to close and stay closed. There was no lasting harm done, but it was extremely annoying, and exposed me to some things I really didn't want to see.

On a positive note, I contacted the webmaster at the site that pointed me to the site that had all the inappropriate material on it. Within hours, the webmaster had blocked access to the problem site, and scoured his links for any additional trouble that had crept in. There are certainly unscrupulous people on the Internet, but this just goes to show that there are lots of decent people out there too. If you stick close to the MP3 sites covered in this chapter and elsewhere in the book, you're unlikely to run into problems.

Downloading MP3 Files from FTP Sites

Trying to download MP3 files from FTP sites can be confusing. Sometimes Internet Explorer or Netscape Navigator can handle the chore with no trouble. At other times, they just can't do it. The solution is to give your Web browser some help. The right utility can sit in the background, waiting until the browser needs help, then pop up and handle the FTP download chores. Go!Zilla is the right utility.

Downloading with Go!Zilla

TIP

This program makes it easy to download MP3 files (and anything else) from FTP sites.

Go!Zilla, from Aureate Media, is a utility program designed specifically for downloading files from FTP sites. It is powerful and flexible, and describing all of its modes and features here would not make sense. Instead, the next few pages show you how to install Go!Zilla, and use it together with your Web browser to make downloading MP3 files easy, whether they are on a Web site or an FTP site. Aureate Media has allowed us to include Go!Zilla on the CD in the back of the book, so installing it will only take a matter of minutes. Then you'll be ready to find the music you want, whatever form it is in.

System Requirements

To use Go!Zilla successfully, your system must meet these requirements: Windows 95 or 98 operating system, and an Internet connection.

Where to Get Go!Zilla

Go!Zilla is included on the book CD. If your computer does not have a CD-ROM drive, you can download the latest copy of Go!Zilla from the Go!Zilla Web site at: **www.gozilla.com**.

What Does Go!Zilla Cost?

Go!Zilla is basically freeware. That is, there is a freeware version—the one included on the book CD—and there is also a registered version. You can use the freeware version without any obligation, and with the author's blessings. With the registered version, you get:

- A version of Go!Zilla with no advertising (the freeware version is sponsored and contains advertising for the sponsor)
- Notification of updates to Go!Zilla
- Free upgrades
- Priority technical support
- Some registered-only program goodies
- The ability to support the development of Go!Zilla.

Use the free version for a while, and if you find it useful, register it. To register, open Go!Zilla, then click **Help**, and either **Register Online** or **How to Register**.

Installing Go!Zilla

Follow these steps to install Go!Zilla:

NOTE

The installation wizard will insist that you close all other Windows applications until you finish the installation. It would be a good idea to do so now, and save yourself the trouble of doing it in the middle of the installation process.

1. Insert the book CD in your computer's CD-ROM drive.
2. Using Windows Explorer, browse the CD until you reach *X*:\Utilities\Go!Zilla, where *X* is the drive letter for your CD-ROM drive.

3. Double-click **Gozilla.exe**. This starts the installation wizard, which guides you through the rest of the process. After a moment, the Welcome! dialog box appears.

4. Click **Next** to continue installing Go!Zilla. The installation wizard displays an Attention dialog box (Figure 11.1), which insists that you close all other programs until you finish installing Go!Zilla. This dialog box also includes instructions for you to follow if you are already using an earlier version of Go!Zilla.

FIGURE 11.1

To ensure a clean installation, follow the directions in this dialog box.

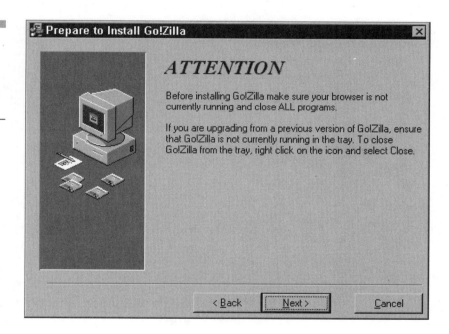

5. If you haven't already done so, close all other programs, then click **Next**. The Select Destination Directory dialog box appears. This dialog box (Figure 11.2) shows where the wizard wants to install Go!Zilla. It also shows the amount of space available on the hard drive before and after installing Go!Zilla. If that number is negative, you need to make room on the hard drive before going further with the installation.

FIGURE 11.2

*Use this dialog box
to make sure there is
enough space for
Go!Zilla on the hard
drive.*

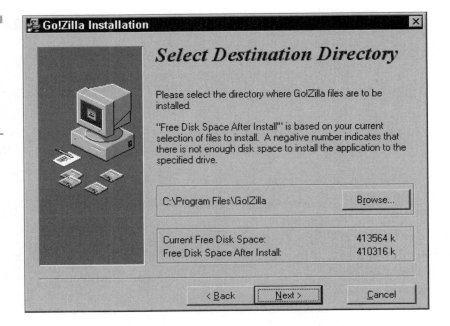

6. Unless you have a specific reason to do differently, you should accept the suggested location by clicking **Next**. The Ready to Install! dialog box appears.

7. Click **Next** to install Go!Zilla. The Installing dialog box appears for a moment, followed by the Go!Zilla Shortcut dialog box.

8. You will want to be able to start Go!Zilla when you're ready to go looking for MP3 files on FTP servers, so select **Yes** to add shortcut to Go!Zilla to your Windows Desktop.

9. Click **OK** to continue. The Browser Integration dialog box appears.

10. Read the text in this dialog box (Figure 11.3) then click **OK**. An Updating System Settings message appears for a few seconds, followed by the Installation Completed! dialog box.

11. View README file should be selected, but not Start Go!Zilla. Click **Finish** to complete the installation process, and view the README file. You're ready to roar (at least, Go!Zilla is).

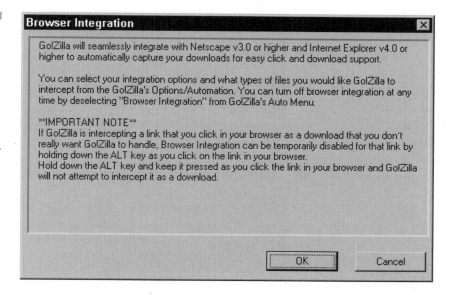

FIGURE 11.3

This dialog box delivers important information on how Go!Zilla works with your Web browser. Read it carefully.

Browser Integration

Go!Zilla will seamlessly integrate with Netscape v3.0 or higher and Internet Explorer v4.0 or higher to automatically capture your downloads for easy click and download support.

You can select your integration options and what types of files you would like Go!Zilla to intercept from the Go!Zilla's Options/Automation. You can turn off browser integration at any time by deselecting "Browser Integration" from Go!Zilla's Auto Menu.

IMPORTANT NOTE
If Go!Zilla is intercepting a link that you click in your browser as a download that you don't really want Go!Zilla to handle, Browser Integration can be temporarily disabled for that link by holding down the ALT key as you click on the link in your browser.
Hold down the ALT key and keep it pressed as you click the link in your browser and Go!Zilla will not attempt to intercept it as a download.

OK   Cancel

Configuring Go!Zilla

The first time you use Go!Zilla, you need to give it some information about your connection to the Internet. Here's how:

1. Double-click the Go!Zilla icon on the Desktop to start the program. If this is the first time you have used the program, the dialog box in Figure 11.4 appears.
2. Enter the speed of your Internet connection, and fill in the settings in the Dial-Up Networking area of the dialog box if necessary.

NOTE

If you have an active connection to the Internet, Go!Zilla can check its Web site to see if there are any updates available. Somewhere around now, the Go!Zilla Monster Update Announcements dialog box is likely to appear, offering you the chance to download announcements and upgrades. For now, just close the dialog box (by clicking the X in the upper right-hand corner). It will be back again at a later date.

3. Click **OK** to finish configuring Go!Zilla. When you do, you get to see the sponsor's ad, and must click a button to end the advertisement for this session.

FIGURE 11.4

The first time you run Go!Zilla, this dialog box appears so that you can give the program infor-mation about your Internet connection and proxy server.

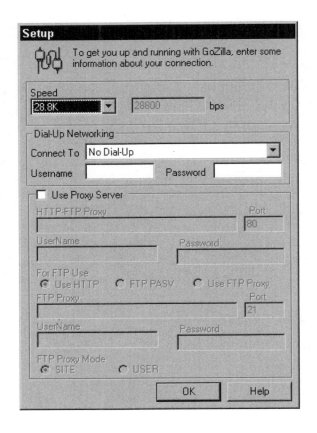

NOTE

If you don't know what to put in any of those boxes, click **Help** for more information. If the help system doesn't do it for you, you can contact the technical support personnel at your Internet Service Provider (ISP). They should be able to help you out.

Using Go!Zilla

It makes the most sense to cover using Go!Zilla in the context of an actual FTP download. The section on Lycos MP3 Search walks you through the process of using Go!Zilla, so be sure to follow along.

Standard MP3 Search Engines

Standard MP3 search engines are search engines that search the Internet looking for MP3 files. When they find a file, they record relevant information about it in a huge database. When you do a search on a standard MP3 search engine, it gives you information from the database, as opposed to searching the Internet while you wait. This approach has advantages and disadvantages. The biggest advantage is that you get an answer in seconds or minutes, instead of hours or days. The biggest disadvantage is that the answer you get may be incorrect.

Again, this is not the fault of the search engines. It is the nature of the Internet, and particularly of smaller FTP sites. Things change constantly on the Net. Just because a particular MP3 file existed at thus and such a location doesn't meant that it is there today. For that matter, thus and such a location might not be there either. Some reasons:

- The computers that host Web sites and FTP sites are not 100% reliable, so sometimes the computer that hosts the site that hosts the song you want will be disconnected from the Net or otherwise unavailable.
- The computer that hosts the site that hosts the song has changed its Internet address (If you're wondering why anyone would do something like that, keep reading).
- The owner of the computer that hosts the site that hosts the song got busted for offering illegal MP3 files. The Record Industry Association of America and similar organizations around the world fight a never-ending battle, not for truth and justice, but to keep pirated music off the Net. These groups continually find sites with illegal music and shut them down, but new ones (or even the unrepentant owner of one that just got busted) pop up again somewhere else on the Net.

Anyway, those three reasons go a long way toward explaining why the results you get from a search engine won't always be 100% correct. These "dead links" as they're called are annoying, but you need to consider them an occupational hazard when downloading MP3 files.

DEFINITION

A **dead link** is a link from a Web page to a non-existent location. The link almost surely led somewhere at some point, but for some reason doesn't lead to anything any more. When you click a dead link, your Web browser displays an error message.

The standard MP3 search engines covered here are Lycos MP3 Search, MP3Board.com, and Musicseek.net.

Lycos MP3 Search

TIP

Lycos MP3 Search is a truly immense search engine, with over half a million files indexed.

Lycos MP3 (**mp3.lycos.com**) Search claims to be the largest MP3 site in the world. Over 500,000 files in the database make a strong case for this claim. Furthermore, Lycos MP3 Search is part of Lycos, one of the leading Internet search engines, so this standard MP3 search engine has a lot of skill and experience behind it. It is definitely a prime destination for those looking for MP3 files. Go right to mp3.lycos.com and explore this search engine's capabilities.

Before you start searching, there are a couple of things you need to do. First, make sure that Go!Zilla is installed. Since Lycos MP3 Search returns links to FTP sites, you will want to let Go!Zilla do the actual downloading of the files you find with your Web browser.

Second, click the disclaimer link that appears below the Artist or Song Name text box. This link leads you to a page that explains Lycos' position on the MP3 files the search engine finds, and reminds you that downloading unauthorized MP3 files is illegal.

Once you finish reading all that, click the Reliability Guide link. This link takes you to a page that explains how Lycos MP3 Search rates the reliability of MP3 sites.

Now that you are finished with all that, click the Back arrow a couple of times to get to the Lycos MP3 Search home page. You should see the search tool. Work through the following example to see a search engine in action and give Go!Zilla a chance to strut its stuff.

*An Example of Downloading a File with
Lycos MP3 Search and Go!Zilla*

Follow these steps to do a search with Lycos MP3 Search, then download an MP3 file from an FTP site using Go!Zilla.

1. If it isn't already installed, install Go!Zilla.
2. If necessary, deal with the Ad window, User Preferences window, Tip of the Day dialog box, and anything else Go!Zilla presents to you. You want Go!Zilla to look something like Figure 11.5 before going on to Step 3.

FIGURE 11.5

Go!Zilla is ready to rumble—or at least download some files for you.

3. Fill in Lycos MP3 Search's Artist or Song Name text box, then click **Go Get It!** to begin the search. For this example, enter the words Moonlight Sonata into the text box, then click **Go Get It!** You should see the results of your search in a few minutes or less.

4. Look closely at the results you received. Remember that the sites with the most stars next to their link are the most reliable sites. Notice also that some of the results may have red stars instead of yellow stars. The links that have red stars next to their names are those that have an upload ratio you must comply with.

5. Look at the first entry in the search results. It probably looks something like this: /MP3/Classical/Beethoven—Moonlight Sonata.mp3. When you see results that look like this, they are 99.9% sure to be links to FTP sites. While you could try to download the file with your Web browser, the best bet is to let Go!Zilla do it for you.

6. Left click the name of the song you want to download. You should hear Go!Zilla roar, then after a moment a Go!Zilla Download box like the one in Figure 11.6 should appear.

FIGURE 11.6

Go!Zilla is ready to download a copy of the Moonlight Sonata.

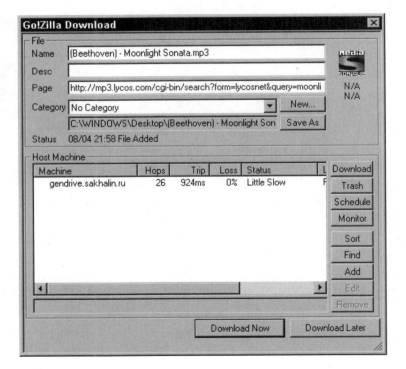

NOTE

If you look closely at the Go!Zilla Download dialog box in the figure, you can see the URL of the machine Go!Zilla is ready to download the file from. The sakhalin.ru at the end of the URL means that the computer Go!Zilla is set to download from Sakhalin Island in Russia. That doesn't particularly have anything to do with the example, but I thought you might find it interesting.

7. Click **Download Now** to retrieve the file. The actual download may or may not work the first time you try it. That's why Go!Zilla will try to connect to a particular FTP site up to 99 times before giving up. If the file won't open for some reason, Go!Zilla will make its 99 tries, then give up and return you to the results page. Click another link to try again.

NOTE

You can also defer downloads to a later time and date, but you will have to figure that one out yourself. Go!Zilla has multiple capabilities there is no room to discuss in this chapter—use the Go!Zilla Help system to teach yourself about them.

8. If successful, Go!Zilla lets out a monstrous roar to let you know it has downloaded the file. By default, Go!Zilla puts the file on the Windows desktop.

NOTE

If you click on the name of an FTP site instead of a specific file at that FTP site, Go!Zilla will start something called the Super Link Leech. The leech lets you gather links to bunches of files at that site quickly and easily. If a Leech File window appears when you're trying to connect to an FTP site, just read the onscreen instructions, then browse the list of folders and files that appears on the left side of the Leech File window and use the Add button to add those you want to the list of files Go!Zilla will download.

That is the end, both of the example and of the list of things you need to know to work successfully with search engines and Go!Zilla.

MP3Board.com

TIP

Find MP3 files you can download with your browser as well as Go!Zilla; no porn anywhere in sight.

MP3Board.com (**www.mp3board.com**) is a member of Pure MP3. That means there is no pornography on the MP3Board.com site, nor is there any on the Web sites MP3Board.com links to. MP3Board is a little more fun to look at than Lycos MP3 Search (see Figure 11.7). It also offers more options for your searching pleasure.

FIGURE 11.7

MP3Board lets you search for music on Web sites as well as FTP sites.

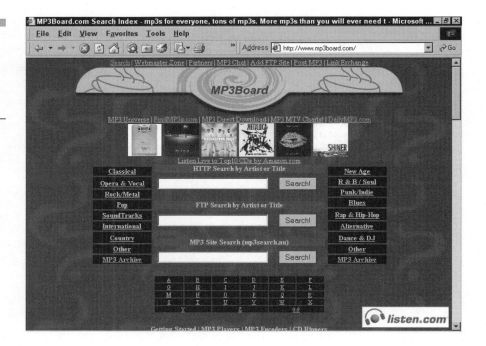

MP3Board.com allows you to do HTTP searches (search Web sites), as well as FTP searches and searches for MP3 sites instead of individual songs. You can also click one of the genres to see what music has been popular at MP3Board.com within that genre.

Musicseek.net

TIP

A site with some unique features, hailing from the land down under.

Musicseek.net (**www.musicseek.net**) is another standard MP3 search engine, but it has a couple of noteworthy features that earned it a place in this book. You can easily customize your searches and there is a list of rare and live music maintained at the site.

As Figure 11.8 shows, the Musicseek.net home page gives you many ways to customize your searches. You can control all of these characteristics:

▪ Number of search results per page
▪ Which file formats to search for
▪ The minimum reliability a site must have to be included in the search results
▪ Whether to include sites with a upload ratio
▪ Whether to use Smart Search.

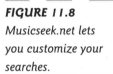

FIGURE 11.8
Musicseek.net lets you customize your searches.

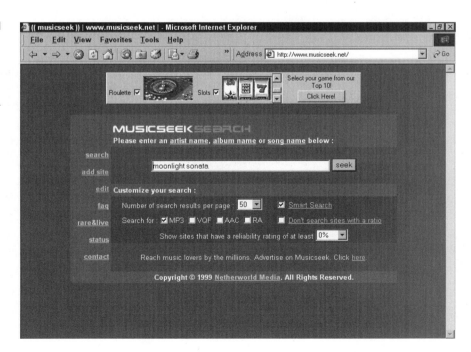

Smart Search is the site's technique for detecting common misspellings of words and searching both for the spelling as entered, and for the correct spelling. Smart Search should increase your chances of finding the files you are looking for.

When you conduct a search, you get back all the information you need to download MP3 files. Musicseek.net returns songs at FTP sites, so make sure Go!Zilla is installed, then left-click the path to the file you want to download. When the Go!Zilla window appears on the screen, click **Download Now** or **OK** to get the song immediately.

To take advantage of the Rare and Live link, just click it. Musicseek.net pops up a page filled with links to big-name artists. Be careful though. The guidelines for avoiding pirated music certainly apply to what you find on this page.

Meta MP3 Search Engines

Standard MP3 search engines continually search the Internet and maintain huge databases of information about MP3 files that they tap when you try to find something on them. Meta MP3 search engines take advantage of the existence of standard MP3 search engines. Instead of creating and maintaining their own databases about MP3 files on the Net, meta MP3 search engines run searches on standard MP3 search engines, and sometimes on sites like MP3.com. They allow you to take advantage of the work done by standard MP3 search engines, without having to visit their Web sites.

The following sections cover four meta MP3 search engines: FindSongs.com, MP3Meta, Palavista, and Scour.net.

Despite each meta MP3 search engine's searching multiple MP3 search engines, if you run the same search on each of these meta search engines, you get different results. The Internet is so vast that no search engine, or combination of search engines, can cover the whole Net and each meta MP3 search engine searches slightly differently. The upshot of all this is that you may need to work with more than one meta MP3 search engine to find what you're looking for.

FindSongs.com

TIP

You can quickly find MP3s, lyrics, CD covers, and more at FindSongs.com, a powerful meta search engine.

FindSongs.com (**www.findsongs.com**) allows you to search the standard MP3 search engines for songs or artists. In addition, you can easily search for music-related materials, all without leaving the FindSongs.com home page.

To conduct a search here, fill in the Enter the Song or Artist Name box. Then, in the drop-down list to the right of that box, select the kind of material you are looking for (MP3s). In the Select Search Engine list, select the search engine you want FindSongs.com to use in the search. Finally, click **Find** to start the search. After a moment, the results appear in a window on the lower right side of the FindSongs.com page, as shown in Figure 11.9.

FIGURE 11.9

FindSongs.com helps you find MP3s and more, all without leaving the FindSongs.com home page.

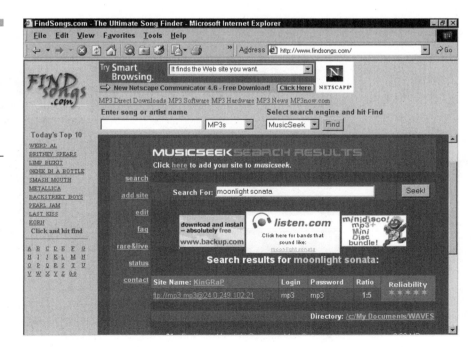

Treat the search results that appear as you would if you were actually at the site the search results come from. By saving you from surfing site to site, FindSongs.com can save you a great deal of time.

MP3Meta

TIP

You can search multiple search engines simultaneously with MP3Meta.

MP3Meta (**www.mp3meta.com**, Figure 11.10) is a powerful meta search engine that goes one step beyond FindSongs.com. Both search for more than just MP3 files. Both also search other search engines, instead of searching the Net. But FindSongs.com searches one search engine at a time. MP3Meta goes one step further and searches multiple search engines simultaneously, then organizes the results into a standard format so they are easy for you to work with.

FIGURE 11.10

MP3Meta lets you search for all sorts of MP3-related materials, not just music files.

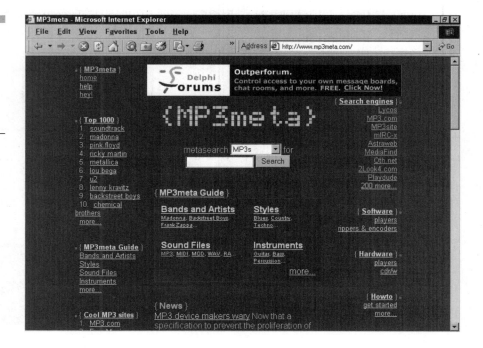

One thing I like about MP3Meta is the way its searches return files from HTTP (Web) sites as well as from FTP sites. Despite the advantages of downloading from FTP sites, I prefer downloading from Web sites. With MP3Meta, I can see if what I want is on a Web site, and if not, check the FTP sites, without having to run another search.

When searching using MP3Meta, your best bet is to work from the home page. Make sure to select MP3s in the pull-down list, then enter the term you want to search for and click **Search**. The results of your search appear on a separate page, which lists the search engines MP3Meta used, as well as the results of the search. For each file MP3Meta found, you can see where it was found, its size, the date it was added, and other potentially useful information.

One thing that can be confusing about this site is that your search results appear on a page with information from a partner site, which may have nothing to do with MP3. For example, my test search for Moonlight Sonata returned its results on a page sponsored by Financemeta, an apparent partner site to MP3Meta. As long as you can ignore sponsors that are unrelated to MP3, you should find this site very useful.

NOTE

While you are exploring MP3Meta, be sure to explore some of the other MP3-related links that adorn the site. MP3Meta gives you access to a huge amount of MP3-related information.

Palavista

TIP

Palavista performs meta searches that return links to the sites that have what you want, as opposed to specific songs.

Palavista (**www.palavista.com**) shown in Figure 11.11, is similar to meta search engines like MP3Meta and Scour.net. It runs your query by a bunch of standard search engines, and returns the combined results of all the searches. Palavista searches FTP sites and organizes the results by which search engine they came from. Furthermore, the link that results from the search takes you to the site that contains the file you want, as opposed to linking you directly to the song you are looking for.

FIGURE 11.11

Combine Palavista searches with Go!Zilla's Super Leech Mode and you get the ability to suck in multiple songs by favorite artists with the minimum of work.

This is an ideal arrangement for Go!Zilla's Super Link Leech dialog box, which pops up automatically when you click on one of the sites. Browse the entire FTP site, and gather links to a collection of songs you want to download. Click **OK** to add the songs to the Go!Zilla download list, then download them as you normally would.

NOTE

If your searches are returning too many links, too few of which lead to what you are looking for, you can narrow your search with Palavista. For complete instructions, click the **Tips on Searching** link that appears below the search term text box.

Scour.net

TIP

Scour.net is a meta MP3 search engine with big-name partners, HTTP (Web-based) downloads, and the ability to browse genres.

If you're interested in downloading legal MP3s, you must visit Scour.net (**www.scour.net/Downloadable_Music**). Scour.net bills itself as a guide to multimedia on the Internet. You can use it to track down videos, images, animations, even multimedia Web sites, in addition to MP3 music. For the purposes of this book, the part of Scour.net you should look at is the Downloadable Music section.

NOTE

I'm not the only person who thinks highly of Scour.net. The company's owners (the oldest of whom was 23 as of August 1999), recently sold 51% of the company to Michael Ovitz in a seven-figure deal.

As far as downloadable music goes, Scour.net is neither fish nor fowl. Perhaps it would be better to say that is both fish and fowl. By that, I mean it is a meta MP3 search engine, but it also allows you to browse music genres as you can at sites like **AMP3.com** and **emusic.com**. Whichever way you find the music, the files are not located at Scour.net. They are at one of Scour.net's partner sites.

The partners include MP3.com, Emusic.com, MusicMatch, Launch, AMP3.com, and Epitonic.com.

This list of partners has important implications for using Scour.net. First, you will get legal music if you download from any of those places, including occasional material from artists like the Beastie Boys, They Might Be Giants, Boston, and others. Second, not everything Scour.net finds for you is available free. Third, not everything Scour.net finds for you is in MP3 format.

To use Scour.net as a meta MP3 search engine, go to **www.scour.net/Downloadable_Music/**. Make sure you enter the URL exactly as shown, including capitalization and trailing / or you might not get in. Once you reach this page, enter the song or artist you are looking for and click **Search**. What you will get back is a list of links to songs. For each link, Scour.net gives you the logo of the partner the link points to, the name of the song, the name of the artist, the file format, and the price.

NOTE

Scour.net incorporates a feature called SmartMatch into the search engine. SmartMatch finds the songs and artists that come closest to the search term you enter. If you misspell the name of an artist, or only know part of the name of a song, Scour.net has a good chance of finding it for you anyway.

When you find a song you're interested in, left click the link to go to the page for that song at the partner site. Then just download it as you would any other song from the partner site.

Chapter Wrapup

In this chapter you learned about two types of MP3 search engines: standard MP3 search engines and meta MP3 search engines. The standard search engines do the heavy lifting, by searching the Net for music, then storing important information in huge databases. The meta MP3 search engines take advantage of all the work the standard MP3 search engines have done by searching the standard engines instead of the Net itself. You also learned a bit about one of the pornographic booby traps that awaits unsuspecting Web surfers when they go too far off the beaten path.

This chapter concludes your tour of Part 3 of this book. Starting in the next chapter, you move from software to hardware. Chapter 12 is a general introduction to upgrading the hardware in your PC. If you have any reason to believe that your PC is lacking some piece of hardware, this coming chapter can tell you what to do about it.

4

The Hardware
You Need

The best software and the hottest music in the world won't do you any good if you can't download, rip, and play it. Most PCs on the market today come with all the hardware, storage space, and processing power you need for MP3. But if you have had your PC for a while, it might not have the guts to do the job. The chapters in this part of the book help you determine if your PC is up to the challenge, and what to do if it's not.

Chapter 12 is the place to start if your PC won't play music, but you don't know why. The information here will help you figure out what's going on. Much of the time you can fix problems by running the right software or doing other things that don't require you to open the case and fool around inside your PC.

In Chapter 13, I take you inside the case of your computer to do more serious upgrades. We're talking about things like installing sound cards and memory, adding a hard drive, even replacing the microprocessor in your PC. While this is not for the faint of heart, many people do similar upgrades on their computers every year.

Chapter 14 goes in a slightly different direction to cover CD-ROM burners. One way to enjoy your MP3 music when you're on the go is to create audio CDs from your favorite MP3s. That way you can use your existing CD players to listen to your MP3 music. This chapter walks you through the installation and use of the PlayWrite MP3.

Chapter 15 is for all the gadget freaks. The number and variety of portable MP3 players is ballooning, as everyone tries to get a player onto the market in time for Christmas '99. This chapter looks at several of the players available or on the way, as well as the even newer crop of car and home MP3 players.

Chapter 16 shows you where to get the best deals on the hardware covered earlier in the book. The short answer is, of course, online stores. Manufacturers' stores, traditional online computer stores, and shopbot sites are all covered. Whether you're after product information, fast delivery, or great prices, the stores in this chapter can deliver.

CHAPTER 12

Pumping Up Your PC for MP3

If you are reading these words, the chances are that you know, or at least suspect, that your computer cannot play MP3 files. This chapter will help you determine your situation and give you advice on what to do next.

Sometimes the fix is simple, like hooking up speakers or clearing old files off your hard drive. Other times, the fix is more difficult and expensive, involving opening your PC and adding new parts. And sometimes the best course of action is simply to donate old Betsy to your local elementary school or a favorite charity and buy a new machine.

This chapter is for out-of-the-box work. By that, I don't mean thinking about the problem in unconventional ways (although there is some of that here). Instead, I mean this chapter covers things you can do without opening your computer's case and poking around inside. The assumption here is that you're looking for the fastest, least expensive solution to your problem. Most people really don't want to go poking around inside the box if they can help it. Wherever possible, the text covers fixes that don't involve opening your PC.

Chapter 13 covers upgrades and fixes that involve working inside the box. While such work is generally harder and slightly more risky than working outside the box, most people, if reasonably handy, can do basic upgrades like adding memory or a sound card.

Here are the high notes you will hit while working outside the box:

▐ Figuring out what your PC needs
▐ Increasing storage space
▐ Sounding off with speakers or headphones
▐ Cranking it out through your stereo
▐ Connecting to the Net: modems and ISPs.

Figuring Out What Your PC Needs

The first thing you need to do is figure out what, if anything, you need to upgrade on your PC. I say "if anything" because sometimes PC problems can be fixed by a little software magic. This is particularly true of PCs that were built in the last year or so. Any machine with the following characteristics has the guts for MP3:

- IBM-compatibility
- Pentium-class processor (AMD K6-2 or Celeron) or better
- 32 MB or more of RAM
- 1 GB or more of disk space
- CD-ROM drive
- Microsoft Windows 95, 98, or later operating system
- Sound card
- Speakers
- Modem.

Virtually any PC built in the last year or so should meet or exceed these requirements. If your PC is pretty new, it's worth trying a few experiments before getting serious about upgrading your hardware.

If your PC has a 486 processor, or is at least two years old, it is probably not worth trying to upgrade it. You will get better results, and likely be happier overall, if you stop right here, go to Chapter 16, "Finding Hardware Online," and find yourself a new PC. Prices are low, and you may be pleasantly surprised at the amount of power you get for your money.

Assuming you are not heading off to buy a new computer, the next section offers a few things you can try.

Doing Some Software Magic

Microsoft Windows comes with diagnostic software that allows you to do some troubleshooting of system problems. In particular, Windows 98 includes the Windows 98 Troubleshooters, a set of fifteen procedures you can work through to resolve problems. Troubleshooters that can come in particularly handy when working with MP3 files are (in the order in which they appear in the Windows help system):

■ Modem
■ DriveSpace 3
■ Memory
■ Sound
■ Hardware Conflict
■ Dial-Up Networking.

If you're having a problem that might fit into one of these categories, give the appropriate Windows 98 Troubleshooter a try. To display the Troubleshooters, click **Start** then **Help**. When the Windows 98 help system appears, click **Troubleshooting** in the Contents list. Next click **Using Windows 98 Troubleshooters**, and follow the directions that appear (Figure 12.1). With any luck, the Troubleshooter will help you to fix the problem.

FIGURE 12.1

The Windows 98 Troubleshooters can help you resolve many problems.

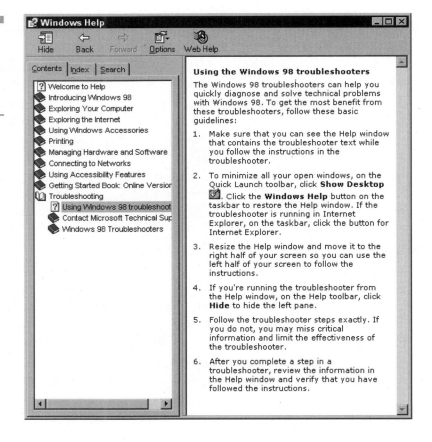

If the Windows 98 Troubleshooters don't resolve your problem, or if you just want heavy-duty ammunition for dealing with system problems, check into Norton Utilities.

Using Norton Utilities

Even if your PC is working perfectly, I heartily recommend you get yourself a copy of Norton Utilities. The box describes the utilities as, "Powerful solutions to fix and prevent computer problems." And that's exactly what you get when you buy this product in the box or download it from the Symantec Web site (**www.symantec.com**).

Grouped together under the Norton Utilities Integrator interface (Figure 12.2) are a slew of utilities that address every aspect of your computer. Norton System Check finds disk and Windows problems that can cause poor performance, including problems that interfere with playing MP3 music or downloading files from the Internet.

FIGURE 12.2

Run Norton Utilities on your PC whenever you suspect a problem.

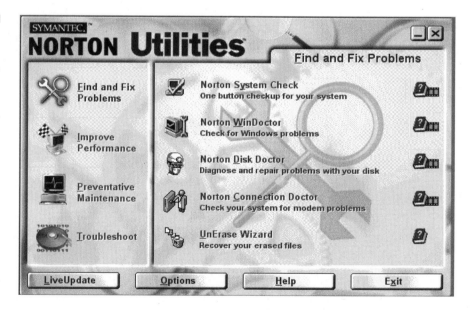

I was amazed when I first ran Norton System Check on my PC. Despite its being a new machine that had only been in use for a few weeks, Norton System Check found something like 146 problems and corrected every one.

Now most of those problems were minor, but you never know what little problem will be enough to foul something up. Even now, perhaps due to all the trial software I've been working with on this book, Norton System Check found 4 problems on the PC I'm using to write this book. Figure 12.3 shows the problem report generated by Norton System Check for my PC.

FIGURE 12.3

The results of running Norton System Check on my PC.

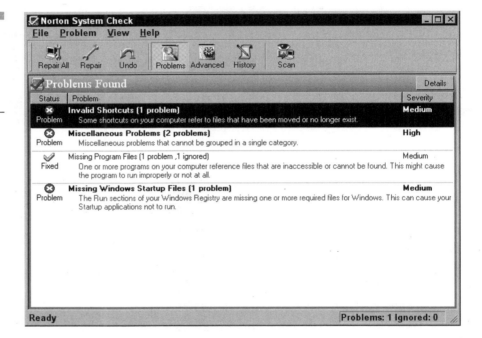

Norton Connection Doctor (Figure 12.4) provides the same kind of in-depth analysis for your modem. Since I have a cable modem (which isn't really a modem at all, but a network interface) I don't use Norton Connection Doctor myself. But it's a must for anyone with a modem.

Once you've run Norton System Check and Norton Connection Doctor (if you have a regular modem), go back to wherever you had a problem with your system and retry whatever it is that you were doing. It's likely that Norton Utilities solved your problem.

FIGURE 12.4

Norton Connection
Doctor can cure
almost anything that
ails your modem.

Now What?

Now that you've run some magic software through your system, it's time to decide what to do next. If the software found and fixed any problems, there's a good chance that you are ready to proceed. Go back to whichever chapter you came from, and try redoing the steps that gave you the problem in the first place. If the problem is fixed, there's no need to come back here.

If the software didn't find any problems, or the fixes by the software didn't solve the problem that brought you here in the first place, it is time for some more specific troubleshooting.

Dealing with Specific Problems

Presumably, you are reading this because your PC still isn't doing what you want it to. This part of the chapter offers specific procedures for dealing with specific problems. In the list that follows, find the description that most closely matches the problem, then follow the directions in the specified topic.

Problem	Topic
I don't have:	
speakers or headphones	Sounding Off with Speakers or Headphones
an Internet account	Connecting to the Net: ISPs
a modem	External Modems (Chapter 12) or Internal Modems (Chapter 13)
a CD-ROM drive	Installing a CD-ROM Drive (Chapter 13)
a sound card	Adding a Sound Card (Chapter 13)
No sound comes from the speakers.	Speaker Basics
The speakers appear to be set up properly, but I don't hear any music.	Checking Multimedia Properties
I can't rip a track from an audio CD, or my CD-ROM drive has trouble reading discs.	The MusicMatch Jukebox Phenomenon
I want to listen to MP3 files on my stereo.	Cranking It out Through Your Stereo
My machine is slow, slow, slow!	Adding Memory (Chapter 13)
I've added memory and my machine is still slow, slow, slow!	Upgrading the Microprocessor (Chapter 13)
I get "disk full" messages.	Increasing Storage Space

Speaker Basics

You've probably already checked all this. Even so, if you're like me, it sometimes takes someone else to point out that obvious thing staring me in the face. So just bear with me and follow along.

First, make sure that the connection between your speakers and PC is correct. If you have the documentation that came with the speakers, use that to confirm that you have everything connected properly. If you don't have any documentation to follow, make sure that there is a connection from your PC to your speakers. That connection should run from the Audio Out jack on the sound card. If the jacks on the sound card aren't labeled, you could be connected to the wrong jack. The Audio Out jack is typically set off by itself. Try connecting to this jack, then play the music again. If you can't find a jack on the back of the PC, you probably don't have a sound card. Go to Adding a Sound Card in Chapter 13, or call in someone familiar with computer hardware to take a look.

NOTE　Many people listen to audio CDs by plugging their headphones in to the jack on the CD-ROM drive. While this works fine for listening to audio CDs, it will not work for listening to MP3 files. Your headphones or speakers must be connected to a sound card, not to your CD-ROM drive.

Still no luck? Well, are the speakers plugged in to the wall? Are they turned on? Almost all PC speakers draw their power from the house current, so make sure the speaker transformer is connected to the speakers and plugged into the wall. Most speaker sets also have an on/off switch on one of the speakers. Make sure that's turned on too, then try listening to a song again.

NOTE　If your speaker system has three or more components, you need to be sure they are all interconnected properly, too. Your best bet in this case is the documentation that came with the speaker system. There are too many variables for me to give you better advice.

If you still don't have any sound, go to Checking Multimedia Settings to find out what's happening.

Increasing Storage Space

No matter how big your hard drive is, eventually you run out of disk space. Given that each new version of major programs is larger than the last, the long-term solution to disk space problems is a bigger hard drive. But if you're not ready to add a new drive to your PC, there are still some ways to squeak more space out of the drive you already have.

Consider this four-step plan for dealing with disk space problems:

1. Delete unused programs and miscellaneous stuff the manufacturer put on the system.
2. Use Windows Disk Cleanup or Norton Space Wizard to eliminate other unnecessary files.
3. Compress your hard drive with DriveSpace and the Compression Agent.
4. Add another hard drive to your PC (this is covered in Chapter 13).

Step 1: Delete Unused Programs and Miscellaneous Junk

Is your computer a name-brand machine, particularly one marketed toward home users? Have you switched from using, say, Word-Perfect to Word? Do you like to download and try various shareware programs? If you answered Yes to any of these questions, it is likely that you have tens to hundreds of megabytes of space on your hard drive tied up storing programs and other files you never use. Every hundred megabytes (100 MB) of disk space you free can store at least 20 MP3 files, so clearing out the old junk can definitely be worthwhile.

While you can turn this into a major project, Windows can help you delete the bulk of the unused material in a few minutes. You can do this using the Add/Remove Programs Properties dialog box. Follow these steps:

1. Click **Start** then **Settings** then **Control Panel** to open the Windows Control Panel.
2. In the Control Panel, double-click **Add/Remove Programs** to open the Add/Remove Programs Properties dialog box (Figure 12.5).

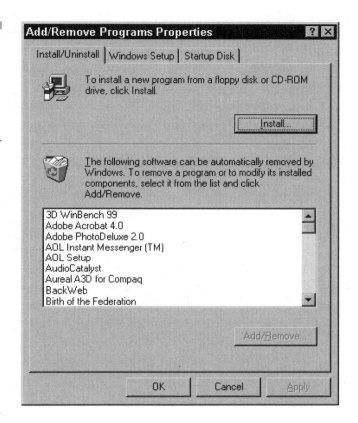

3. In the list on the bottom of the dialog box, select a program that you know you no longer use. When you select the program, the Add/Remove button beneath the list becomes active.

4. Click **Add/Remove** and follow the directions that appear on the screen to delete the program.

5. Many programs use a utility named unInstallShield to remove their files and data. Often, there will be files or folders that unInstallShield cannot remove automatically. When this happens, a message to that effect appears at the bottom of the Remove Programs From Your Computer dialog box (Figure 12.6) that unInstallShield displays.

FIGURE 12.6

The unInstallShield Remove Programs From Your Computer dialog box tracks the removal process and reports on its success or failure.

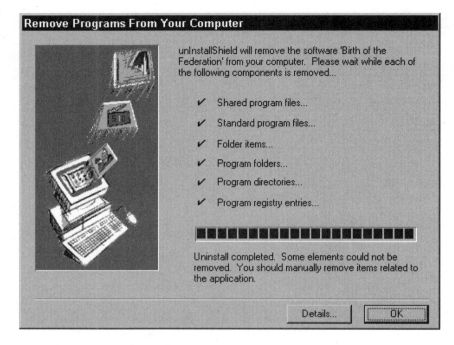

6. If unInstallShield tells you it could not remove all files or folders, you should click **Details...** to see what got left behind. In most cases, you can go in and delete the leftovers manually, using standard Windows file-manipulation techniques.
7. Repeat this process for each program you are sure you don't use.

Step 2: Use Windows Disk Cleanup or Norton Space Wizard

Deleting entire unused programs can free up huge chunks of disk space quickly, but so can cleaning out temporary or leftover files. Windows 98 includes a utility named Disk Cleanup that can list temporary files, Web browser cache files, and unused program files that you can safely delete.

NOTE

Norton Space Wizard does a similar job to Windows Disk Cleanup, while offering more features and flexibility. However, you need to exercise good judgment when using Space Wizard, as some of the files it offers for possible deletion may be files you shouldn't delete.

Follow these steps to clear out unused files with Disk Cleanup:

1. Double click **My Computer** on the Windows Desktop to open it.
2. Right click the icon for the disk drive you want to free space on, then click **Properties**.
3. On the General tabbed page, click **Disk Cleanup**. Disk Cleanup scans that drive and determines which files you can delete, as well as how much space this will free. The results appear in a dialog box (Figure 12.7).

FIGURE 12.7

Disk Cleanup can free plenty of space on your hard drive.

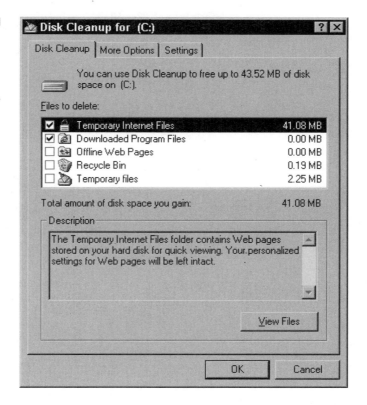

4. Click the name of a file type (Downloaded Program Files, for example) to see what kind of files are included in that type.
5. Check the types of files you want Windows to remove.
6. Click **OK** to let Disk Cleanup delete the types of files you selected.

Step 3: Use DriveSpace and the Compression Agent

If you still don't have enough space on your hard drive, it is time for more drastic measures. Windows comes with DriveSpace, a program that compresses the data on your hard drive so you can fit more in the same space. While DriveSpace can often "create" huge amounts of additional space, using it involves tradeoffs.

Lossy vs Lossless Compression

DriveSpace compresses files using a lossless algorithm. If you compress a file using a lossless algorithm, then decompress it, the resulting file is identical to the original.

The MP3 format, by contrast, uses a lossy compression algorithm. As a result, if you compress a file to MP3 format, then decompress it, the resulting file is not identical to the original file. Because MP3 discards data that people normally can't hear, you don't notice the loss. Lossy compression algorithms typically result in smaller files than lossless algorithms, hence their popularity.

Your computer's processor must do the work to compress and decompress the files on the hard disk, which takes time. If you have a slow processor, using DriveSpace will likely result in it taking longer than before to read from and write to the hard drive. On the other hand, if you have a fast processor, it is possible that disk access be slightly faster after using DriveSpace. How? While you add some processing time to compress and decompress files, you save some disk access time because compressed files are smaller than uncompressed ones.

Also, the gains you get from DriveSpace vary. Text files compress a lot. MP3 and ZIP files, which are already compressed, hardly compress at all.

Despite these negatives of using DriveSpace, the end result is usually worth it. After applying DriveSpace to a typical 4 GB drive, Windows might now be able to store 6 GB or more of data on the drive.

NOTE

If you use Windows 98, you may not be able to use DriveSpace. Windows 98 supports FAT32, a very efficient system for storing files on a hard disk. FAT32 can free up hundreds of megabytes of disk space relative to older file storage systems, and it is faster while using fewer system resources. However, if your hard drive is using FAT32, you cannot use DriveSpace.

Follow these steps to use DriveSpace. You will notice that the screen shots all pertain to a floppy disk. My computers all use FAT32 for the hard drives, so that left only the floppy drive. Anyway, here are the steps you need to follow:

1. Click **Start** then **Programs, Accessories, System Tools, DriveSpace**. This starts DriveSpace (Figure 12.8).

FIGURE 12.8

DriveSpace can compress your hard drives or floppy disks.

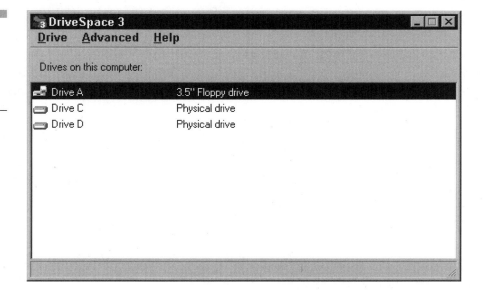

2. To compress a drive, select it, then click **Drive** followed by **Compress....** DriveSpace analyzes the disk and reports the expected results of the compression operation using the Compress a Drive dialog box in Figure 12.9.

FIGURE 12.9
*The expected results
of compressing a
floppy disk.*

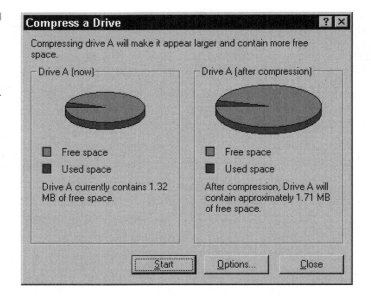

3. Click **Start** to begin the compression process. Windows gives you one last chance to back out (Figure 12.10), and advises you to back up your files before beginning to compress the drive.

FIGURE 12.10
*One last chance to
back out of com-
pressing the disk, or
to back up your files.*

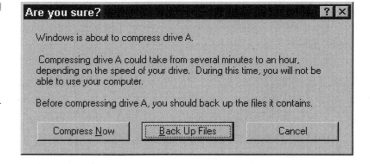

4. After DriveSpace compresses the drive, it displays the Compress a Drive dialog box again. This time, the dialog box contains the actual results of the compression operation. Compare Figures 12.9 and 12.11. The actual results of the compression are much more impressive than the expected results, and are more in line with what you would expect from running DriveSpace on your hard disk.

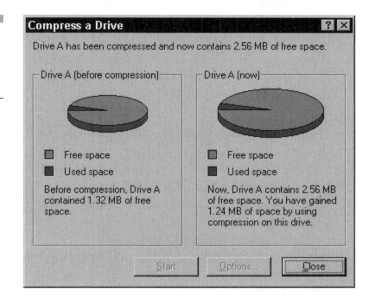

FIGURE 12.11
The actual results of running DriveSpace on a floppy disk.

5. Click **Close** to return to the main DriveSpace window.

Step 4: Adding Another Hard Drive to Your PC

This is definitely an inside-the-box job and is covered in Chapter 13 under "Increasing Storage Space Revisited."

Checking Multimedia Properties

If it seems you have all your audio hardware (speakers or headphones, and sound card) set up properly, but still don't hear anything, your multimedia properties may be incorrect. To work with the multimedia properties, the best approach may be to go through the Windows help system.

The first thing to check is the playback volume. Follow these steps:

1. Click **Start** then **Help**. This opens Windows help.
2. Select the **Index** tab, then enter the term **multimedia** in the keyword box.

3. Double-click the **Audio** tab topic under the Multimedia Properties heading. A Topics Found dialog box appears.
4. Double-click **To adjust the playback volume**. The procedure for doing this adjustment appears in the right panel of the Windows help window (Figure 12.12).

FIGURE 12.12
Windows help contains procedures for checking the multimedia settings on your PC.

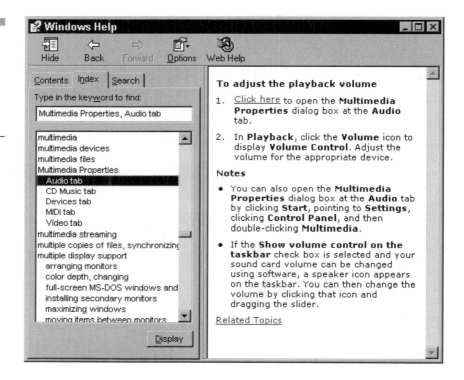

5. Follow the procedures listed here to adjust the playback volume. If you changed this setting, return to what you were doing before and see if this change has fixed your problem.
6. If you still have the problem, return to Windows help and double-click the **CD Music** tab topic.
7. In the Topics Found dialog box, double-click **To send CD audio directly to a digital output device**.

The instructions for this topic may not exactly match what you see on the CD Music tabbed page.

NOTE

8. Make sure that the Default CD-ROM drive for playing CD music corresponds to the drive letter of your CD-ROM drive (if you are not sure which drive letter corresponds to your CD-ROM drive, leave this one alone). If the drive letter was incorrect, return to what you were doing before and see if this change has fixed the problem.

9. If you still have the problem, slide the CD Music Volume control all the way to the right. This sets full volume.

10. If the CD Music Volume was not set to full volume, return to what you were doing before and see if this change has fixed the problem.

11. If you still have the problem, look for a digital CD audio checkbox at the bottom of the CD Music tabbed page. If this box is dimmed, you are done here.

12. If the digital CD audio checkbox is not dimmed, it may be set incorrectly. Try clearing this checkbox if it is set, or setting it if it is cleared. Return to what you were doing before and see if this change has fixed the problem.

13. If the problem persists, return to the digital CD audio checkbox and set it back to the original setting, and call the local computer store or a computer-savvy friend for help.

The MusicMatch Jukebox Phenomenon

As noted in an earlier chapter, when you install MusicMatch Jukebox, one of the first things it does is configure your CD-ROM drive. I don't know what it does when it configures your CD-ROM drive, but it sure is good. On one PC, I was unable to rip audio tracks. The software would go through the motions, but end up recording several minutes of nothing. I couldn't get that drive to work right no matter what I did.

Then I installed MusicMatch Jukebox on that system. The program did its "configure the CD-ROM drive bit" and that PC has been able to rip tracks ever since.

If you're thinking the MusicMatch Jukebox phenomenon is just a fluke, think on this. Another of my machines had terrible trouble with a particular game CD. It could install and run the game about

25% of the time, while returning data errors reading the CD-ROM drive the remaining 75% of the time. I ran MusicMatch Jukebox on that machine, and from then on it could read the problematic CD. The moral of the story is, run MusicMatch Jukebox on any machine that has CD-ROM drive problems for a quick and dirty shot at fixing those problems.

Sounding Off with Speakers or Headphones

If you don't have speakers of headphones connected to your computer, you're going to have a very hard time listening to MP3s. Since you are reading this section, you're probably getting ready to buy some speakers or headphones. You may realize that it doesn't matter how good your sound card is or how high-quality your MP3 files are; if your speakers or headphones are not high quality, the music will sound bad. All you need is some advice on which equipment is best for you.

You can go to one of the online stores mentioned in Chapter 16 and shop for speakers or headphones based on the information you find there. But let me throw in my two cents worth here, and tell you which speakers and headphones I use.

Speakers

I love my Boston Acoustics speakers. I started out with their BA635 Powered Speaker System and was really happy with it. The system has two compact satellite speakers (less than three inches on a side) and a compact subwoofer. The system gave me great sound and didn't take up much space at all.

When I got serious about MP3, it only made sense to try more serious speaker systems. I tried both the Boston Acoustics Micro-Media system and their top-of-the-line MediaTheater system.

MicroMedia offers more power and a wider frequency response than the BA635 system. Not surprisingly, it sounded somewhat better too. In a review, *PC World* described the MicroMedia speakers as among the best they had heard, and as the best for their compact size.

After the BA635s and the MicroMedia, I had to try the MediaTheater system. MediaTheater is a larger, more powerful system with two satellite speakers and a serious subwoofer. When I turn this system up, it makes my entire office vibrate. Even better, the power doesn't come at the cost of clarity.

MP3.com gave MediaTheater a five-star rating, and *PC Magazine* called it the ticket for putting together a PC-based home theater system.

NOTE

But what's really wonderful about the MediaTheater is its surround-sound capabilities. After you take a couple of minutes running through the simple surround-sound calibration process, MediaTheater engulfs you in the music. In the basic three-speaker configuration, MediaTheater uses Virtual Dolby® Surround to simulate a five-speaker system. With the optional surround speaker installed, the system switches to true Dolby Pro Logic for even greater 3D sound.

The three systems make up the Boston Acoustics Multimedia series. You can order any of them direct from the Boston Acoustics factory-direct Web site at **www.bostondirect.com** (Figure 12.13).

Headphones

I have always had problems with headphones. I have gone through cheap headphones, expensive headphones, noise-quieting headphones, you name it. The problem only got worse when I started playing with portable MP3 players. Who wants to hook a 2.5-ounce MP3 player up to a set of 8-ounce speakers?

MP3 players now come with the little ear-bud type of headphones, where you tuck the phone inside your ear. Those are fairly good, but I found that they got uncomfortable after a while, and would sometimes fall out while I was jogging or cutting the lawn. They might well work fine for you, but I still was not entirely happy.

Finally, I found my dream headphones, the Koss sportclip KSC 35s. Imagine a set of Koss headphones, the lightweight ones that fit over a large portion of your ear. Now take the headband away, and replace it with curved plastic clips that fit behind your ears.

You need to see them to understand exactly what I mean, but when you wear these, you can't feel the clip at all. It is as if the headphones are just attached to the outside of your ear. Thanks to the design of the clips, they won't fall off. I've got the cord caught on my bicycle handlebars and given it a good solid yank without losing the phones. Investigate them the next time you are at the store, or visit the Koss Web site at www.koss.com. You will find the KSC 35s under portable stereophones.

FIGURE 12.13

Shop here for Boston Acoustics Multimedia speaker systems.

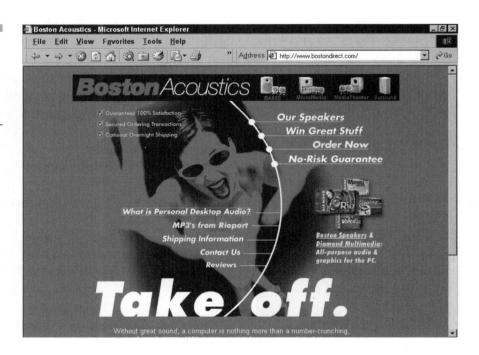

Cranking It Out Through Your Stereo

You may feel the need to connect your PC to your stereo system so as to play MP3s through all that wonderful equipment you bought when music didn't come from the Internet. You can do this even if your stereo and computer are in different rooms (or on different ends of the house). MusicMatch sells special cables for exactly this purpose.

Available in 100' and 300' lengths, these cables are designed to prevent audio distortion, while still being thin enough to install in your house. To order cables, go to **jukebox.musicmatch.com/ connects/**.

Once you have the cable, plug the stereo mini-plug (the one that looks like the connector on a set of headphones) into the Line Out connector on your sound card. If the card doesn't have a Line Out connector, plug the cable into the Audio Out connector. Set the PC to play several MP3 files so you have a signal to work with at the stereo end. Now go to the stereo, and turn it off. Then plug the RCA plugs on this end of the cable into the connectors for an unused input source on the stereo. That's all it takes.

With the volume turned all the way down, turn on the stereo and set it to use the input source connected to your PC. Slowly turn up the volume, listening for the MP3 files you're playing on the PC. If you hear the music, adjust the volume level normally—you are set.

If you don't hear any music, even after turning up the stereo, you probably have the cable connected incorrectly. Turn the volume back down, check your work, and get the cable plugged into the right connectors. That should be all you need to do to get this connection working.

External Modems

You have two choices when adding a modem to your system: external or internal. You need to consider a few factors when deciding which kind of modem to use:

- External modems cost more, and require that your machine have a spare serial port, but don't require you to open the box to install them.
- Internal modems cost less, but take up an expansion slot inside your PC, and require that you open the PC to install them.

Whichever type of modem you use, you need one additional facility: a live phone jack near your computer. The modem connects your computer to the telephone system and from there to an Internet Service Provider (ISP).

NOTE

If you are lucky enough to live in an area where cable modem services are available, you may not want to buy a conventional modem at all. Call the company providing the cable modem service for more information before buying anything. Cable modems typically download information from the Internet at 20–50 times the speed of a conventional modem. The time you save downloading MP3 files can easily make up for the higher cost of cable modem. For an unbiased view of the cable modem service in your area, read about CNET's Ultimate ISP Guide under the heading, "Connecting to the Net: ISPs."

This topic assumes that you are considering an external modem. The first thing to do is check to see if your PC has a spare serial port. Turn off your computer and take a look at the connectors on the back. You're looking for an unused 9-pin connector that's named Com 1 or Com 2, Modem, RS-232, or Serial. Serial ports normally have male connectors—that is, there are pins on the connector that stick out toward you. The PC's manual can help you identify the serial port or ports on your particular machine.

If your PC has a spare serial port, you are in good shape and ready to go shopping for a modem. If your PC doesn't have a spare serial port, you might as well go for an internal modem. Skip to Chapter 13 for advice on buying and installing internal modems.

Because the speed and features of modems are constantly improving, your best bet is to go to the online computer stores covered in Chapter 16 and check their modem selections. Read the product descriptions and buying guidelines to get a feel for the speed and characteristics of the current crop of modems. If you already have an ISP, check to see which modems they recommend. Your best bet is generally to buy the fastest modem you can afford, as long as your ISP can work with it. Come back to this topic when you have your modem in hand. In the meantime, you can go to the next topic and shop for an ISP.

NOTE

PC Card modems are a third type of modem, but are designed for laptop computers. Unless you're using a laptop, you should stick with internal or external modems.

Now that your modem is here, you are probably itching to install it. You should have no problem doing so. Follow the instructions that came with the modem and you should be connected and running in minutes. The installation process will go something like this:

1. Turn off your PC.
2. Connect the cable that runs between the PC and modem.
3. Connect the modem to the phone jack.
4. Connect the modem's power supply to an outlet and to the modem.
5. Turn on the PC and the modem.
6. Microsoft Windows will detect the modem and ask you to insert the disk with the modem software.
7. Windows runs a setup wizard that guides you through the rest of the installation process.

Once you finish the installation process, your modem should be ready to go. Many modems allow you to register them online. This not only eliminates the need to fill out a registration card, but if successful, shows you that the modem functions properly.

Connecting to the Net: ISPs

Shopping for an ISP can be a hard job. There are local mom and pop outfits, regional ISPs, national ISPs like AT&T WorldNet or PSINet, and combined online service/ISPs like AOL (America Online), CompuServe, and Prodigy. How do you decide which service to use?

DEFINITION

ISP is short for Internet Service Provider. An ISP provides the connection (through the phone system) between your PC and the Internet.

If you can beg, borrow, or steal a little time on someone else's Internet connection, browse to CNET's Ultimate ISP Guide at **www.cnet.com/Content/Reports/Special/ISP/index.html**. This site provides information on over 4,000 ISPs worldwide. It also features dozens of special reports, as well as an ISP checklist to help you shop.

Chapter Wrapup

Upgrading your PC for MP3 can mean many different things, depending on the characteristics of your particular PC. Whether the upgrade involves adding new hardware or just tweaking things to make it all work properly, you can divide the work into two categories: inside the box and outside the box.

This chapter started by addressing some "upgrades" you can make to your system without any new hardware at all. By running various Microsoft Windows utilities, you can make your machine work better than it used to, even making your disk drives act as if they had grown much larger. By installing and using Norton Utilities in conjunction with the Windows utilities, you can really revitalize your old PC.

For cases where those steps aren't enough, the text included a table of specific problems. For each problem there was a reference to a topic in Chapter 12 or Chapter 13 that dealt with that problem. Use of this table and running Windows utilities and Norton Utilities should resolve most problems you might have playing MP3 files on your PC.

Once you get past the table, this chapter addressed upgrades you can make outside the box. A few of the upgrades explained here were purely software fixes, while others involved adding hardware like speakers or an external modem to your machine. None of them required you to open the case of your computer and poke around inside it.

The case-opening and around-poking is all reserved for Chapter 13, "Working Inside the Box." In that chapter you get to open the case and install memory, disk drives, and expansion cards like internal modems.

Working Inside the Box

Chapter 12 looked at ways to upgrade your PC without actually opening the case. In this chapter, you pull open the case and play around with the guts of your machine. While working inside the box isn't for the faint-hearted, it isn't terribly hard, either. If you are reasonably handy, and good at following directions, you can do the upgrades covered in this chapter.

Of course, if looking at what's involved in some of these upgrades makes you uncomfortable, you know to get some help before tackling them.

Without further ado, here are the high notes of working inside the box:

- Getting ready to open the box
- Adding memory
- Adding a sound card
- Adding an internal modem
- Increasing storage space revisited
- Installing a CD-ROM drive
- Upgrading the microprocessor.

Getting Ready to Open the Box

Before you open your computer's case for the first time, there are a few things you should do and a few tricks you should know.

Things You Should Do

There are three things you should always do before you change the hardware inside your computer. Although they might be a pain to do, consider them good insurance should disaster strike and you need to reconstruct your software environment.

Create an Emergency Boot Disk

An emergency boot disk is a special floppy disk that allows you to restart your computer when it won't start normally. Windows can create an emergency boot disk (a startup disk, in Microsoft parlance) for you, as can Norton Utilities. The disk Windows creates will allow you to restart your system in DOS so you can start troubleshooting it. The Norton Utilities Rescue Disk tool (Figure 13.1) also allows you to restart your system in DOS, but includes DOS versions of some Norton Utilities tools to help you diagnose and fix the problem.

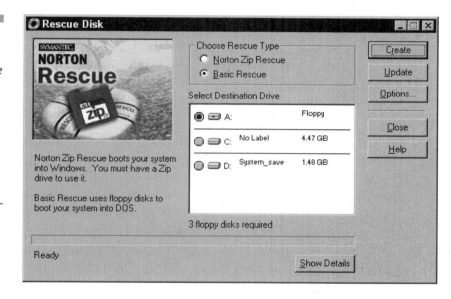

FIGURE 13.1

Use Norton Utilities Rescue Disk to create a set of floppy disks that will help you recover should something go wrong while you are working inside the box.

DEFINITION

DOS stands for Disk Operating System. It is a low-level, non-graphical operating system that has been largely superseded by Windows.

To create an emergency boot disk using Windows, click **Start** then **Settings** then **Control Panel**. In the Control Panel, double-click **Add/Remove** Programs and select the Startup Disk tabbed page. Then just follow the instructions.

To create a rescue disk set with Norton Utilities, click **Start** then **Programs**, **Norton Utilities**, **Rescue Disk**. Then just follow the instructions.

Back Up Your Data

This is good advice that is honored more in the breach than anything else. It is always a good idea to back up your data before you do anything significant to your computer, but it is also a pain in the neck; particularly in these days of multi-gigabyte hard drives on home PCs that have only a floppy disk drive for backup. At least back up your most important files, those that would be really hard to re-create if you had to. Also record any registration codes you might have trouble finding if you had to start over. Finally, if you have any really important e-mail messages, either print them, or e-mail them to yourself and don't check your mail again until you finish the upgrades you are doing.

Prepare Your Work Area

You can make working inside the box a lot easier if you prepare your work area. If you have plenty of open space on the desk where your computer normally sits, you can work there. If you don't, or the lighting isn't that great, consider moving to someplace big and flat, like the kitchen table, for the steps where you are actually poking around inside the computer.

If you put some newspaper under the computer, you won't have to worry about the finish on the table. And you will really appreciate the wide-open spaces when you start pulling the guts out of the machine. Just remember to unplug all the cables from the back of the computer before you move it.

Tricks You Should Use

Here are some tricks you should apply when you work inside the box. The first, Ground Yourself, is a necessity whenever you are working inside the computer's case. The second trick is Don't Touch Those Contacts. The third trick, Use an Old Towel, comes in very handy when (not if, when) you drop one of those tiny screws you find inside the case of your PC. The fourth, Have the Proper Tools, comes from years of bitter experience.

Ground Yourself

Many of the components inside your PC are sensitive to static electricity. A little spark in the wrong place and you can fry a component. To avoid this, you need to ground yourself to the computer. Simply touch the metal frame of the computer before touching any components, card, cables, connectors, or the like. This virtually eliminates the chance of static discharge.

Don't Touch Those Contacts

This trick plays along with the previous one. When you are working with memory chips, circuit cards, or connectors, you will see rows of shiny metal pins and surfaces. Those are contacts. Don't touch them. They carry electrical signals to and from whatever they're attached to, and will carry static discharges too. You greatly reduce the risk of damage if you avoid touching anything that looks even vaguely like a contact or an electrical circuit. Hold memory chips and cards by the circuit card whenever possible.

Use an Old Towel

Lay an old towel on the floor beneath your work area. I find it almost impossible to work inside a PC without dropping at least one screw on the floor. They usually stay put when they land on the old towel, instead of bouncing across the room and going under the refrigerator.

Have the Proper Tools

You don't need a lot of fancy tools to work inside the box. I usually work with a small Phillips-head screwdriver, a small flat-head screwdriver, a pair of tweezers (in case I drop a screw somewhere in the case), and a small flashlight. The flashlight is key. Even if you have good lighting in your workspace, computers are full of nooks and crannies. A small flashlight can be just the ticket to see what you're up to in such spaces.

That's the last of the things you should do and the tricks you should use when working inside the box. Now turn to the topic that applies to the upgrade you want to do, and read the instructions carefully before starting work. You'll do fine.

Adding Memory

The easiest and most effective in-the-box upgrade is adding memory (RAM, or random access memory). Unless you bought a high-end system, your PC probably came with 16 or 32 MB of memory. If you have 16 MB, you will likely notice an amazing improvement in the performance of your Windows PC by adding at least another 16 MB of memory. Having 32 MB of memory puts you at the bottom of the usable range as far as I'm concerned, particularly when you're going to be working with multi-megabyte MP3 files. If possible, you want to get your system up to at least 64 MB of RAM.

Virtually all PCs today come with some room for additional RAM. The sockets for RAM are usually on the computer's motherboard, which is the main circuit board in the PC and holds the majority of the electronics and circuitry.

The specifics of adding memory to a PC vary from machine to machine. Once you start talking about memory, you can quickly descend into buzzword hell, spouting terms like SIMM, DIMM, EDO, fast-page, parity, and the like. The people who make PC memory chips know this, and have taken steps to simplify adding memory. Many computer stores offer memory selection programs from the chipmakers, where you can enter some information about your computer and the program spits out the model number of the memory you should buy.

PNY is one company I've bought memory from several times. In addition to memory selection programs in computer stores, PNY has great tools on its Web site at **www.pny.com**. The Retail Memory Configurator is the online equivalent to those computer-store programs, while the Memory Wizard is closer to an online course in choosing and installing memory.

To give you an idea of the power of these tools, here are the topics covered by the Memory Wizard:

▐ What is memory?
▐ How much memory do I need?
▐ Configure my computer
▐ Where to purchase
▐ Installation help
▐ Problem solver.

As you can see from this list, the information at the PNY Web site covers all aspects of buying and installing memory. In the vast majority of cases, you can get exact instructions for installing memory in your make and model PC from this site, so instead of walking through a typical memory installation, I recommend you head over to the PNY Web site and investigate their detailed instructions for your specific PC.

NOTE

PNY isn't the only memory maker with great tools on the Web. Kingston Technology is another manufacturer I have used in the past. Their site (**www.kingston.com**) also offers an online memory configurator, as well as detailed information about PC memory in general.

Adding a Sound Card

A key computer component for anyone who wants to play MP3 files on their PC is a quality sound card. Although most PCs these days come with a sound card installed or built into the mother-board, those sound cards are seldom top of the line. Although such equipment is fine for most uses, if you're reading this book, it is likely that you'll want better sound quality than you get with the original equipment. This is particularly true if you invest in a decent set of multimedia speakers.

Go to Chapter 17 to see a collection of online stores where you can learn about sound cards and order the one you will install. Come back here when you have your card in hand.

Installing a sound card is fairly easy. To illustrate the process, the rest of this topic takes you through the installation of a Montego II Quadzilla PCI – 3-D Audio Accelerator from Voyetra Turtle Beach Inc. This capable card is designed to provide 3D audio effects in cutting-edge computer games. It also makes a superior sound card for playing MP3 files on the PC.

NOTE

You can see the full line of Voyetra Turtle Beach sound cards and audio software at their Web site (Figure 13.2), **www.voyetra-turtle-beach.com**.

FIGURE 13.2

Voyetra Turtle Beach offers a line of quality sound cards that make great music and add 3-D sound to your games.

The following procedure recounts the steps I took to install the card and get it running under Windows 98. Other quality cards require a comparable amount of time and effort—not much at all. If you are comfortable under the hood of your PC, figure on being up and running again in less than 30 minutes.

Here are the steps I followed:

1. Uninstall the sofware drivers for the existing sound card, then remove the card. Make sure you turn off the PC and unplug it from the wall before doing this.

2. Look inside the PC for a free PCI expansion slot and any other free slot. Like many high-end sound cards, the Montego II requires two slots. Consult your computer's manual for information on what the slots look like.

3. Remove the slot covers from the two slots.

4. Insert the Montego II board in the PCI expansion slot and screw it down.

5. Insert the breakout bracket (a small subcard that contains additional circuitry and connectors) in the second slot and screw it down.

6. Connect the Montego II board to the breakout bracket and the CD-ROM drive using the supplied cables.

7. Close the system up, plug the speakers into the Line Output 1 connector, then plug the PC in and turn on the power.

8. Insert the Montego II CD-ROM in the CD-ROM drive while Windows 98 is starting. Windows detects the new hardware and walks you through a series of steps designed to get the hardware working smoothly with Windows.

9. Follow the directions that appear on the screen until they are complete. The Montego II should now be ready to play music.

Because I didn't properly delete the sound drivers from my machine before installing, I did need to do one additional thing before the sound card would make so much as a peep. By installing the new drivers without removing the old, I left Windows not knowing which sound drivers to use—so it kept using the old ones.

Fortunately, the fix for this is straightforward, requiring only that I adjust the Windows multimedia settings to use the proper drivers. In case you ever need to do this, here are the steps:

1. Click **Start** then **Settings** then **Control Panel**. This opens the Windows Control Panel.

2. In the Control Panel, double-click **Multimedia** to open the Multimedia Properties dialog box, then click the **Audio** tab to open to the Audio tabbed page (Figure 13.3).

FIGURE 13.3

The Audio tabbed page of the Multimedia Properties dialog box controls which sound card Windows talks to.

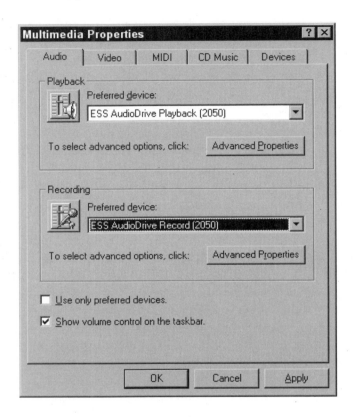

3. Click the down arrow to display a list of the available play-back devices and select the correct device.
4. Click **OK** to apply the change and return to the Control Panel. Windows should now begin communicating with the proper sound card.

If you play an MP3 file right now, you should hear the sound. If you don't, open the Windows help system (click **Start** then **Help**) and search the Index for a Troubleshooting subtopic under the Sound Cards topic. This will help you debug the sound card.

Adding an Internal Modem

Adding an internal modem to your system is much like adding a sound card. You need to plug the modem card into an unused expansion slot, connect some cables (in this case the phone line) to the back of the modem, then restart your computer and run some configuration software to get the modem and Windows talking to each other.

As noted in Chapter 12 under the heading of External Modems, your best bet for choosing a modem is to go to the online computer stores covered in Chapter 16 and check their selections. Read the product descriptions and buying guidelines to get a feel for the speed and characteristics of the current crop of modems. If you already have an ISP, check to see which modems are recommended. Go for the fastest modem you can afford, as long as your ISP can work with it.

To choose a modem that will work in your system you need to know what kinds of unused expansion slots your PC has. Shut down the PC, unplug it from the wall, and remove the cover from the case. With the help of the computer's documentation, identify the types of spare slots available. Record this information, and have it handy when you shop for a modem.

The installation process for an internal modem goes something like this:

1. Turn off your PC, unplug it from the house current, and remove the cover from the case.
2. Unscrew and remove the cover plate that closes the opening where the back of the modem card will protrude from the computer.
3. Insert the modem card in the unused slot, and screw it into place using the screw that held down the cover plate.
4. Close the case, then connect the modem to the phone jack.
5. Turn on the PC.
6. In most cases, Microsoft Windows detects the modem and automatically installs appropriate driver software.

Once Windows finishes installing the software drivers, your modem should be ready to go. Many modems allow you to register them online. This not only eliminates the need to fill out a registration card, but if successful, shows you that the modem functions properly. Installing an internal modem is likely to take you less than an hour.

Increasing Storage Space Revisited

Chapter 12 explored ways to increase the storage space on your PC without adding any new hardware. Although you can often achieve dramatic increases in storage space using those techniques, eventually you reach limits. That is when you might consider adding additional storage to your system. With drives available today (Summer '99) holding 10s of GBs of data, you can make storage space a non-issue for a long time.

Most PCs are designed with the cables, circuitry, and open space needed to add a second hard drive. To see if your PC is so designed, start with the computer's documentation. Sometimes that will tell you what you need to know. With other systems, the documentation tells you something like, "Depending on the computer model you have, you may be able to upgrade the system by adding a second hard drive." Not much help there.

The next step is to let Windows System Information tell you if the computer can support a second hard drive. Here's how:

1. Click **Start** then **Settings** then **Control Panel**. This opens the Windows Control Panel.
2. In the Control Panel, double-click **System** to open the System Properties dialog box, then click the **Device Manager** tab to open to the Device Manager tabbed page (Figure 13.4).
3. If it is not already selected, select **View devices by type**.
4. The first thing to do is to check on the available hard-disk controllers. Find Hard Disk Controllers in the list, and click the plus sign to the left of the name to view the hard-disk controllers installed on your PC. Figure 13.5 shows the controllers on my PC.

FIGURE 13.4

The Device Manager tabbed page in the System Properties dialog box has lots of information about the hard drives and hard drive controllers in your machine.

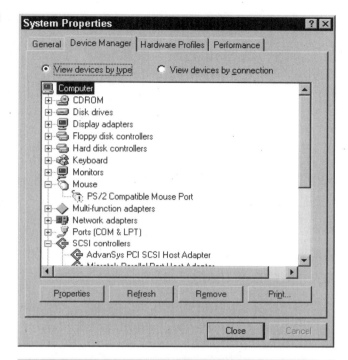

FIGURE 13.5

My PC has three hard-disk controllers, a Primary IDE controller (dual fifo), a Secondary IDE controller (dual fifo), and an SiS 5513 Dual PCI IDE controller.

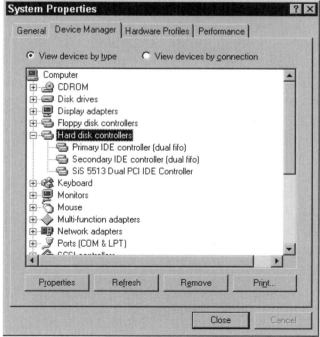

5. Make sure that your computer has at least a dual primary controller and a dual secondary controller. With that configuration, your computer can support up to a total of four hard drives and CD-ROM drives. The other important thing to note here is the type of hard drive, IDE or SCSI. The vast majority of home computers use IDE drives, but it never hurts to check. The new drive you buy must be the same type as the existing drive and controllers, or you need to replace them too.

NOTE

When you refer to IDE these days, you normally mean EIDE, Enhanced IDE.

6. Now you need to check on the hard drive or drives already installed in your PC. To do this, click the plus sign next to Disk Drives. This shows you all the floppy and hard drives installed in your computer. Figure 13.6 shows the two drives, one floppy and one hard, that are installed on my computer. The selected one is the hard drive.

FIGURE 13.6

Open Disk drives to see all the hard drives and floppy drives installed in your computer.

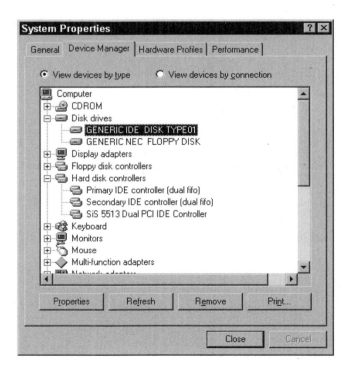

7. If you only have one hard drive installed in your computer, you are ready to go. If you already have two, you can still add another, but it gets trickier.

8. Now you need to open up your PC. You know that you have the controllers to support another drive, but you still need to be sure there is a place to put the thing inside the computer. So turn off the PC and unplug it from the wall, open it up, and look for the hard drive that's already installed. You're looking for an unused internal drive bay, which will be an open rectangular space near the current disk drive.

9. Once you know you have room for an additional drive, close up your computer, and turn to Chapter 16, where you can find some places to order your new drive online. You need to know the drive type, IDE or SCSI. If you want help making your selection, try shopping at CNET Shopper (**www.shopper.com**) or Computershopper.com (**www.computershopper.com**). Both sites offer extensive advice on shopping for all sorts of computer hardware.

10. Once you have a drive in hand, the best thing I can tell you is to follow the instructions that come with the drive. Most hard drives today come with extensive instructions that walk you through the process of installing the hardware and software in great detail. I will tell you that you can save yourself a lot of work by making your current drive the master (primary) drive, and the new drive the slave (secondary) drive. That way, you won't need to reinstall all your software after you install the new drive.

Figure on less than two hours to install your new hard drive.

Installing a CD-ROM Drive

CD-ROM drives have been standard equipment on PCs for a few years now. If your PC doesn't have one, you should think hard about whether upgrading your PC is even worthwhile. The lack of a CD-ROM drive could well indicate that your machine will need other upgrades too, things like more memory, a faster processor, and an additional hard drive. At that point, it is probably cheaper and more effective to buy a new machine.

NOTE

Another reason to consider installing a new drive is if you want to create your own audio CDs from your MP3 files. In this case, I recommend you buy a CD-R (CD-Recordable) drive. There is a more detailed discussion of CD-ROM versus CD-R versus CD-RW (CD-Rewritable) drives in Chapter 14. For simplicity, the rest of this chapter uses the term CD-ROM drive to refer to any of these drive types.

Assuming you decide that installing a new CD-ROM drive is still in order, the next step is to determine what kind of drive and how fast it should be. To see what type of drive you need, use Windows System Information:

1. Click **Start** then **Settings** then **Control Panel**. This opens the Windows Control Panel.
2. In the Control Panel, double-click **System** to open the System Properties dialog box, then click the **Device Manager** tab to open to the Device Manager tabbed page.
3. If it is not already selected, select **View devices by type**.
4. Find Hard Disk Controllers in the list, and click the plus sign to the left of the name to view the hard-disk controllers installed on your PC. The hard-disk controllers also control any CD-ROM drives.
5. Make sure that your computer has at least a dual primary controller and a dual secondary controller. With that configuration, your computer can support up to a total of four hard drives and CD-ROM drives. Make note of the type of hard drive controller, IDE or SCSI. The vast majority of home computers use IDE drives, but it never hurts to check. The new drive must be the same type as the existing drive and controllers, or you must replace them too.
6. Now you need to make sure you have a place to put the drive. Since you need to insert and remove CDs, the front of a CD-ROM drive must be accessible from the front of your computer. Therefore you need an unused external drive bay to hold the drive. Check your computer's documentation for information.

7. If you can't find anything in the documentation about an external drive bay, you can do a little prospecting yourself. Shut down the PC, unplug it from the wall, and take the cover off the case. Take a look around inside. Unused external drive bays are almost always near the used external drive bays (which hold things like floppy disk drives). They have plastic knock-out covers that provide external access to the bay. If you've got one of those available, you should be all set. The majority of PCs have spare internal power and data connectors expressly for the purpose of adding new devices.

8. Assuming you know the drive type (IDE or SCSI), and have a spare external drive bay to hold the drive, you're ready to buy your new CD-ROM drive.

9. Computershopper.com is an excellent source of advice and information related to buying your new drive. Find the CD-ROM drive section for Expert Picks, Buying Guides, Research and comparison shopping tips. Chapter 16 has more information on computershopper.com.

10. As with a hard drive upgrade, the best advice at this point is simply to follow the instructions that come with the CD-ROM drive. If you follow the hardware and software installation instructions carefully, the work should go smoothly.

Figure on less than two hours to install your new CD-ROM drive.

Upgrading the Microprocessor

What do you do when your PC is just too slow, even after you've added memory? You have two choices to remedy the problem. If your machine is more than a couple of years old, you should think seriously about buying a new PC. Upgrades can bring new life to old computers, but at some point it will cost more to do all the needed upgrades on your old machine than it will to buy a new one. Besides, newer computers incorporate newer technologies like USB, which you really can't add to your old machine. Another issue to consider is that much of the newer software won't run on machines with anything less than a Pentium-class processor. For example, Sonique and MusicMatch Jukebox both require Pentium-class processors to run.

If your PC is less than two years old, and its speed or compatibility are your only complaints, consider becoming a PC brain surgeon. In many PCs, you can remove the microprocessor and replace it with a faster one.

I did exactly that on one of my PCs, upgrading a machine with a Pentium 100 processor using an MxPro 200 upgrade kit from Evergreen Technologies. The upgrade didn't give me the equivalent of a PC with a 200-MHz Pentium processor, but it did give a significant performance boost and added the ability to take advantage of MMX-enabled multimedia programs.

Evergreen Technologies has continued to improve its processor upgrade offerings. Today it offers products like the Spectra 400, which replaces your old Pentium processor with a 400-MHz AMD K6-2 processor that supports the MMX and 3DNow multimedia and graphics instruction sets. Visit the Evergreen Technologies Web site at **www.evertech.com** to see their latest creations.

DEFINITION

MMX is an Intel trademark for a multimedia instruction set added to Pentium processors to improve multimedia performance. Early Pentiums, like the one in my machine, did not support MMX.

Two things are vitally important if you're considering a processor upgrade. The first is to realize what a processor upgrade can and cannot do for you. A processor upgrade can speed up your system, often significantly. A processor upgrade can give your PC the ability to use some new technologies, like MMX and 3DNow. A processor upgrade cannot make your PC comparable to a new machine with the same processor.

When manufacturers design a new PC, they do a lot more than just drop in a faster processor. Faster processors call for faster memory, sometimes a faster system bus and peripherals, a new motherboard that is optimized for the processor, new non-processor technologies like USB, maybe a new BIOS, and so on. So an upgrade like the Spectra 400 will not make your PC as fast as a brand-new machine with a 400-MHz AMD K6-2 processor.

The **BIOS** is the lowest level software in your computer, providing basic services to Windows and controlling the computer when you first turn it on.

The second vitally important thing you must do before attempting a processor upgrade is to determine whether your computer can be upgraded in this way. Not all PCs can support all (or any) processor upgrades.

Evergreen has some information that can help you determine if your PC will support their products. Go to their Web site and view the FAQ (frequently asked questions) document for the upgrade processor you are interested in. In the FAQ you will find a section on compatibility. Follow the instructions in this section to determine if a processor upgrade will work for your computer. I went through this process, and eventually settled on the MxPro 200 for my computer. The installation took less than an hour, and the machine has worked without a hitch, running perfectly anything I could throw at it.

To give you an idea of what's involved in a processor upgrade like this (and to show you that this isn't rocket science), here are the steps, as laid out on the easy-to-follow instruction sheet that came with the upgrade processor:

1. Insert the INSTALL disk in the floppy drive, then restart the computer. The INSTALL software runs a suite of diagnostic and performance tests.
2. Follow the instructions that appear. These tell you whether the software will upgrade the BIOS in your system, and which jumpers, if any, you will need to change on your motherboard.
3. Exit INSTALL and turn off the PC.
4. Unplug the computer from the wall, disconnect all the cables connected to the PC, and remove the case cover.
5. Find the CPU on the motherboard. Use the photos on the installation guide to help you identify it.

DEFINITION

The **CPU (Central Processing Unit)** is the integrated circuit that programs run on. It is the most important single contributor to the performance of your PC.

6. Carefully note the placement of any cables, wires, or components that will need to be moved to remove the CPU.

7. Remove the CPU. If necessary, remove the heatsink or cooling fan located on top of the CPU chip itself. This typically involves removing a retaining clip for a heatsink, and undoing some connections for a cooling fan. Consult your computer's documentation for more information on removing the CPU.

8. Set the system bus speed if necessary. Depending on the speed of the upgrade processor you install, you may need to change the speed at which data travels through the rest of your system. See the installation guide for the proper speed to set, and the computer's documentation for instructions on how to set that speed.

9. Install the upgrade processor. Insert the upgrade processor in the socket that previously held the old processor. Follow the directions on the installation guide carefully to ensure that you don't bend a pin or otherwise damage the upgrade processor or your PC.

10. Reconnect any connections you had to remove when removing the old processor (Step 7).

11. Reconnect all cables and power connections you removed in Step 3, but do not put the cover back on the computer yet.

12. Make sure the INSTALL disk is in the floppy disk drive and restart the computer.

13. Check to see that the fan on the upgrade processor is spinning, then look at the information displayed by INSTALL. If the fan spins and INSTALL runs, you should be all set.

14. Turn off the computer, put the cover back on the case, and remove the INSTALL disk from the floppy disk drive.

15. Restart the computer. It should start normally, which tells you that the upgrade was a success. From this point on, your machine should seem the same as before, except noticeably faster.

Chapter Wrapup

Upgrading your computer by working inside the box tends to be relatively expensive, and is more difficult than working outside the box. However, working inside the box is the way to get the most significant performance boosts. This chapter showed you how to do these upgrades:

■ Adding memory
■ Adding a sound card
■ Adding an internal modem
■ Increasing storage space
■ Installing a CD-ROM drive
■ Upgrading the microprocessor.

Where a specific example made sense, it walked you through one. Where the options are too varied for an example to be of much value, the chapter referred you to an online source of information, or to the documentation that comes with the upgrade hardware.

This chapter touched very lightly on a variation on the CD-ROM drive. CD-R drives allow you to create (burn) your own CDs, while still being able to act just like a standard CD-ROM drive. Chapter 14 is dedicated to the hardware you need to burn your own CDs. It features the PlayWrite MP3, an external CD-R drive system that comes with software optimized for creating audio CDs from MP3 files. There are some big advantages to burning your own CDs, and this coming chapter shows you how it is done.

CHAPTER 14

Burning
Your Own CDs

Listening to MP3s on your PC is fun, as long as you are near your PC. Assuming you have a life away from your PC, you will sometimes have to be away from your digital music machine. You might actually have to sit in the living room, where your PC could look out of place. You might even have to ride in a car sometimes, and where can you put your mouse, keyboard, or monitor in a car?

Obviously, someone needs to build MP3 players that fit everywhere—and a group of someones have. If, however, you don't have an MP3 player wherever you go, there is another solution. Rehabilitate your old-fashioned CD players by burning your favorite MP3s onto audio CDs.

This chapter covers everything you need to know to burn your own audio CDs. To illustrate the process, I walk you through the installation and use of the PlayWrite MP3 Pro, a hardware and software system designed to allow you to create professional-quality audio CDs from your favorite MP3s and other sources.

NOTE

Please remember that most music is copyrighted. You cannot just record your favorite MP3s, burn them onto an audio CD, then give copies to all your friends. If you are going to burn audio CDs, be responsible and respect the rights of others.

High notes you'll hit in this chapter include:

▌ Burning your own CDs: the basics
▌ About PlayWrite MP3 Pro
▌ Installing the hardware and driver
▌ Installing the software
▌ Using the PlayWrite MP3 Pro software
▌ Burning a CD

Burning Your Own CDs: The Basics

The information on an audio CD consists of patterns of microscopic pits in the surface of the disc. The laser in your CD-ROM drive reads the data by reflecting off that pattern and translating what it "sees" back into data. The audio CDs you buy in the record store are stamped with a die. This is a great way to mass-produce CDs, but not one conducive to creating your own CDs. For that, you need a different approach.

With the right kind of drive, you can burn the microscopic data pits into the surface of special discs yourself. The right kind of drive is known as a CD-ROM burner.

DEFINITION

A **CD-ROM burner** is a CD-ROM drive equipped with a laser that can be used to burn data into the surface of a special kind of disc.

Two Options: CD-R and CD-RW

Of course, in the PC world nothing stays simple for long. Today there are two types of CD-ROM burner. One, a CD-R burner, burns the data into CD-R discs. That data are permanent—you cannot write new data onto a part of the disc you have already used.

DEFINITION

CD-R stands for CD-Recordable. A CD-R is a special type of CD you can write data onto using the laser in a CD-Recordable drive. You can read the data on a CD-R as many times as you like, but you cannot erase the data and write something new later.

The second type of CD-ROM burner is a CD-RW burner. This burns data onto special CD-RW discs. That data is rewritable. You can write data to this kind of disc, then erase and write new data to the same disc.

DEFINITION

CD-RW stands for CD-Rewritable. A CD-RW is a special type of CD; you can write data, read the data, erase the data, and the reuse the CD. Not all CD-ROM drives can read CD-RW CDs.

Each type of disc has advantages and disadvantages:

▌ The standard CD disc can be produced quickly in large volumes, but can only be created in a special facility. This is the last you will hear about them in this chapter.

- The CD-R discs are inexpensive to produce in small quantities and are compatible with virtually any CD-ROM, CD-R, or CD-RW drives. However, you cannot reuse them.
- The CD-RW discs are more expensive to produce than CD-R discs (both the discs and the burners cost more), and are not as compatible with other drives as CD-R discs. However, you can reuse them.

Taking these factors into account, for the near term, if you want to create your own audio CDs, CD-R is the best approach. Once you settle on CD-R as the best approach for burning your own CDs, you need to choose the tools to do the job. Those tools consist of special hardware and software:

- The hardware is the CD-R burner, as well as any cards and cables required to connect it to your PC.
- The software is the software required for the interface between the PC and the CD-R burner, special software you need to choose the files you will burn to the disc, as well as the software that does the actual burning.

You can assemble your CD-R tools piece by piece, getting the CD-R burner from one source, the interface cards and cables from another, and compatible software from yet another source. Or you can go for the all-in-one approach and choose a bundle that contains everything you need.

For something like this, I advocate the all-in-one approach. If you are willing to invest a little more money, you can get an all-in-one package optimized for copying MP3 files to audio CDs. That package is PlayWrite MP3 Pro, from Microboards Technology, Inc.

About PlayWrite MP3 Pro

The PlayWrite MP3 Pro package consists of:

- An external CD-R drive
- An adapter card that fits inside your PC and allows it to communicate with the CD-R drive

- Cables to interconnect the CD-R drive and the adapter
- Software that allows the PC to communicate with the adapter
- PlayWrite MP3 software with special features for working with MP3 files
- Backup software for backing up your hard drive to CD-ROM
- Watermarking software for copyright protection
- Documentation
- Two CD-R discs to get you started.

While this is an impressive collection of goodies, a mere list doesn't do the PlayWrite MP3 Pro justice. The most impressive part of the package is the PlayWrite MP3 software. This allows you to create a custom playlist, convert the MP3 files that comprise the individual tracks into Red Book audio format on the fly, and burn the CD in as little as a quarter of the playback time. Once the software burns a track to the CD, it automatically deletes the Red Book audio format file from your PC. This is important, since Red Book audio files can be more than 10 times the size of the MP3 file they came from.

DEFINITION

Red Book audio format is the format of the music tracks on an audio CD. You must convert MP3 files into Red Book audio format if a regular audio CD player is to be able to play them.

Furthermore, the PlayWrite MP3 software allows you to massage the tracks before you record them to the CD. You can remove clicks and hisses from the audio, trim the length of a track to fit it into the available space, adjust the length of the silence between tracks, and more. In most cases though, you should be able just to specify the playlist and let the PlayWrite MP3 Pro system have at it. Within 20 minutes or so, you will have a full-length audio CD.

To get there, you need to install the PlayWrite MP3 hardware and software.

PlayWrite MP3 Pro System Requirements

To use PlayWrite MP3 Pro successfully, your system must meet these requirements:

- Windows 95 or 98 operating system
- Pentium 166 or faster processor
- 32 MB or more of RAM
- 2.2 GB or larger hard drive
- SoundBlaster-compatible sound card.

Where Can I Get PlayWrite MP3 Pro?

The best way to get PlayWrite MP3 Pro is to contact your local Microboards dealer. Call 1-800-646-8881 for the name and number of the nearest Microboards dealer.

Installing the Hardware

The PlayWrite MP3 Pro does not come with a printed manual for the external PlayWrite 4080 CD-R drive assembly. It does include a printed manual for the CD-R drive unit mounted in the drive assembly, and you can download a copy of the PlayWrite 4080 manual from the Microboards Web site. Fortunately, for anyone running Microsoft Windows 95, or even better Windows 98, installing the hardware is easy. The following procedure details how I got the hardware installed and running in under 20 minutes.

NOTE

If you have never installed any hardware on your PC, installing the PlayWrite MP3 Pro hardware is not the way to start. Get a computer geek friend to come over and help, or consider hiring a computer technician to do the job.

Follow these steps:

1. Turn off your computer and all SCSI devices connected to it. (If you don't know what a SCSI device is, your PC almost certainly doesn't have any of them.)
2. If your PC does not already have a SCSI adapter installed, install the Advansys 3925 Bus Mastering Host Adapter in an unused PCI slot in your PC, then close your system up again.
3. Connect the SCSI cable to the Host Adapter and the PlayWrite 4080 external CD-R drive assembly. You can use either of the SCSI connectors on the back of the assembly.

4. Place the terminator on the other connector, unless this is not the last device in the SCSI chain. Be sure to place the terminator on the last device in the chain.

5. Check the SCSI ID. The assembly comes from the factory set with a SCSI ID of 6. If this conflicts with the ID of another SCSI device in the chain, change it to an unused ID by pressing the (–) button near the SCSI ID switch with a pointed object.

6. Connect the power cord to the drive assembly and plug it in.

7. Turn on the PlayWrite 4080 CD-R drive assembly and any other SCSI devices in the chain.

8. Turn on the PC.

9. When Windows starts running, it should automatically detect the Advansys 3925 Bus Mastering Host Adapter, then install and configure the appropriate driver software. The correct drivers for the Host Adapter are included on a floppy disk, in case Windows asks for them during the installation and configuration process.

10. Follow the directions that appear on the screen to complete the installation and configuration of the Host Adapter.

Once the installation and configuration process is complete, you should be able to insert the CD that came with the PlayWrite MP3 Pro into the PlayWrite 4080 drive assembly, and browse the CD using Windows Explorer. You are ready to install the software that lets you burn your own audio CDs.

NOTE

The PlayWrite MP3 Pro hardware may use the drive letter that previously belonged to the CD-ROM drive that came installed in your PC. In a typical installation, the CD-ROM drive that came with the computer will have a drive letter of D:. When you install the PlayWrite Mp3 Pro hardware, drive letter D: will normally be the PlayWrite MP3 Pro CD-R drive, while the CD-ROM drive that came in the PC will move to E:.

Installing the Software

Follow these steps to install the PlayWrite MP3 software:

NOTE

During the installation process, the PlayWrite MP3 Pro Setup will recommend that you close all other Windows applications until you finish the installation. It would be a good idea to do so now, and save yourself the trouble of exiting Setup, closing everything, then restarting Setup.

1. Insert the PlayWrite Backup CD into the PlayWrite MP3 external drive.

2. Using Windows Explorer, browse to the PlayWrite MP3 external drive. Its name is Mp3pro and will be the D: drive on most systems. On mine it appears as drive E:.

3. Click the **Mp3pro** drive. The PlayWrite MP3 CD has 3 folders on it (Figure 14.1). For now, only the one named Pwmpro3 is important.

FIGURE 14.1

The Pwmpro3 folder contains the PlayWrite MP3 software you need to burn your own audio CDs.

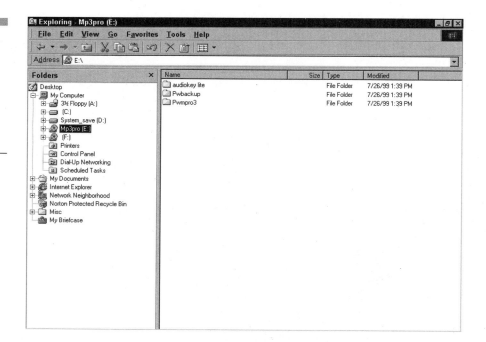

4. Double-click the **Pwmpro3** folder to open it. The folder (Figure 14.2) contains the PlayWrite MP3 software setup program, as well as the manual for the software, stored as an Adobe Acrobat .PDF file (MP3proman.PDF).

Working with .PDF Files

Adobe Acrobat .PDF (Portable Document Format) files are a way to include documentation on a CD-ROM. PDF files retain the formatting and fonts of the original document, and can be viewed on virtually any PC with decent results. If you don't have Acrobat Reader on your PC, you can download the latest version from the Adobe Web site (**www.adobe.com**) or install it from the PlayWrite Backup CD. On the CD, Acrobat Reader is in *X*:\Pwbackup\Acrord32, where *X* is the drive letter for the drive containing the PlayWrite Backup CD. Run AcroRd32.exe from this folder to install Adobe Acrobat Reader on your PC.

FIGURE 14.2

The files you need to be concerned with right now are Setup.exe and MP3proman.PDF.

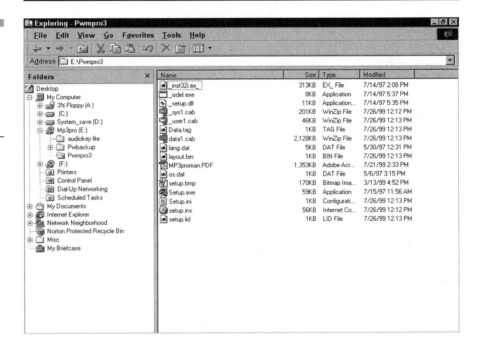

5. Double-click **Setup.exe** to begin installing the PlayWrite MP3 Pro software. After a moment, a PlayWrite MP3 splash screen appears, along with a dialog box telling you that Play-Write MP3 Pro Setup is preparing the wizard that will guide you through the rest of the installation process. After a few moments, the Welcome dialog box replaces these items.

6. Read this dialog box, then click **Next** to continue the installation process. The Choose Destination Location dialog box

appears. Unless you have a strong reason to change it, allow the Setup program to install the software in the suggested Destination folder.

7. Click **Next** to continue. The Select Program Folder dialog box appears. Unless you have a strong reason to change it, allow the Setup program to add the icons to the suggested Program folder.

8. Click **Next** to continue. The Setup program copies files to your PC for a while. Then, depending on your PC configuration, you may see a dialog box asking you about installing a program named ActiveMovie (Figure 14.3).

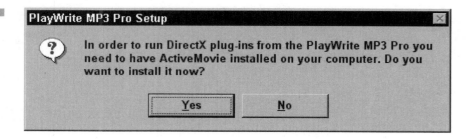

FIGURE 14.3

You should install ActiveMovie so you can take advantage of various DirectX plug-ins that add capabilities to the basic PlayWrite MP3 Pro package.

9. Click **Yes** to install ActiveMovie on your PC. Once the ActiveMovie installation is complete, the Setup program displays the Setup Complete dialog box, where Setup asks if it can restart your PC.

10. Click **Finish** to restart your computer immediately. Once the system finishes restarting, you should be able to use the Play-Write MP3 Pro software.

Using the PlayWrite MP3 Pro Software

To use the software, find the PlayWrite MP3 Pro Program Group in the Windows Programs list, and click **PlayWrite MP3 Pro**. When the program starts, it asks you to specify the drive letter for the CD-R drive. Select the appropriate drive letter and click **OK** to open the PlayWrite MP3 Pro software (Figure 14.4).

NOTE

This guide to using the PlayWrite MP3 Pro software is geared toward automatically recording audio CDs from MP3 files. It doesn't cover any of the software's other capabilities, like the ability to record from virtually any audio source, the DeClick and DeHiss features for cleaning up noisy tracks, and various other features. If you are interested in these kinds of capabilities, read the software manual (the MP3proman.PDF manual mentioned earlier in the chapter) for detailed instructions.

FIGURE 14.4

The PlayWrite MP3 Pro software's main window is where you will create your playlists.

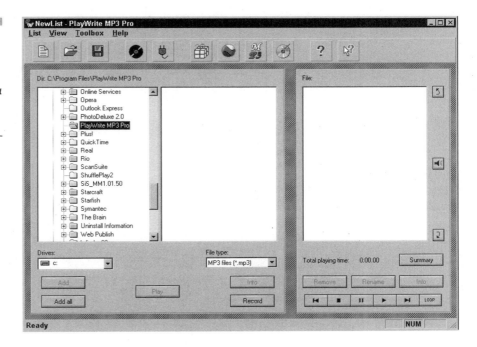

The main PlayWrite MP3 Pro software window has two panels, the File panel (on the left) and the Playlist panel (on the right). The list on the left side of the File panel is a standard directory tree for your PC. To the right of that is the Music list. When you select a folder that contains MP3 files in the left directory tree, the names of all the MP3 files in that folder appear in the Music list.

NOTE

You can right-click a file in the music list to see a shortcut menu that allows you to Copy, Move, Rename, or Delete the file.

Beneath these two lists is a set of controls for working with files and adding them to the playlist. Use the Drives list to see the directory tree for a different drive, and the File Type list to view files other than MP3s. Select a file in the Music list and click **Add** to add it to the playlist. You can also drag files from the Music list and drop them in the playlist. Click **Add All** to add every file in the Music list to the playlist. The Play button plays the currently selected file, or the first file if several are selected.

When you add files to the Playlist panel, its controls become active. The panel keeps a running total of the amount of time the tracks in the playlist will take to play. Click **Summary** to see a summary of the playlist and how much of the CD-R it will occupy (Figure 14.5).

FIGURE 14.5
This playlist summary helps you create your audio CDs.

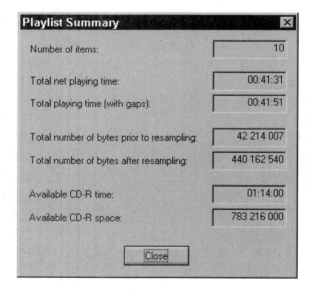

The Remove and Rename buttons perform those actions on the selected file, while Info opens the File Info dialog box (Figure 14.6). This dialog box provides detailed information about the selected track, as well as controlling the gap time (the length of the silence) between the selected track and the following track. You can set the gap time you want to use, then click **Apply to All** to set that gap time for every track on the CD.

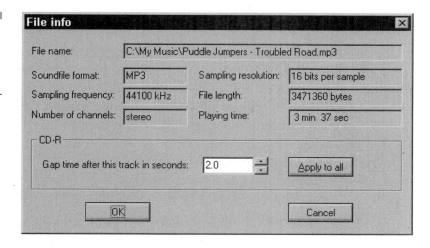

FIGURE 14.6

Set the gap time for your tracks using the File Info dialog box.

The controls at the bottom of the Playlist panel allow you to play your playlist as if it were already recorded as an audio CD. You can see how the tracks will work together when arranged in the order you have specified. If you aren't happy with the order of the tracks, use the Move Up and Move Down buttons on the right side of the playlist to rearrange the tracks.

Burning a CD

There is more to burning a quality audio CD than just throwing songs onto a disc. You need to consider how the tracks fit together. Putting all the slow songs together, followed by all the fast songs, won't make for the best CD. I think designing a CD is an art, not a science. The best approach may be to see how your favorite CDs have their tracks arranged and use those arrangements for inspiration.

Once you decide how to arrange the tracks on the CD, use the PlayWrite MP3 Player Pro software to find the tracks you need, drag them into the playlist, and arrange them in the order you want. Then use the playback controls beneath the playlist to listen to the resulting list and make any adjustments you need.

Once you are happy with the arrangement of the tracks, click **List** then **Write to CD** (or click the **Write to CD** button on the toolbar). This begins the process of burning the audio CD.

Since you are working with MP3 files, the first thing that happens when you click **Write to CD** is that the Check CD Format dialog box appears. This dialog box contains the names and paths to all the MP3 files that are to be converted then included on the audio CD.

The PlayWrite MP3 Pro software knows how to convert MP3 files to audio CD format automatically, but it needs significant disk space to do so. If you look carefully at Figure 14.7, it shows that I don't have enough disk space to store the temporary files created when the software does the conversions from MP3 format. I had to click Cancel, clear enough space on my hard drive, and try again.

NOTE

The PlayWrite MP3 Pro software automatically eliminates the temp files after it is done with them.

FIGURE 14.7

The Check CD Format dialog box appears when needed and tells you which files it will add to the audio CD, as well as whether you have enough disk space to perform the conversion.

Check CD Format

The following soundfiles are not CD format compatible. They need to be 16 bit 44 kHz stereo files:

Albert Einstein Dreams.mp3 (C:\My Music\Albert Einstein D
Alien Fashion Show - Secret Pill.mp3 (C:\My Music\Alien Fa
Apollos Popsters - - Captured By You.mp3 (C:\My Music\Ap
Cats - Rum Tum Tugger.mp3 (C:\My Music\Cats - Rum Tur
Combustible Edison - Lauras Aura.mp3 (C:\My Music\Comb
Dire Straits - Money For Nothing.mp3 (C:\My Music\Dire Str
Eye Of The Storm111[1].mp3 (C:\My Music\Eye Of The Sto
JoyToWorld (C:\My Music\Various - Three Dog Night - Joy
Loreena McKennitt - Mummers' Dance.mp3 (C:\My Music\L

It is possible to perform a conversion of these files to a CD format, however this requires additional disk space. Temporary files will be placed in a directory shown below:

c:\windows\TEMP\   [Change]

Space needed: 674 MB

Space available: 356 MB

[Convert]   [Cancel]

When I clicked **Convert**, the software took a few minutes to convert each track to the format it needs for writing to the CD. Once the conversion was complete, the software opened the Write to CD dialog box shown in Figure 14.8. This dialog box shows the type of CD-R drive, the maximum speed at which it can burn the disc on this drive, as well as a summary of the disc that will result.

FIGURE 14.8

The Write to CD dialog box is the last stop before actually burning the CD.

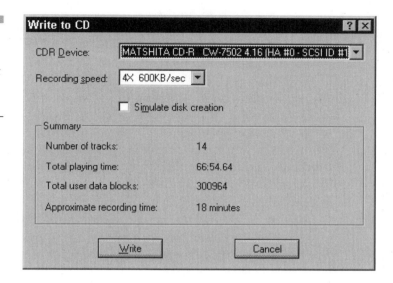

NOTE

If you're feeling extra cautious, you can click **Simulate Disk Creation** before actually burning the CD. The simulation makes the software do everything it would do, except for actually burning the disc. Once you are satisfied that this works, you can do the real thing.

Make sure you have the blank CD-R in the CD-R drive. Insert the disc with the gold side up, and click **Write** to burn the CD. After the approximate recording time shown in the Write to CD dialog box, the CD-R drive will open, and the message box shown in Figure 14.9 appears on your screen. Your CD is now ready to play in any audio CD player or CD-ROM drive.

FIGURE 14.9

When you see this message box, your new audio CD is finished.

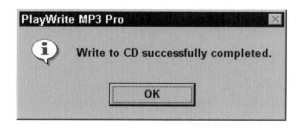

Chapter Wrapup

Once you get hooked on MP3, you can run into a new dilemma: most of the music-playing devices in the world don't yet support MP3. Lugging your PC wherever you go isn't a practical solution. Adding a CD-R burner to your PC and putting your favorite music on audio CDs can be.

While the PlayWrite MP3 Pro is not the least expensive way to get your MP3s onto an audio CD, it is a comprehensive solution, designed with the needs of the MP3 crowd in mind. The included software makes creating playlists, testing their sound, and burning them to CD about as simple as possible. In addition, if you ever need to massage your MP3s to improve their sound quality, the PlayWrite MP3 Pro software can do that, too. The PlayWrite MP3 is a fine choice for anyone who wants to burn audio CDs.

Burning your MP3s onto an audio CD is one way to take your music with you. There is another way. Get yourself gizmos that let you take your MP3s with you wherever you go. The next chapter is dedicated to those gizmos: portable MP3 players, car players, players that plug into your home stereo system. While many of these devices are new, or scheduled to arrive in time for Christmas '99, I have been able to get my hands on a few of them. Read on to see what they are like and how these little portable devices are changing my daily life.

CHAPTER 15

Other Gizmos for Making Music

You've used your PC to make MP3 music. You may even have run cables from your PC to your stereo so you could sort of play MP3 music on your stereo. But MP3 can't really flourish as a widely accepted music format until you can take your MP3 music anyplace you can take the rest of your music. That means around the block, on a hike, in the car, and as an integrated part of your stereo system.

Dozens of companies are working furiously to solve this problem, with many targeting Christmas '99 as the time to ship their first products. To give you an idea of what's coming, this chapter looks at portable MP3 players, as well as home and car players. Where I was able to get my hands on a device, you will find my impressions of it. Where I wasn't, I've given you a description based on the press kits and other materials I was able to gather.

Here are the high notes you'll hit in this chapter:

▮ Portable players
▮ Home and car players.

Portable MP3 Players

The small size, ease of use, and high sound quality of portable MP3 players can really make a difference in the way you listen to music. I've owned portable radios, tape players, and CD players. They are all fun and useful, but somehow never became a part of my day-to-day routine. Portable MP3 players have.

Living with Rio

I was psyched when I got my Rio PMP300. I had been playing with MP3 music for some time, and knew that being able to take my music with me would make listening to this stuff even better. It certainly did. I take my Rio with me wherever I go. To the gym, on hikes, cutting the grass. It never skips, never hiccups, never lets me down in any way—except when I forget to change the battery.

At times it's like my life is a movie (low-budget) and I've got the sound track in my pocket. I've listened to Blue by Nature while sitting stranded in a tent during a downpour, and Big Sky while standing on top of a fire tower on a mountain in the middle of a state forest. When I'm lifting weights, I put on some hard rock and pump a little more iron than normal.

> And the Rio is great when my family and I go on trips. My daughter can listen to her music in the back seat, while my wife and I can talk without competition from a children's CD.
>
> For a computer geek like me, a portable MP3 player offers the perfect blend of my favorite music, high technology nerdiness, and cool computer toy.

I was able to get my hands on three of the portable MP3 players currently available. Each has advantages and disadvantages, and each is appropriate for certain kinds of users. Even so, unless you use Linux or Macintosh computers, your best overall choices right now are the Diamond Rio family of players, and the Creative Nomad.

NOTE

One thing you don't need to worry much about is sound quality. I can't notice any difference in playback quality between the portable MP3 players I have. They all sound great.

Diamond Rio Family

TIP

Diamond Rio is the reigning king of portable MP3 players.

While it wasn't the first portable MP3 player to hit the market (that honor appears to belong to the little known MPMan from Saehan) the Diamond Rio PMP300 (**www.rioport.com**) was definitely the first to make a real impact. The launch of the Rio in 1998 triggered a lawsuit by RIAA (Recording Industry Association of America) attempting to get the Rio pulled from the market. The failure of that suit was one of the contributing factors leading to the music industry's creation of the SDMI (Secure Digital Music Initiative), which aims to impose controls over the use and distribution of all forms of digital music, including MP3. Not bad for a little gizmo that can only hold about 30 minutes of near-CD quality music.

The Rio family began with the original device, the PMP300, with its 32 MB of memory. Next out of the chute was the Rio SE, with 64 MB of memory and a cool translucent case. Most recently came the Rio 500, with 64 MB of memory and a slew of new features. Each of the devices can support an additional 32 MB of memory, in the form of a Smart Media flash memory card.

DEFINITION

Flash memory is a type of memory that retains its information, even when the memory card has no power. This makes it ideal for low-power devices like portable MP3 players. It also makes it possible (if you have the money to spend) to gradually move your music collection onto flash memory and carry a virtually limitless amount of music around in your shirt pocket.

I'm still using my Rio PMP300. It may not be as small as a Nomad, or have as much memory as its younger siblings, but the thing works well. There are five buttons on the front of the player, arranged around the rim of a circular control. These are increase volume, decrease volume, random play order, repeat, and A to B (which repeats the music between the first point where you press the button and the second).

You press the edges of the control to get the play, pause, stop fast forward, and rewind functions. There's a hold button on the side, and three more buttons on the top. The top buttons are the menu (which shows you the status of the memory in the device), the equalizer (four settings, normal, classical, jazz, and rock), and intro, which plays short snippets of each song.

In addition to the player, the package comes with:

▊ Software (including a limited version of MusicMatch Jukebox)
▊ A CD full of MP3s to get you started
▊ Headphones
▊ A battery
▊ All needed cables, including a pass-through connector to the PC's parallel port, so you don't have to disconnect your printer whenever you want to download music to the Rio.

The Rio Manager is the software you use to transfer music into the player. Rio Manager has four windows, as shown in Figure 15.1:

- The main window, which looks like a CD player and allows you to play audio CDs or MP3s
- The CD window, which displays the contents of the audio CD in the CD-ROM drive
- The Playlist window, where you create the playlist you want to download into the Rio
- The Internal Memory window, which shows what's loaded into the Rio's memory.

FIGURE 15.1

The Rio Manager software makes the care and feeding of your Rio a snap.

The Rio PMP300 may have been one of the first players to ship, but I've found it to be a polished, professional product.

When you are shopping for a portable MP3 player, I recommend you check into the Rio 500. It has all the features of the PMP300, plus twice as much memory, a USB port connection for extremely fast music downloads to the device, and special software to work with spoken audio content from Audible.com. The Rio 500 also supports MetaTrust security (allowing for copy protection of music), and has upgradable firmware so you can be confident it will work with evolving music standards.

DEFINITION

Firmware is a term for some of the software that runs a device like the Rio. It is firmware instead of software because it is stored in a read-only memory or flash memory, making it into a combination of software and hardware.

The Rio PMP300 and SE only work with PCs running Microsoft Windows. The Rio 500 works with Macs too.

Creative NOMAD

TIP

Small, light, stylish, and packed with capabilities, Creative NOMAD is a worthy contender for the title of most popular portable MP3 player.

At the very moment I wrote this (late August 1999), the Creative NOMAD (**www.nomadworld.com**) was the smallest, most capable, coolest-looking portable MP3 player I could lay my hands on. The NOMAD features 32 MB of built-in memory and a 32 MB flash memory card (on some models) for a total of 64 MB of memory. In addition, the NOMAD has a built-in voice recorder and an FM radio tuner.

All this comes in a tiny, retro-looking brushed magnesium case (Figure 15.2). All the controls are on the sides of the player, with the volume control, mode and equalizer buttons, and the hold button on the left, and the play/pause, stop, fast forward, rewind, and erase/record buttons on the right. Some of the buttons on the right side do double duty as controls for the voice recorder as well as the MP3 player.

The NOMAD display panel is in the circle on the front center of the device. It shows you everything going on including the name and number of the track you're playing (in MP3 mode), and the state of the battery.

To communicate with your PC, NOMAD comes with a PC Interface/Charger and the cable and AC adapter needed to make it run. You place the NOMAD in the cradle to recharge its batteries and activate the NOMAD Manager software (Figure 15.3). NOMAD Software Manager is a little more complicated than Rio Manager, since it must deal with the voice recorder and the additional flash memory. Even so, the NOMAD Manager software is easy to use.

FIGURE 15.2

*The Creative
NOMAD.*

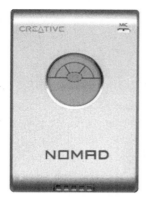

FIGURE 15.2

*The Creative
NOMAD.*

FIGURE 15.3

*Use NOMAD Manager to download
music and upload
voice recordings.*

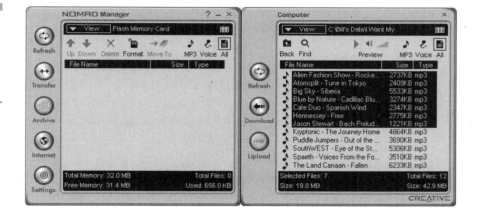

In addition to the NOMAD Manager, the device comes with a version of MusicMatch Jukebox called the Creative Digital Audio Center. This software has the features of MusicMatch Jukebox, plus additional capabilities dealing with Creative's Environmental Audio technology. Use the software to manage your MP3 collection, rip tracks from your CDs, and generate playlists (manual or automatic lists, as in MusicMatch Jukebox) to load into the NOMAD.

In addition to all these goodies, the NOMAD comes with headphones and a CD full of MP3s you can play on your device. It is a great package, and certainly worth your consideration.

Samsung Yepp

TIP

Yepp is a series of portable MP3 players that are close cousins to the Creative NOMAD.

Samsung (**www.yepp.co.kr**) produces the Yepp series of portable MP3 players. These come with a minimum of 32 MB of flash memory, built in, and sport a SmartMedia card slot so that you can upgrade them to 64 MB (or more if the right SmartMedia cards become available).

The E series, visible in Figure 15.4, is the base model for the Yepp family of devices. The B series and D series share the same case and most of the same features, with the D series being top of the line, and virtually identical to the NOMAD.

FIGURE 15.4

The E series (shown here) is the base model Yepp player.

Expect at least one of the Yepp portable MP3 players to be available in the United States by the time you read this.

Pontis MPlayer3

TIP

Expandability and compatibility are key features of MPlayer3.

Here is another player I've had the opportunity to use for a while now. MPlayer3 (**www.mplayer3.com**) shown in Figure 15.5, from the German company Pontis, lacks the visual appeal of the Rio or NOMAD, but in exchange offers expandability and compatibility. The device does not have any built-in memory. Instead it supports one or two MultiMediaCard flash memory cards. Currently, only 8 MB and 16 MB cards are available. However, MultiMediaCards with a capacity of 128 MB have been announced, and even larger cards are likely. MPlayer3 is designed to support up to 4 GB of memory—something like 800 songs. It also supports the Linux and Macintosh operating systems, as well as Windows 95/98 or NT.

FIGURE 15.5

MPlayer3 works for Macintosh and Linux users, as well as every current flavor of Microsoft Windows.

NOTE

The MPlayer3 is sometimes sold without a flash memory card. Because the player has no built-in memory, if you buy it this way, you will not be able to use it until you get at least one MultiMediaCard.

MPlayer3 comes with software on CD-ROM, the player, perhaps a MultiMediaCard, and headphones. The player itself is larger and heavier even than the Rio PMP300. It uses two AA batteries, and gets around 10 hours of use out of them. It also has a power connection so you can add an external power supply. The two slots for memory cards are at the bottom, protected by a simple sliding cover. MPlayer3 has five control buttons on the front, beneath a two-line alphanumeric display. When the machine is in playback mode, the buttons control the music. You can also use the buttons and display to pick from a menu controlling the mode the device is in (playback, information, download, bass/treble adjustment). Submenus control the specific playback mode (normal, repeat all, repeat single, shuffle) as well as the treble and bass.

My player came with a serial port connection which is fairly slow. For faster music transfers, consider investing in the Card Station, which connects to your computer's parallel port.

The software that comes with the MPlayer3 can rip and encode tracks from audio CDs, as well as create playlists and transfer them to MultiMediaCards. You may want to use MusicMatch Jukebox or the other programs covered in this book to perform the ripping etc., and just use the MPlayer3 software to transfer data to the memory cards.

Sensory Science MP2100 RaveMP

TIP

A curvy hour-glass shape, lots of memory, and some unique features make the RaveMP a promising player.

With the heart of the portable MP3 player market staked out by products like the Rio and NOMAD, later entrants are looking for ways to stand out from the crowd. The RaveMP product family (**www.ravemp.com**) stands out in both form (Figure 15.6) and function.

FIGURE 15.6

RaveMP has the looks and the features to challenge the leaders in the portable MP3 player market.

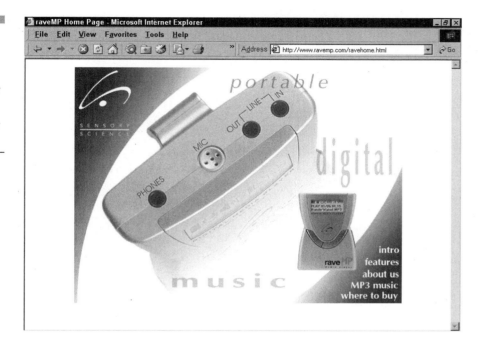

According to the literature, the RaveMP comes standard with 64 MB of memory, and you can expand it to 96 MB. Striking looks and more memory are both plusses. So are the built-in voice recorder, and the ability to use the device as an external data store. In other words, you can do things like load your huge presentation into your RaveMP at work, carry it home, and transfer the presentation onto your home PC. Unfortunately, due to legal considerations, you cannot use the RaveMP to transfer MP3s from computer to computer.

The RaveMP is also striking out into new territory by including a basic electronic organizer and personal memo feature linked to the voice recorder. We'll have to see whether consumers will choose this all-in-one approach, as opposed to getting separate specialized devices for playing music and organizing their lives. Whichever way it goes, Sensory Science deserves credit for taking a chance.

There are two models in the RaveMP family, although the only difference appears to be that the MP2100, the top-of-the-line model, comes with Sennheiser Mx4 Earbud earphones. Both models come with MP Manager software to handle music and the electronic organizer, as well as a parallel port cable to connect the device to the PC.

Home and Car Players

It is clear that there are viable answers to the need for portable MP3 players, and that even more options are on the way. But what about MP3 for the home and car? While these areas are lagging behind the portable players, there are some options to consider, and there should be significantly more in the year 2000.

OSCAR

TIP

Replace your audio CD player with one that plays audio CDs and MP3s on CD-ROM.

Here's a simple question with interesting ramifications for your home stereo system: "What if my CD player could also play MP3s stored on CD-ROM?" The answer is that your stereo would be the same as always, except you could also listen to over 100 of your favorite songs on a single CD-ROM. This was the original premise behind OSCAR (Optical Storage Compressed Audio Replay). OSCAR (**www.oscar-mp3.com**) started life as a student project, and the original prototype had a definite home-grown look to it (Figure 15.7).

Starting from that student project, OSCAR has evolved into a home stereo component you can buy directly from the manufacturer, BayCom Hard- und Software GmbH. During its gestation, OSCAR gained space for a standard 3.5 inch hard drive, giving it even more flexibility.

As you've probably gathered, OSCAR is not a mass-produced device. It is, however, one solution to the problem of getting your MP3s onto your home stereo.

FIGURE 15.7

*The OSCAR
prototype under
development.*

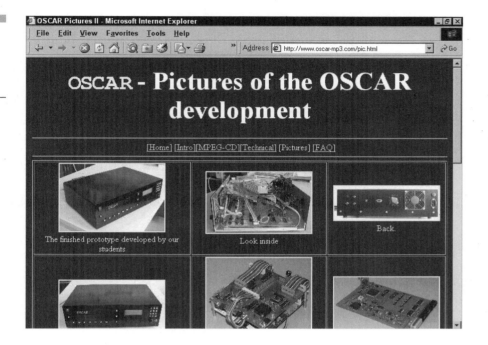

FIGURE 15.7 *The OSCAR prototype under development.*

AudioReQuest

TIP

Can you play MP3s on your stereo, and control the player from your TV?
AudioReQuest says "Yes."

AudioReQuest (**www.audiorequest.com**), like OSCAR, combines an MP3 player with an audio CD player. But it adds several
useful and fun capabilities, thanks to its interfaces with your
stereo, PC, and TV.

According to the AudioReQuest literature, the device has the
capabilities to:

- Play audio CDs
- Play MP3s from CD-R and CD-RW discs
- Rip and encode audio CDs as MP3s
- Download MP3s from your PC
- Create and manage playlists using your TV as the interface
- Store enough MP3s to play 300 hours of music

- Create MP3s from any audio source: LP, cassette tape, eight-track, radio…
- Display light shows that move to the beat of the music on the TV
- Import your own images to display with the music.

It also has:

- Upgradable software so that you can keep up with changes in music formats
- Parallel and USB ports for high-speed connections to your PC
- Optional wireless keyboard for easier data entry.

Basically, it looks like the AudioReQuest can do it all. Mind you, I haven't actually used this device, so I can't tell you how well it fulfills its promise, but if this device can do what it says, I think these folks have a real winner.

Impy3

TIP

Impy3 is a pricy MP3 solution for the car and home.

The Impy3 (**www.impy3.com**) is an in-car MP3 player that can also be used as a home stereo component. According to the manufacturer's literature, you can set things up so that you can move the player between the car and house quickly and easily. The Impy3 comes in several models, with hard drives ranging from the base model 8.4 GB drive to a 17.2 GB model (somewhere around 6000 songs). You can also upgrade the memory from a base of 32 MB up to 256 MB. Finally, you can add a CD-ROM drive to the system.

When you add the CD-ROM drive, the Impy3 gains the ability to automatically rip and encode any audio CD you feed it. Every track from the ripped CD gets added to the hard drive, and Impy3 generates a playlist for that CD. You control the Impy3 using a T-shaped hand-held controller that looks a lot like the gizmo in Figure 15.8.

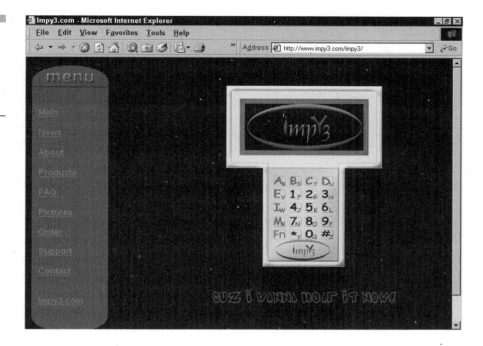

FIGURE 15.8

The Impy3 Web site, with a drawing of the hand-held controller.

Impy3 runs Microsoft Windows, and uses a version of WinAmp as the music controller/player software. To get MP3s into the device in the first place, you can connect it to your PC's parallel port or Ethernet card (depending on the version of Impy3 you buy) and transfer the data directly to the Impy3 hard drive.

The Impy3 comes with all the hardware needed to connect it to your home stereo and PC. To connect to your car stereo, the Impy3 uses a cassette adapter device that plugs into your car cassette player.

Three models of the Impy3 are currently available, each of which can be customized as described earlier. Prices range from around $1300 on up.

Chapter Wrapup

MP3 is starting to move into the mainstream of consumer electronics. The devices continue to gain additional memory and new capabilities (voice recording, FM radio, electronic organizers, for example). It seems that another major manufacturer announces plans to build a portable MP3 player every week. If everyone who has announced portable players actually gets them done, by Christmas 1999 there could be more than two dozen players to choose from.

The market for home and car MP3 players is not so well developed. Devices like the AudioReQuest and Impy3 are available, but the consumer electronics giants don't have anything available yet. Expect this to change in the year 2000, as the number of people listening to MP3 grows to levels great enough to attract the attention of the big boys, and the whole SDMI situation shakes out.

Now that you've learned about the various kinds of hardware you can get to improve your MP3 experience, you're probably wondering where you can get a good deal on all this. Chapter 16 has the answer: shop the Net.

CHAPTER 16

Finding
Hardware Online

In this part of the book, you have learned how to tell if your PC needs a hardware upgrade. You watched me walk through upgrades for sound cards, CD-ROM drives, memory, speakers, and just about anything else you might need to replace to make your PC into an lean, mean MP3-playing machine. You also learned something about the amazing hardware MP3 players, from portables like the Nomad and the Rio, to the home and car players that are just coming into production. You even learned how to burn your own audio CDs from MP3 files (or other sources).

But there is still one thing missing—advice on where to buy all this. This chapter is a guide to getting the best price and selection by shopping for your computer hardware online.

You can shop for MP3-related hardware at three types of Web sites. The first type is manufacturers' sites, places like the Creative Online Store, where you can buy products direct from the manufacturer. The second type is what most people think of when they think of online computer stores. These sites sell brand-name and sometimes house-brand hardware from many manufacturers. You can often get better prices here than at the manufacturers' stores, and it is easier to comparison shop, because you can compare products from several manufacturers without surfing all over the Net.

The third type of online store is not really a store at all. Instead, places like the Lycos Shopping pages are the home of shopbots, a type of software that makes shopping on the Internet simple. These shopbots take your order, then visit numerous online stores to see if those stores can supply what you're looking for. Once the shopbot finishes checking the stores, it generates a report that you can use to compare the deals at the various stores.

DEFINITION

A **shopbot** is a tool that shops in numerous online stores for you, gathering the results into a report that you can scan for the best deal.

Since there are three types of stores you can shop for MP3-related hardware, the chapter is divided into three sections:

▌ Manufacturer's stores
▌ Traditional online computer stores
▌ Shopbot sites.

NOTE

Please remember that change is continuous on the World Wide Web. There will likely be some differences between the way the sites looked when I wrote this, and what you will see today if you visit those same sites.

Manufacturers' Stores

Manufacturers' stores sell their own hardware. They are particularly good places to shop for really new items, gizmos, and gadgets that might not have made it into the retail channel yet. You may not be able to get whatever you're looking for before it is available elsewhere, but you can often pre-order products. If you need to be the first kid on the block to own that new sound card or portable MP3 player, you should definitely check the manufacturers' stores.

Another advantage of shopping a manufacturers' store is that you can sometimes get more information about a product than you can at other types of sites. After all, who knows that modem or MP3 player better than the manufacturer?

This section looks at two manufacturers' stores that are in the thick of the MP3 action:

▌ Creative Online Store
▌ Diamond Multimedia eStore.

Creative Online Store

TIP

Some of the hottest MP3 hardware including SoundBlaster, NOMAD and more, is for sale at the Creative Online Store.

Creative has been a force in the computer world for years, with their SoundBlaster sound cards. They've now taken a big jump into the forefront of the portable MP3 player filed with the NOMAD.

The Creative Online Store home page (**buy.creative.com**) features several key products that you can order immediately by clicking Buy Now. From the home page, you can perform keyword searches, or manage your shopping cart. The shopping cart here fits the standard Web shopping cart model: it's a way to keep track of the items you want to buy while you browse around the site. The cart keeps track of the number of items you are buying and the total price. When you're finished shopping, you click Checkout to make the purchases.

The products at this store are divided into six shopping categories. Categories of particular interest for MP3 fans are:

- **Audio**, where you can shop for the famous SoundBlaster sound cards
- **Speakers**, with a selection of SoundBlaster and Cambridge SoundWorks speaker systems
- **Modems**, with a small collection of Modem Blaster products
- **Portables**, where you can order NOMADs and accessories.

NOTE   While there were no accessories available at the store when I wrote this, Creative did provide me with samples of some of the accessories they will make available. I particularly like the sportclip headphones. They're convenient, comfortable, don't fall off, and don't muss your hair.

One last touch is that you can track the status of your order at any time, using the Track Your Order link that appears on every page.

Diamond Multimedia eStore

TIP   Shop the eStore for Rios, monstrous sound cards, and modems.

The Diamond Multimedia eStore (**store.diamondmm.com**) is a place to shop for superior sound cards and modems, as well as the entire Rio portable MP3 player family. Like the Creative Online Store, this site has a home page with featured products you can order immediately, a shopping cart you can use while you browse in the site, and a half-dozen sections you can shop in. The sections of particular interest for readers of this book are:

■ **Rio/Audio**, where you can buy Rios, Rio accessories, and the highly regarded Monster Sound cards

■ **Modems**, with a complete line of Supra brand products

■ **Steals & Deals**, where discontinued and otherwise value-priced hardware of all sorts pops up.

NOTE

You can become a member of the eStore free, using a super-simple sign-up form. If you join, the site will automatically enter your address for you when you place future orders, and you are entitled to special members-only discounts.

Not surprisingly, the big feature at the eStore when I wrote this was the Rio 500 64MB MP3 player. The device itself was not available, but you could pre-order it.

One place where Diamond was definitely ahead of the pack when I visited the eStore was with accessories for the Rio. While the competition was still lining up accessories, Diamond already had a full line, including memory upgrades, leather cases, travel kits, headphones, and a car stereo adapter.

Traditional Online Computer Stores

Traditional online computer stores are places to go when you want to comparison shop. Because they sell competing products from several manufacturers, you can compare individual products and see for yourself which ones best suit your particular needs. At these stores you may also be able to tap into unbiased reviews and buying advice. This can be invaluable when you're not sure exactly which features or capabilities you should be looking for.

Once you decide which products you want to buy, a traditional online computer store can usually give you a better price than the manufacturer's site will. Here are two traditional online computer stores you may want to visit: eCOST.com and PC Connection.

Either one of these online stores will give you access to a huge selection of products for any kind of upgrade your tired old PC might need. I recommend you shop at them both, as the specific products they offer, the specific information they provide, and the specific prices can all vary.

eCost.com

TIP

The benefit of eCost.com is that it allows you to save money and time while getting the knowledge you need to make the best buying decisions.

The focus at eCost.com (**www.ecost.com**) is saving you time and money. They claim you will pay wholesale or lower prices for everything you buy here, thanks to their focus on reducing costs. Prices are updated daily, both for the featured products and for the rest of the selection.

eCost.com's focus on saving you time means that they carry a huge (nearly a billion dollar) inventory to make sure you get your products as soon as possible. They say even back orders normally ship in one to three business days.

The wider selection at eCost.com, as compared to a manufacturer's site, is evident in the number of product categories; eCost.com offers nearly two dozen categories of computer hardware alone. Shopping in the categories is easy too. Within each category are subcategories, and sub-subcategories, and so on. To shop for a particular kind of product, you just keep working your way down through the categories by making the selection that best matches your needs at each level.

For example, I wanted to look at hard drives here, so I clicked Storage on the main page to identify the category I was interested in. The first subcategory asked what kind of storage I was looking for. The second asked about the interface I needed. Once eCost.com digested that information, it spit out a long list of disk drives that met the criteria I had clicked on my way. In this example, the result was a list with 38 drives from six different manufacturers. Once you have things narrowed down to a list of hardware, you can do a little comparison shopping. eCost.com allows you to compare between two and five products from the list. Mark the check boxes of the products you want to compare, scroll down to the bottom of the page, and click Compare!. Another browser window appears, containing a side-by-side comparison of the products. The depth of this comparison varies from product to product, as you might suspect. Whatever amount of information you receive is likely to be of use, so make liberal use of that Compare! button.

Like the manufacturers' stores, eCost.com has a shopping cart to hold your selection while you continue browsing in the site. You must create an account with eCost.com before you can actually purchase products, but the process is just as painless as it is with Diamond Multimedia eStore.

PC Connection

TIP

Tons of product, super-fast delivery, and award-winning service make PC Connection a great place to shop.

The one thing that is annoying about shopping for hardware online is that whatever you buy must physically travel to your house. That takes time. I don't know about you, but I'm living on Internet time these days, and waiting 3–5 business days to get a piece of hardware seems like forever.

PC Connection (**www.pcconnection.com**) can make this problem go away. If they have what you want in stock (in my experience, most of what they sell appears to be in stock most of the time) you can order as late as 2:00AM, and receive your order on the following business day. For example, order an in-stock sound card at 1:30 AM (EST) Tuesday, and you'll likely have it by the end of the day Tuesday. Can't ask for much faster service than that.

But PC Connection offers more than just fast delivery. If you visit their Web site (Figure 16.1) you will see that they have a wide selection of products (a browse through the sound card section turned up 20 different cards), with a range of ways to find what you're looking for. You can browse in the product categories (eight of them for hardware), or conduct all sorts of searches. The basic search lets you find specific terms (like product names) on the site. The advanced searches are where it really gets interesting. Click Advanced Searches below the basic search to get to these two powerful tools:

■ The **Feature Search**, which helps you track down products that have specific features

■ The **Power Search**, which is good when you're looking for a specific product or manufacturer.

FIGURE 16.1

PC Connection features delivery and service for all your computer hardware and software needs.

FIGURE 16.1

PC Connection features delivery and service for all your computer hardware and software needs.

PC Connection is also known for customer service. The company has won numerous awards, including *PC World* Best Mail Order Service awards in eight of the last ten years.

Shopbot Sites

Suppose you know exactly what you want to buy, and want to get the best possible deal. Or you know what features and capabilities you need, but are flexible as to the make and model of the hardware. Using a shopbot could be the perfect way to find what you're looking for. Below I will cover the following shopbots:

- CNET Shopper
- Computershopper.com
- Excite Search
- Lycos Shopping
- mySimon.

CNET Shopper

TIP

CNET Shopper offers a vast collection of any hardware your MP3-playing PC might need.

CNET Shopper (**www.shopper.com**) is one place to go whether or not you know exactly what you're looking for. The site offers 18 categories of computer-related hardware and software, including categories for Sound, Storage, and Modems.

But really, you can find any kind of hardware you might need. CNET Shopper isn't just a massive list of products, although you can use it that way if you wish. A particularly useful tool here is the Interactive PC Scoreboard. To reach it, click **PC Databoard** on the main Shopper page.

NOTE

The Interactive PC Scoreboard requires that you have the Macromedia Shockwave player installed to view the Macromedia Flash content in the scoreboard. If you don't have this installed, follow the links from the Interactive PC Scoreboard home page to download and install it, then return to the scoreboard and continue. You can also use the non-Flash version of the scoreboard if you don't want to install Shockwave.

Take a moment to read about the scoreboard, then click **Start the Interactive PC Scoreboard Now** to begin. From here, click **Peripherals** to start shopping for hardware. Now choose the category of peripheral you're interested in, out of the eleven categories available. The better to see how the tool works, click **Sound**.

Within the Sound category are two subcategories: sound cards and speakers. In addition to the list of subcategories, the scoreboard includes a sound product buyer's guide. This provides useful background information on the category. To continue the exploration, click **Sound cards**.

The Sound Cards page contains links to, and information about, 67 sound cards. For each card, you can get product information, a review by CNET (if available for this particular card), and pricing. You can also apply a set of filters to narrow the selection, if you wish.

To see the amount of information that can be available for popular products, I clicked Creative Labs SoundBlaster Live. For this card, there are a CNET rating, summary information, full reviews, user ratings, quick facts, specs, and pricing. When I clicked Compare Prices, the scoreboard gave me prices, vendor information, and Buyit! links to over 40 vendors carrying this card. You can't ask for much more from an online store.

Computershopper.com

TIP

Check out the expert picks and shopping advice from the experts at *Computer Shopper* magazine.

Computershopper.com (**www.computershopper.com**) is the online cousin of *Computer Shopper* magazine. Like CNET Shopper, computershopper.com has a wide range of categories, covering every kind of hardware you might want to buy for your PC. The site also has a research section, featuring how-to-buy guidelines, smart shopper columns, reviews, and discussion forums.

NOTE

Computershopper.com is part of ZDNet, the immense collection of online resources run by Ziff-Davis. If you go up one level from computershopper.com, to the ZDNet home page, you can jump to MP3 Central, a section of ZDNet's software library dedicated to MP3 software and news.

In keeping with my exploration of CNET Shopper, I decided to explore the Sound Cards category at computershopper.com. The first page I came to included all these options:

- A link for people who already know which features they want. This link allows you to run a variety of searches.
- Links to two expert picks

■ How-to-buy guidelines answering questions like, "Is 3-D audio important?"
■ The ability to shop and compare by manufacturer
■ The ability to shop and compare by price range
■ Related products.

Eventually you will find your way to a specific product or a group of products. Once you do, computershopper.com presents you with the pricing for all the vendors that carry the product, along with any available reviews. If you are on a page containing multiple products, you can choose from two to five of them and run head-to-head comparisons.

Lycos Shopping

TIP

Let Lycos help you comparison shop for the features that are important to you.

Some online stores only sell their own products. Others sell many products, but give no advice on which to choose. Still others give suggestions, but those suggestions are based on criteria chosen by others. Lycos Shopping (**www.lycos.com/Shopping/Compare_ Products/**) (Figure 16.2) lets you choose among a wide range of products, with those products sorted by the criteria you think are important.

Go to the computer hardware pages of Lycos Shopping and you can choose from eight categories of hardware. Of particular interest for MP3 fans are the components and storage areas. To understand what this service can do for you, you need an example. Try following the links from computer hardware to components, then from there to memory.

On the memory page, Lycos presents you with a wide range of features, including key things like size and speed. For each feature, you can specify how important it is to you by clicking at points along the scale. When you run your search, Lycos returns a list of products, sorted by how well they match your preferences.

FIGURE 16.2

Lycos uses the preferences you specify to comparison shop for all types of computer hardware. © 1999 Lycos, Inc. Lycos® is a registered trademark of Carnegie Mellon University. All rights reserved.

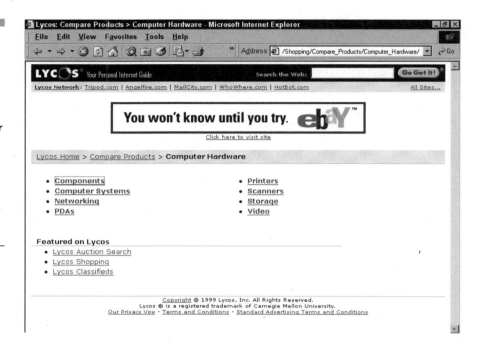

mySimon

TIP

Simon says he is the world's smartest shopping agent. Try him out and see what you think.

Whatever you are looking to buy online, mySimon (**www.mysimon.com/computers_and_software/**) (Figure 16.3) can help. This site claims to be the largest comparison shopping site on the Web, providing real-time pricing information from over 1000 merchants in categories ranging from apparel to toys, including computers. The computers and software section of mySimon includes 22 hardware and five software categories. Within the hardware section are categories covering all the hardware you could want when upgrading your PC for MP3, including sound cards, modems, and memory.

Perhaps because mySimon covers such a wide range of products, there is very little specialized information about specific products. For example, clicking Sound Cards leads to a simple page with a pull-down list for choosing a manufacturer and a text box for entering the model for a card. You click Go Shop! to start the process, which returns a long list of sound cards that match your entries, along with vendor information and a Buy! button to purchase the product. You can sort the list of cards in various ways, including by price.

mySimon is best considered a place to visit once you know exactly which item or items you want. You can search for the items at this site, and compare the prices against those you found at other sites. Find the product you want on each of these shopbot sites, and you can be fairly sure you will get the best price available online.

FIGURE 16.3

mySimon helps you buy virtually anything online, not just computer equipment.

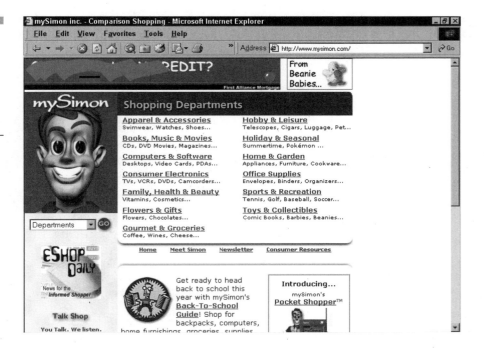

Chapter Wrapup

In this chapter we covered the final piece of the PC upgrade puzzle—where to shop for the hardware you need to perform your upgrade. You learned that the best place to buy computer hardware is on the Internet, and that there are three kinds of online stores for you to shop in: manufacturers' stores, traditional online computer stores, and shopbot sites. Each kind has pros and cons:

- The manufacturers' stores are the place to go when you're looking for products that may not even be shipping yet, or for the maximum amount of information about a specific product.
- Traditional online computer stores let you comparison shop because they carry a range of competing products. They may also have distinguishing characteristics like in-depth reviews, flashy tools, low prices, or super speedy delivery.
- Shopbot sites take online shopping to a new level. These sites scour other online stores to find you the best deal on whatever it is you're looking for. They are ideal when you have your decision narrowed to just a few products (or even a single product), and want to get the best deal you can.

Among all the sites covered in this chapter, you will certainly find at least one that suits your hardware upgrade needs.

This chapter wraps up Part 4: The Hardware You Need. You now have, or know how to get, everything you need to acquire and play MP3 music on your PC or when you are on the go.

But as the cliché goes, "Change is the only constant on the Net." Things change rapidly on the Internet, even more so for hot topics like MP3. You need ways to keep track of what's going on in the MP3 scene. Part 5: Keeping Up with the MP3 Scene shows you how.

PART 5

Keeping Up with the MP3 Scene

Keeping up with everything happening in the world of MP3 music is pretty hard. I know, because I've tried to do it for the past year. Fortunately, there are some resources that make the job easier.

Chapter 17 takes you to the "newsrooms" of several of the popular MP3 Web sites. These make it their business to keep up with the action, so are great sources for MP3 news—from who is doing what deal, to which artists just released their first MP3, to where you can get the best prices on portable MP3 players.

Chapter 18 covers MP3 newsgroups, mailing lists, and electronic newsletters. Surprisingly, if you aren't looking for pirated music, there aren't that many sources to choose from. This chapter contains information on the best of these sources, including the *I Want My MP3* electronic newsletter, published by the author.

CHAPTER 17

MP3 News
Web Sites

Keeping up with the action in MP3 can be a real job. There is so much going on, so many people involved, so much hype that you almost need an MP3 news service. Fortunately, several sites run what are, in effect, daily MP3 news services. You can visit these sites to find out about the latest megadeal, see which famous artist has released a new song in MP3 format, or just enjoy the noise as the big boys in the music industry try to cope with MP3. The Web sites covered in this chapter are great resources for following all the action.

Here are the high notes you'll hit in this chapter:

■ MP3.com
■ 20–20Consumer
■ RioPort
■ Emusic.com
■ MP3Now
■ MP3 Place.

MP3.com

As you know, MP3.com (**www.mp3.com**) is the center of the MP3 movement. So of course it has an extensive news page. Unlike many MP3 news pages, the one at MP3.com features news stories written by the MP3.com team, not just links to stories on other sites. These stories are often done in depth, with interviews and analysis, not just straight reporting. There is also a searchable archive of past news stories.

NOTE

For big stories, you will find links to sources like MSNBC and Yahoo! News.

To find out more about the MP3.com news page, go to Chapter 9, "The Heart of the Movement: MP3.com."

20–20Consumer

TIP

Looking for the best price on a Rio, a NOMAD, a RaveMP, or any other portable MP3 player? Visit 20-20Consumer.

20-20Consumer (**www.20-20consumer.com**) is a free service designed to provide independent and unbiased comparison shopping information. The site lists the best prices on all sorts of techie goods, digital camcorders, scanners, printers, and the like. For each category, the site covers several popular products. Select one, and 20-20Consumer gives you a sorted (lowest price to highest) collection of links to stores carrying that product.

For any store carrying a product, you may find a set of icons next to its name. Those icons can be things like a thumbs-up, which means the store is highly rated, or a globe, which means the store ships internationally. The ratings are particularly interesting, as they come from consumers. 20-20Consumer allows you to rate stores on a variety of criteria, from overall experience to slimy sales practices. The site also posts specific consumer comments received in the last 30 days.

Recently, 20-20Consumer added coverage of portable MP3 players (Figure 17.1). This part of 20-20Consumer is very new, and still under development. Even so, 18 different brands of MP3 player and accessories are listed (a few that I never even heard of), with photos for most. For the products that are shipping, you can get the same kind of information you get for a camcorder or monitor, namely lowest prices and the stores that offer those prices.

To further enhance this site's value, 20-20Consumer includes various notes within the price listings. For example, when I visited the site last, there was an icon for a note that warned consumers of hidden extra "processing fees" charged by one of the online retailers. The note went further, to explain that 20-20Consumer includes the processing fees in the prices it lists for that retailer, so you get a better price comparison than you would otherwise.

Another note pointed out a special time-limited deal, direct from the manufacturer, that offered $50 off on a certain well-known MP3 player. 20-20Consumer can do things like this because they are an independent service. They don't accept money to review products, so they can be critical of stores, or recommend that you go direct to the manufacturer for a product and bypass any of the stores selling the same product.

When you are ready to shop for a portable MP3 player (and you will be soon), visit 20-20Consumer to look for the store with the best price and service.

FIGURE 17.1

This page at 20-20Consumer.com links to current pricing on every portable MP3 player available.

RioPort

TIP

There's more news than meets the eye at RioPort.

At first glance, RioPort (**www.rioport.com**) doesn't seem like a promising place to go for music news. If you go to the News column (next to the music and tools columns near the bottom of the home page), everything is spoken content from Audible.com. The News heading near the top of the page only shows a couple of stories. However, click the link to one of those stories near the top of the page, and the situation changes drastically.

When you click one of those links, you get the story you expect, but you also get a massive amount of today's music news, as provided by SonicNet, Inc. Next to the main story are dozens of links to general music news, as well as MP3-specific news. Many of the stories have associated photographs. Some have links to audio or video clips.

NOTE

You can always get the news "direct from the horse's mouth," as it were, by going to the SonicNet Web site yourself. The URL is: **www.sonicnet.com**.

If you don't feel like reading your music news, you don't have to. At the end of the news links there is an Audio News link. Click this to hear the top music headlines in RealAudio format. To get the full details on these and other stories, the Audio News commentator refers you to the SonicNet Web site (no big surprise there).

Finally, there's another link that takes you to the SonicNet Web site's news archives, which hold stories all the way back to 1995.

Emusic.com

TIP

Emusic.com is another quality source of music news on the Web.

Emusic.com (**www.emusic.com**) is rightly known as a place to buy MP3s from older groups like Bachman-Turner Overdrive, but it also has a solid music news page. Click the **Music News** button on any emusic.com Web page to get there.

Emusic.com gives you a short lead-in to a selection of music news stories. Each lead-in introduces you to a particular story, then gives you a link to follow to get the rest of it. Many of the story lead-ins have pictures associated with them. The stories at emusic.com are provided by Onradio.com, a company that provides branded content to more than 550 radio station Web sites.

If you compare the music news available at Emusic.com to that available at Rioport.com, you will find some overlap, but a lot of differences too. It makes sense to visit both sites if you really want a full view of the music news of the day.

Emusic.com has an archive for past music stories. The stories are sorted by month, not by day. The titles of all the stories appear on the main archive page, so it is easy to find a particular story or subject.

MP3now.com

TIP

MP3now.com offers links to MP3 news highlights across the Web.

MP3now (**www.mp3now.com**) offers a collection of MP3-specific news stories. Or perhaps I should say, it provides a collection of links to MP3-specific news stories. The news page at MP3now (Figure 17.2) consists of links to information at other sites on the Web. Click one of those links and MP3now opens a new browser window that displays the story at whichever Web site it comes from. As you might expect, MP3now also offers an archive of links to past news.

This approach works well as long as the links remain valid. Because MP3now news links point to other peoples' Web sites, there is always a risk that the link will break over time. So don't be surprised if you sometimes find that you can't reach the story a news link describes.

NOTE

Dead links are a common problem for search engines, too. While the major search engines police their links, now and then you do stumble across a dead link. It's one of the unavoidable side effects of the dynamic, even frantic pace of action on the World Wide Web.

Another useful resource at MP3now is the Articles page, which contains articles that are not news, but do deal with the issues in the MP3 news. For example, when the SDMI chose ARIS as its provider of digital watermarking technology (a way to tell whether your MP3 file was created by an approved source) MP3now posted an article about the impact of giving ARIS a monopoly in this area.

The articles at MP3now are written by the staff of MP3now, as well as by David Weekly, an online audio consultant for companies like Time-Warner and Casio Research.

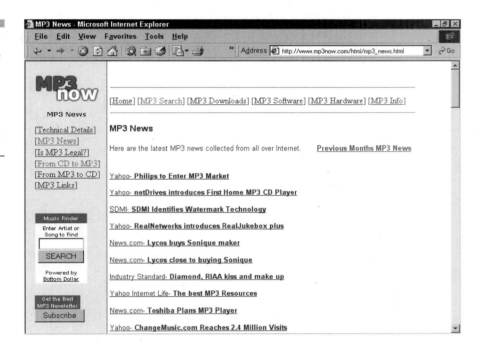

FIGURE 17.2

The MP3 News page at MP3now is not fancy, but it has links to major news stories plus a news archive.

MP3 Place

TIP

MP3 Place offers yet another angle on the news. It is part of the Change Music Network.

The team at MP3 Place (**www.mp3place.com**) gives you its interpretation of the Daily Audio News from around the world. Audio news stories appear in the center of the MP3 Place home page. As at other sites, each story gets a lead-in on the main audio news page. The stories normally have links to related resources, with stories about a new Web site linking to that site, or perhaps to MP3 Place's own resources, like their Top 15 Chart (the top 15 downloads from MP3 Place).

These people report the news with a bit of attitude. Talking about an article on the CBC Infoculture site, they report that it should have included a quote like this: "Hype: MP3.com is a good website. Reality: MP3.com sucks, visit MP3Place.com."

You won't find a news archive here, and you won't find the kind of polished prose you get at places like MP3.com. What you will find is audio news, as reported by people in the trenches.

An additional newsy feature at MP3 Place is the Music News section. Get there by clicking any of the links under the News heading. These stories are updated every weekday by Van Kapeghian, a guitarist in a band named 13 Stories. The stories in this section are straight factoids, typically two or three sentences long.

NOTE

MP3 Place is part of the Change Music Network, an organization that intends to "revolutionize the way music is made, promoted, distributed, and consumed." I don't know exactly what this means for MP3 Place, but after looking at the beta ChangeMusic.com Web site, expect some interesting activity.

Chapter Wrapup

I love listening to MP3 music. But as I've followed the growth of MP3 over the last year, I've discovered that just watching what's happening is a lot of fun. Things move so fast in MP3 land that almost every day brings news of a new controversy, success story, breakthrough, something. In other words, the news about MP3 is in itself highly entertaining.

In Chapter 9 you learned about MP3.com's huge collection of daily news stories and timely articles, some written by Michael Robertson himself. In this chapter, you learned that MP3.com isn't the only place to go for MP3 news and information. The sites covered in this chapter each have a different slant on the news, making each of them worth investigating. Try reading the news at a few different sites every day for a week or two. See if you don't become hooked, too.

Web sites aren't the only source of MP3-related news. MP3 newsgroups and mailing lists abound. While some are little more than channels for people to exchange pirated music, others provide legitimate news and information. Turn to Chapter 18 and find out more.

CHAPTER 18

MP3 Newsgroups, Mailing Lists, and Newsletters

Although the World Wide Web is certainly the most visible part of the Internet, here is plenty of action in the world of newsgroups and mailing lists. You can find tens of thousands of newsgroups on the Net, covering virtually any topic conceivable. The same is true for mailing lists and newsletters, which are just a specialized type of mailing list. These Internet services are popular and efficient ways to share information.

If this is true, there should be tons of newsgroups, mailing lists, and newsletters dedicated to MP3. There are, but there's a catch. The majority of MP3 newsgroups and mailing lists are either tiny or are means for distributing pirated music.

If you do a search for newsgroups, you can find more than 60 of them. In most of those I have visited, the bulk of the messages are illegal copies of songs (broken into smaller chunks for ease of downloading) and requests for songs ("Anyone got the new Alanis stuff?"). One notable exception to this trend is alt.music.mp3, which is covered later in this chapter.

When it comes to mailing lists and newsletters, there aren't very many of them at all. You can find some lists being run by sites like MP3.com or Listen.com. These lists provide useful and interesting information, but, not surprisingly, are geared toward promoting the sites that create them. A couple of these are described in the following pages.

Since I couldn't find a general-interest MP3 information source that I liked, I've created one myself. The "I Want My MP3" electronic newsletter is designed to be your free source for news, reviews, and general information about the world of MP3 music. Why chase all around the Net to find out what's happening when you can get the highlights delivered right to your electronic mailbox? The last part of this chapter covers the newsletter. If you have enjoyed this book, you will enjoy my newsletter. Please subscribe.

Here are the high notes you'll hit in this chapter:

- alt.music.mp3
- MP3.com Music Newsletter
- EMusic.com mailing lists
- Listen.com Weekly Newsletter
- I Want My MP3 newsletter.

alt.music.mp3

TIP

alt.music.mp3 is a place to ask questions and discuss MP3 products.

Where can you go if you have a question about an MP3 player, or are looking for the latest ripper (assuming, of course, you couldn't find the answer in this book)? The alt.music.mp3 newsgroup (Figure 18.1) is one place you can ask your questions, and can reasonably expect an answer. A lot of the action in this newsgroup is just this kind of question and answer.

FIGURE 18.1

alt.music.mp3 is a high-volume newsgroup where you can ask questions and discuss issues, not just exchange pirated music.

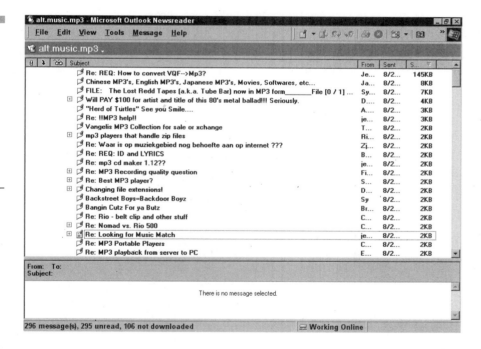

Given the unregulated nature of most newsgroups, and the prevalence of music pirates on the Net, it is inevitable that you will run into a significant number of requests for pirated music. But all in all, this is a good place to take your questions without running into too much dubious activity.

You can use your newsreader to subscribe to alt.music.mp3. You can also go to Deja.com (**www.deja.com**) and search the discussions for alt.music.mp3. Doing so gives you a Web view of this newsgroup.

MP3.com Music Newsletter

TIP

MP3.com Music Newsletter is a personalized music picks and information from the heart of the MP3 movement.

One of the problems with MP3 music is that there is so much of it. With over 100,000 songs at MP3.com alone, finding material you like can be a real pain. That is where the MP3.com Music Newsletter comes in. It is primarily a means for MP3.com to pass along music recommendations to you. The recommendations are created specifically for you, and are based on the music you have downloaded from MP3.com in the past, along with the top favorites at MP3.com.

To take advantage of this newsletter, you must start a free My MP3 account. Once you create an account, the music you download is tracked, and used to determine other songs you would probably like. To open your My MP3 account, click **My MP3** from any page at MP3.com, and follow the instructions that appear.

NOTE

You can get more information about starting a My MP3 account in Chapter 9.

Once you have your account, go to the My News page of My MP3 (Figure 18.2). Select MP3.com Music Newsletter (and any of the other e-mail subscriptions you are interested in), then click **Save Changes**. Your first newsletter should arrive in a week or less.

Other features of the MP3.com Music Newsletter include news updates from your favorite artists, reports on the latest hardware and software, tips, and information about the MP3.com Web site.

FIGURE 18.2

Subscribe to the personalized MP3.com Music Newsletter here.

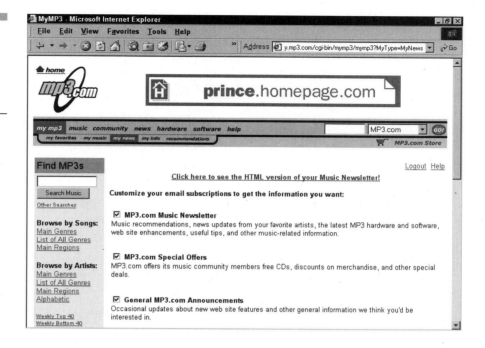

EMusic.com Mailing Lists

TIP

EMusic.com mailing lists are a collection of newsletters on many aspects of online music.

EMusic.com sells MP3s. They are also plugged in to what is happening in the MP3 world, so they can be a good source of information. The EMusic.com mailing lists give you a range of information having to do with EMusic.com, MP3, artists, and products.

The types of mailing lists you will find here include:

■ Corporate announcements, geared toward investors and media
■ Artist announcements, telling you what's up with various groups
■ Product announcements, reporting the latest on Rio and other products.

To subscribe to any of EMusic.com's newsletters, you need to join Emusic.com. Click **Join EMusic** and follow the directions. Once you join, go to your account page (click **My Account**) and then click **Join Various Mailing Lists**. This takes you to the Mail List page. Click **Add Me** for each mailing list you want to join, and you are set.

Listen.com Weekly Newsletter

TIP

The Listen.com Weekly Newsletter is a weekly report on what's new at Listen.com and in the world of downloadable music.

Listen.com offers digital music, some pieces free, some with a fee. The newsletter gives you the story on what's new and interesting at the site, as well as in the world of downloadable music. In particular, the newsletter tells you which Big Shot artists have posted music on the Web this week, points you to interesting Web sites, and tunes you in to new music of all types.

To subscribe, go to Listen.com (**www.listen.com**). Near the top of every page is a newsletter text box. Type your e-mail address into the box and click **Subscribe**. As soon as you return the confirmation e-mail message the site sends you, you are on the list.

I Want My MP3 Newsletter

TIP

My electronic newsletter of MP3 news, reviews, and much more is called "I Want My MP3."

It has become simple to start your own mailing list or electronic newsletter. Companies like Topica and ONElist host tens of thousands of them. If you nose around a bit at these sites, you can find a couple of dozen MP3-related mailing lists or newsletters. But if you look closely, you'll find that most of them are tiny, some are abandoned, and quite a few of them are for exchanging MP3s of dubious origin.

Since I couldn't find any lists or newsletters that excited me, I decided to create one. "I Want My MP3" is a free electronic newsletter hosted at Topica (Figure 18.3). Each issue will feature a product review, a write-up on a great new MP3 Web site, or some other meaty article. You'll also get links to the biggest news in the world of MP3, reports on what's happening with the artists that contributed music to this book, and whatever else you want that we can reasonably provide.

One thing you won't find in the "I Want My MP3" newsletter is coverage of, or support for, music pirates. If your main interest is in getting pirated MP3s, don't bother subscribing.

FIGURE 18.3

The free "I Want My MP3" electronic newsletter is born.

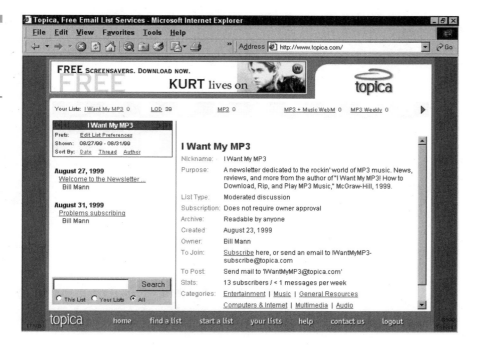

My goal for this newsletter is to make it into something that suits the needs and interests of the subscribers. You will get the chance to tell me what you would like to see included, and I'll be asking your opinion on the hot MP3 issues of the day, so be ready to make your voice heard.

If the "I Want My MP3" electronic newsletter sounds interesting to you, give it a try. Just send a blank e-mail message to **iwantmymp3–subscribe@topica.com**. When the confirmation message arrives in your mailbox, just click **Reply** and **Send**. It's that simple. Within minutes you will be subscribed and ready to receive the next edition of the I Want My MP3 newsletter.

I hope to hear from you.

Chapter Wrapup

At first glance, newsgroups, mailing lists, and newsletters look like they should provide a wealth of MP3-related information. But once you start digging into what is out there, you find that many newsgroups and mailing lists are used primarily for sharing pirated music. alt.music.mp3 is a welcome exception, as are the mailing lists and newsletters produced by specific MP3 companies. Of course, mailing lists and newsletters produced by a particular MP3 company must serve the needs of that company, as well as those of its subscribers.

For unbiased coverage of the MP3 music world, delivered direct to your electronic mailbox, the I Want My MP3 electronic newsletter is the answer. It is designed to serve the needs of its subscribers, not push a particular company or product (it will, however, occasionally include plugs for this book). Every issue will include a feature story, news, reviews, and whatever else we can collectively agree on. Please subscribe.

You've reached the end of the book proper. I hope and believe that you've picked up a lot of useful information along the way, and are happily listening to MP3 music as you read this. Whatever you are listening to now, please try out the music included on the CD. In the Music folder on the CD, you will find over a dozen quality songs, covering everything from classical to electronic opera with transhumanist influences (?!), to power pop. The Appendix has the full scoop on the music and the software that lives on the CD.

Have fun, and thanks for reading *I Want My MP3*.

MP3 on a
Silver(y) Platter

Thanks to the generosity of a number of software developers, MP3 companies, and artists, the CD that comes with this book is loaded with great material, including:

- The Sonique and MusicMatch Jukebox MP3 players
- A number of utilities
- Skins for Sonique
- Some great music.

Everything is organized into folders on the CD, so it is easy to find what you're looking for. All the software is covered in the appropriate chapters, including full instructions on how to find it on the CD. Not all of the skins and the music are explicitly covered in that way, so you can find out more about them in this chapter.

The Folders and Their Contents

Here are the folders on the CD and what you'll find in them. For simplicity, assume that the CD-ROM drive on your PC is the D: drive. If it isn't, just replace D with the appropriate drive letter when you access the CD.

D:\All-in-One Players\MusicMatch Jukebox

Contains mmjb4526.exe, a self-extracting executable that installs MusicMatch Jukebox on your PC.

D:\Rippers and Encoders\WinDAC32

Contains wdac149.exe, a self-extracting executable that installs WinDAC32 on your PC.

D:\Stand-alone Players\Sonique

Contains s105wma.exe, a self-extracting executable that installs Sonique on your PC.

D:\Stand-alone Players\Sonique\Skins

Contains two Sonique skins: Eight and Exclusive.

D:\Utilities

Contains a collection of MP3 utilities.

D:\Utilities\Go!Zilla

Contains gozilla.exe, a self-extracting executable that installs Go!Zilla on your PC.

D:\Utilities\ID3 Editor

Contains ID3Editor.exe, the ID3 Editor program, and its associated Readme file; no extracting is necessary.

D:\Utilities\MP3 PopUp!

Contains Mp3popup.exe, the MP3 PopUp program, and its associated Readme and other files; no extracting is necessary.

D:\Utilities\MP3 Renamer

Contains MP3Renamer.exe, the MP3 Renamer program, and its associated Readme and other files; no extracting is necessary.

D:\Utilities\ShufflePlay

Contains the ShufflePlay Setup program and associated Readme and other files; no extracting is necessary.

D:\Utilities\WavNormalizer

Contains Norm10.exe, the WavNormalizer program, and its associated Readme file; no extracting is necessary.

D:\Music

Here are over a dozen MP3s to get you started. The artists listed here are all pioneers. They had the courage to give away their music in hopes of creating a new way to distribute and play music.

They deserve your support. The music is sorted by artist or band here and on the CD.

Alien Fashion Show–Rocket 95 (Space Age Swing)

Alien Fashion Show has toured with the Brian Setzer Orchestra, and their song "Crazy Moon" was featured in the 1998 Parthenon Entertainment Film, "The Thin Pink Line." Their music mixes swing, cocktail, surf, and rockabilly.

Web site: **www.babsboys.com** (Figure A.1).

"Rocket 95"—Proud Mary Entertainment/Mary L. Aloe, manager.

FIGURE A.1

The Aliens have landed!

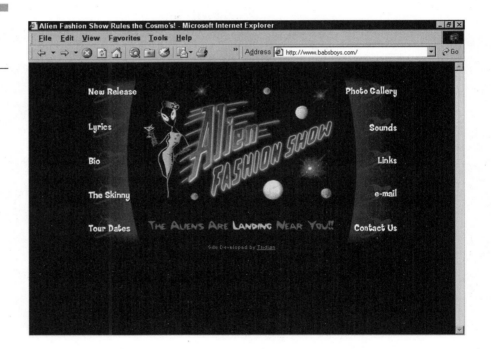

Atomsplit–Tune in Tokyo (Power Pop)

Atomsplit delivers power pop from Atlanta, GA. "Tune in Tokyo" is part of the soundtrack of the book *Coming of Age in Babylon*.

Web site: **www.atomsplit.com** (Figure A.2).

"Tune in Tokyo"—Atomsplit

FIGURE A.2

There's some serious shockwave work at the Atomsplit Web site.

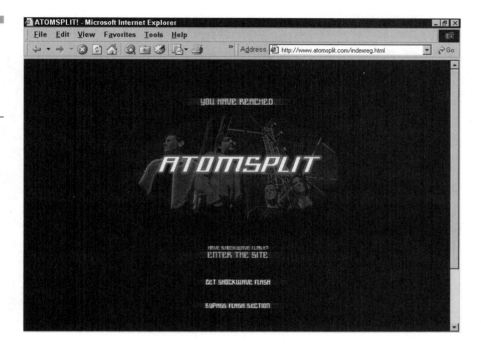

Big Sky – Siberia (Rock)

Vocalist Johnna Morrow has been compared to a young Grace Slick, while guitarist Steve Sklar may be the only performer in the United States doing Tuvan throat-singing.

Web site: **www.tc.umn.edu/~skla0003/Big_Sky.html** (Figure A.3).

"Siberia" Music & lyrics by Johnna Morrow © 1996 Taiga Music © 1997 Skysong Productions, Inc.

Blue By Nature–Cadillac Blues (Blues)

"Cadillac Blues" has reached all the way to #1 on the MP3.com Blues chart, and Blue By Nature lead vocalist Karen Lawrence sang backup for Supertramp on their platinum release "Some Things Never Change." *Blues Revue* magazine called the band's "Live at the Lake" "gritty, realistic, bar blues."

Web site: **www.bluebynature.com**

"Cadillac Blues"—Hostel Records/Karen Lawrence.

Café Duo–Spanish Wind (World Fusion)

A Spanish-influenced ballad by two guys from Austria.
Web site: **meltingpot.fortunecity.com/latvia/869/**
"Spanish Wind" written by Marcus Babler and Toni Kaiser.

ENIS–G.M.C. (Garage Man's Conspiracy)

ENIS is a favorite from NYC. They make their way using a slow-ish, pounding tempo, pushed along by mushrooming chords and decorated by squealy guitar frills and creamed harmonies. Their full album, *Songs from the Bin*, is available through Thicksole Publications.
Web site: **www.thicksole.com**

Hennessey–Free (Space Opera)

This is something a little different; a transhumanist opera from Scotland.
Andrew Hennessey: Aeon, Epic Space Opera: "Free": **pegasus@easynet.co.uk**

Jason Stewart–Bach Prelude 2 (Classical)

This quote says it all. "Jason Stewart has a style and brilliance that has to be heard to be believed. He plays with the soul of a poet and the fire of a virtuoso."—Mark Mantilla, *CD Review*.
Web site: **jss.webjump.com**
"Bach Prelude #2"—Jason Stewart is under the management of Lance Records.

Kryptonic–The Journey Home (Film Music)

Kryptonic specializes in film music, dance, and techno. One piece was used in an NBC special on NASA zero-G training. It was inspired by an episode of the TV show, "Star Trek: The Next Generation."
Web site: **members.aol.com/KRYPTIXX**
"The Journey Home"—Lawrence M. Jarquio/Kryptonic Productions.

Mock Turtle–Stage Fright (Rock)

Mock Turtle plays melodic, groove-based rock out of NYC. "Stage Fright" is from its upcoming debut album and from the forthcoming film "The Dead Part of You."
Web site: **www.homestead.com/mockturtle/**
"Stage Fright"—Newark & Jackson Records, 1999.

Puddle Jumpers–Out of the Shadows (Rock)

These Seattle-area artists are known for their unique brand of music that critics are calling "progressive folk." Whatever you call their music, the Puddle Jumpers have just released their second full-length CD.
Web site: **www.puddlejumpers.com**
"Out of the Shadows" Title track by the debut album from The Puddle Jumpers. Words and Music by Rick Vartian, Performed by The Puddle Jumpers.© 1996 Pontoon Publishing (BMI).

SouthWEST–Eye of the Storm (Country Blues)

SouthWEST calls themselves a bunch of Hill Billies from Central Pennsylvania. See what you think. The band's debut CD, Eye of the Storm, is available through Amazon.com.

Web Site: **www.southwestmusic.com** (Figure A.4).

"Eye of the Storm"—SouthWEST

FIGURE A4

The SouthWEST home page.

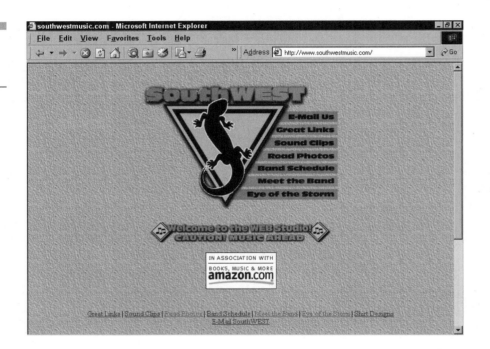

Spaeth–Voices From the Forest (New Age)

Paul Spaeth's first full-length CD is available now through Riffage.com.

Web site: **spaeth.homepage.com**

"Voices From the Forest"—Composed and performed by Paul Spaeth. © 1999 Paul Spaeth.

SugarfriedsuperOs–You're the One (Alternative)

How's track this for short and to the point?
Web site: **www.sugarfried.com** (Figure A.5).
"You're the One"—Jim Birch/Caffeinated Recordings.

The Land Canaan–Fallen (Neo-Classical)

An electronic opera, sort of, about the tragedy of mortality. From
the Planet Canaan, by way of Australia.
"Fallen"—The Land Canaan

Glossary

bannerware

Bannerware is a form of software distribution. The software can be used free of charge. However, if you find the software useful, the author (of the software, not this book) asks you to go to the Web site associated with that software and click the banner ad located there. In other words, bannerware is sponsored software, where the software author encourages users of the software to visit the sponsor's Web site.

BIOS

The BIOS (Basic Input Output System) is the lowest-level software in your PC. It allows the computer to start and provides low-level services to the operating system (Microsoft Windows).

bitrate

Bitrate is the average number of bits of data it takes to produce one second of audio.

CDDB

CDDB is an online database containing information about thousands of albums, including information about the artists and the names of each track. A CD player or other program can use the CD's serial number to search CDDB and import all title, artist, and track data. This allows you to have the data without typing them in yourself.

CD quality

CD-quality recording is recording done at 128 kbps or faster. It gives high-quality sound, but takes up more disk space than lower-quality recording rates.

CD-R

CD-R stands for CD-Recordable. A CD-R is a special type of CD onto which you can write data using the laser in a CD Recordable drive. You can read the data on a CD-R as many times as you like, but you can't erase the data and write something new later.

CD-ROM burner

A CD-ROM burner is a CD-ROM drive equipped with a laser that can be used to burn data into the surface of a special kind of disc. There are two kinds: one burns CD-R discs, and one burns CD-RW discs.

CD-RW

CD-RW stands for CD-Rewritable. A CD-RW is a special type of CD onto which you can write data, you can read the data, erase the data, and reuse the CD. Not all CD-ROM drives can read CD-RW CDs.

CPU

The CPU (Central Processing Unit) is the integrated circuit that runs programs and does the bulk of the computations in your PC.

dead link

A dead link is a link from a Web site that doesn't lead to a valid destination. Dead links are fairly common on the Web to begin with, and perhaps more so in the MP3 world, where things change like lightning, and many sites are run by volunteers who don't have the time and resources to check all their links regularly.

digital audio extraction

Digital audio extraction (DAE) refers to the ability of a CD-ROM drive to transfer audio data (the song you are ripping) in digital format. If a CD-ROM drive supports DAE, it can transfer digital audio data without error. If your PC and CD-ROM drive are up to it, DAE may allow you to rip tracks from CDs at faster than their normal playback speed.

DOS

DOS stands for Disk Operating System. It is a low-level, non-graphical operating system that has been largely superseded by Windows.

download

To download a file is to transfer it from another computer to your computer. With respect to the Internet, downloading a file means to transfer it from your computer to some other computer to which yours is connected through the Internet.

encoder

An encoder is a program that can convert a Windows WAV file into MP3 format. You need an encoder if you are going to convert music from your audio CDs or other sources into MP3 format.

File Transfer Protocol (FTP)

File Transfer Protocol is an early way to transfer files across the Internet. Many MP3 files, including most of the illegal ones, are available through FTP sites.

firmware

Firmware is a term for some of the software that runs any computer-controlled device. It is firmware instead of software because it is stored in a read-only memory or flash memory, making it into a combination of software and hardware

flash memory

Flash memory is a type of memory that retains its information, even when the memory card has no power. This makes it ideal for low-power devices like portable MP3 players. It also makes it possible (if you have the money to spend) gradually to move your music collection onto flash memory, and carry a virtually limitless amount of music around in your shirt pocket.

freeware

> Freeware is copyrighted software that is distributed free of charge. You can use it for an unlimited time without paying a cent. Some freeware authors do request that you send them e-mail or a post card if you like and use their product.

FTP

> *See File Transfer Protocol.*

gateway

> A gateway is a Web site that connects you to other sites.

hyperlink

> A hyperlink is a phrase or picture on a Web page that, when you click it, takes you to another location on the Web. Hyperlinks are the primary method for getting around on the Web. Text hyperlinks are typically underlined and colored blue, though this rule is not followed as rigorously now as it was in the past.

ID3 tag

> The ID3 tag is a short chunk of data attached to the end of many MP3 files. The tag contains space for the title of a song, the artist or artists who performed the song, the name of the album it is from, the year the song was recorded, the musical genre, and a short comment. Most MP3 players can read the information in an ID3 tag and display that information while playing the song.

Internet

> The Internet is a worldwide network of interconnected computers. The Internet (a.k.a the Net) is the system that e-mail, newsgroups, and the World Wide Web run on top of.

ISP

ISP stands for Internet Service Provider. Typically, your PC uses your modem and the phone lines to connect to an ISP, which provides a connection to the Internet.

link

See hyperlink.

lossless compression

Lossless compression refers to compression techniques that do not discard any of the information in a file during compression. When you decompress a file that has been compressed using a lossless algorithm, the resulting file is identical to the original file.

lossy compression

Lossy compression refers to compression techniques that discard some information in the process of compressing a file. When you decompress a file that has been compressed using a lossy algorithm, the resulting file is not identical to the original file.

MMX

MMX is Intel's trademarked term for the multimedia instruction set added to newer Pentium processors.

modem

Modem stands for modulator/demodulator. A modem converts signals from the digital form used by your PC to the analog form used by the phone system, and vice versa.

motherboard

A motherboard is the primary circuit board in a computer. It holds the bulk of the electronics and circuitry, and may support various connectors and expansion slots.

MP3

MP3 is the name of a file format for storing information in digital form. MP3 is important because the format makes it possible to store music (other sounds, too) in a compact-enough form so that it is practical to transfer music files over the Internet and store music on your home computer and portable playback devices like the Diamond Rio. MP3 stands for MPEG 1, layer 3, if you really must know.

near-CD quality

Near-CD quality recording is usually considered to be recording at 96 kbps. Files recorded in near-CD quality take up less disk space but don't sound as good as CD-quality recordings.

Net

Short for Internet.

normalize

To normalize a sound file means to adjust the peak sound level of the file. By normalizing all files to 100%, you eliminate the differences caused by the varying volume levels at which audio CDs are recorded.

playlist

A playlist is a list of songs grouped together in a way that means something to you. Group mellow songs into one list, classical songs into another, and those your 8-year old can listen to into another playlist. Playlists take the hassle out of managing large collections of music.

plug-in

A plug-in is computer code that can be added to (plugged-into) a program to give it new capabilities. For example, Sonique uses plug-ins to add new visual effects and support for different audio file formats.

proxy server

The proxy server is a server that is located between your Web browser, or other client program, and the server that client program wants to communicate with. The proxy server tries to respond to information requests from the client before passing them on to the target server. Only requests that the proxy server cannot fill get forwarded to the target server.

Red Book audio format

Red Book audio format is the format of the music tracks on an audio CD. You must convert MP3 files into Red Book audio format if a regular audio CD player is to be able to play them.

ripper

A ripper is a program that can read an audio track from a CD and convert it into a file (a Windows WAV file, specifically) on your hard drive.

shareware

Shareware is software marketed on a try-before-you-buy basis. Test it out, see if you like it, then pay to register it if you decide to keep using it.

shopbot

A shopbot is a tool that shops numerous online stores for you, gathering the results into a report that you can scan for the best deal.

site

Short for Web site.

16-bit color

16-bit color is also known as high color. It means that each pixel (dot) on the screen can have any of 65,535 colors.

skin

A skin is a set of graphics that replace the normal user interface of a program. Sonique is an MP3 player that supports skins.

standalone MP3 player

A standalone MP3 player can play music and have many other capabilities, but it lacks the audio CD rip and encode capabilities of an all-in-one player.

timebomb

A timebomb is code in a program that causes it to stop running if you use it too much or too long without registering it.

Uniform Resource Locator

A Uniform Resource Locator (URL) is the address of a document on the World Wide Web.

upload

To upload a file is to transfer it from your computer to another computer. With respect to the Internet, uploading a file means to transfer it from your computer to some other computer that yours is connected to through the Internet.

upload ratio

An upload ratio is the number of songs you must upload to an Internet site (usually an FTP site) before you are allowed to download a song or songs.

URL

See Uniform Resource Locator.

user interface

A user interface is the means by which you (the user) control your software.

VBR

VBR is short for Variable Bit Rate. This is a recording technique, supported by certain MP3 players, that varies the number of bits per second used in encoding, depending on what's going on in the music at any given instant. VBR can give you extremely high quality sound, but does so at the cost of compatibility and increased file size.

virtual drive

A virtual drive is a way to represent storage media that aren't always present on your system. With virtual drives, your software can keep track of MP3s that are stored on floppy disk, CD-ROM, or some other removable storage medium.

Web

Web is short for World Wide Web, the hyperlinked and graphically-inclined portion of the Internet.

Web page

A Web page is a single document on the World Wide Web. Each page has its own URL, or address.

Web site

A Web site is a collection of Web pages. Every Web site has a home page, which is typically the page a visitor first sees when visiting the site.

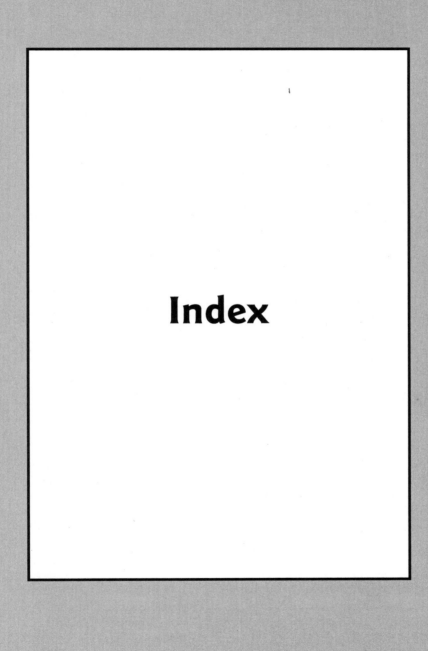

Index

Note: Boldface numbers indicate illustrations.

About the Author

BILL MANN is a freelance writer with eleven books and numerous magazine articles to his credit.